ALLERTON PARK INSTITUTE

Number 21

Papers Presented at the Allerton Park Institute

Sponsored by

Forest Press, Inc.

and

University of Illinois
Graduate School of Library Science

and

University of Illinois
Office of Continuing Education and Public Service

held

November 9-12, 1975

Allerton Park

Monticello, Illinois

Major Classification Systems: The Dewey Centennial

edited by

Kathryn Luther Henderson

University of Illinois
Graduate School of Library Science
Urbana-Champaign, Illinois

CONTENTS

Foreword

One hundred years ago, in 1876, Melvil Dewey anonymously published the first edition of his classification system. Forest Press, publisher of the Dewey Decimal Classification since 1931, could think of no more suitable way to honor the DDC and its author during this centennial year than to bring together librarians interested in classification. It was with great pleasure, therefore, that Forest Press welcomed the opportunity to cosponsor with the University of Illinois Graduate School of Library Science the twenty-first annual Allerton Park Institute. Held on November 9-12, 1975, the topic of the institute was, most appropriately, "Major Classification Systems: the Dewey Centennial."

The goal of the Allerton conference was to provide a forum for an in-depth discussion of classification systems in general and of the DDC in particular. Experts in the field from the United States, Canada, and England presented papers on a variety of topics ranging from a look at recent editions of the DDC and a comparison between Dewey and the Library of Congress Classification, to an examination of the role of classification in subject retrieval. The first report on the survey of DDC use in the United States and Canada was also given at the conference. These papers, all original contributions to the classification field, have been collected in the present volume.

Forest Press wishes to thank in particular the two people whose diligence and care made the conference possible: Kathryn Luther Henderson,

Associate Professor, Graduate School of Library Science, University of Illinois at Urbana-Champaign, and Chairperson of the Planning Committee; and Herbert Goldhor, Director and Professor, Graduate School of Library Science. We are also very grateful to the participants in the conference, for their essays provide an excellent introduction to the study of classification and constitute a fitting centennial tribute to the Dewey Decimal Classification.

RICHARD B. SEALOCK
Executive Director
Forest Press

June 1976

Introduction

Not the least of the important events in library history occuring in 1876 was the appearance of a (then) anonymous publication entitled: *A Classification and Subject Index for Cataloging and Arranging the Books and Pamphlets of a Library*. We now know that the author was Melvil Dewey and, through the years, the work has become known as the *Dewey Decimal Classification* (DDC). The twenty-first annual Allerton Park Institute of the University of Illinois Graduate School of Library Science honored this modest beginning of modern library classification on the eve of its centennial. Forest Press (Albany, N.Y.), publisher of the DDC, served as cosponsor of the conference held from Sunday, November 9, through Wednesday, November 12, 1975, at Allerton Park (the university's conference center) near Monticello, Illinois.

From the first conversations concerning the conference, the intention was that the conference concentrate on classification in general and that it should be critical and objective, and not simply expository and laudatory with regard to DDC. Since Dewey's classification scheme has had a major impact on library classification and subject retrieval systems throughout the world, it was felt that the conference should include papers and discussions from leading experts in the field from the United States, Canada, and England. While the focus remained on Dewey, past, present and future, other major systems were to be noted and compared with DDC.

Only the formal papers can be included in the published proceedings. Missing is the flavor of the give and take of discussions among the speakers, the more than ninety registered participants and the colleagues from the local library community and library school. Since we were fortunate to have most of the speakers with us for the entire conference, there were many opportunities to learn from them as they gave freely of their time and expertise.

In the formal papers that are published here, C. David Batty's keynote address focuses on library classification in general one hundred years after Dewey. He notes the different developments which have contributed to our present philosophy and model of classification as being more similar than dissimilar. The new theories are less a new structure founded on the work of a century than they are a "validation and realization" of the earlier work. He proposes a theoretical model that he finds "at the heart of all fruitful classification and indexing developments of the last one hundred years." Batty traces developments in the works of Dewey, the Universal Decimal Classification, Cutter, Brown, the Library of Congress, Bliss, Ranganathan, and the Classification Research Group.

John P. Comaromi concentrates on the history and development of the first sixteen editions of DDC, giving emphasis to the factors which have affected the scheme and to the persons (especially the editors) whose work is reflected in the various editions but who often have remained unrecognized for their influence. The role of the Decimal Classification Editorial Policy Committee and other advisory committees is also noted.

Continuing the story of the editions of DDC, Margaret Cockshutt analyzes the trends toward faceting in the most recent editions of the scheme. She points out the influence of Ranganathan and the Classification Research Group. Cockshutt also explains the organization by which the structure of DDC is molded and maintained as it moves more and more toward an international classification.

But how is the DDC used? To answer that question, Mary Ellen Michael reports on a study sponsored by Forest Press and which she conducted under the auspices of the Library Research Center, University of Illinois Graduate School of Library Science. This study attempted to assess the use of DDC by libraries and processing centers in the United States and Canada, as well as to determine the extent of the use of DDC by libraries of different sizes and types; to obtain information about the application of DDC to library collections; to determine problem areas in the scheme; and to ascertain to what extent DDC is a part of the educational experiences of library school students. Results pertaining to all aspects except the last are included in her paper.

Joel Downing describes the growing interest in and use of DDC in Great Britain since the late 1960s and relates the acts of study and collaboration both within Great Britain and in the United States which have taken place since that date. In addition, he briefly discusses the possibility of DDC establishing a foothold in Europe.

Gordon Stevenson compares DDC with the Library of Congress classification scheme (LCC), finding them competing systems even though the competition has never been fostered by those responsible for either scheme. Stevenson fears that LCC's entrenchment in existing network data bases (geared primarily to the needs of university libraries) will be used as a rationale for structuring similar networks for public and school libraries. He feels that those libraries which have adopted LCC have locked themselves into a system "from which it will be nearly impossible to extricate themselves." To Stevenson, an important problem for the future of classification is how we perceive classification as a tool for subject retrieval. He feels that no person should be given the responsibility for choosing between systems until that person has a thorough grounding in classification and knowledge of the dimensions and structure of the systems, a grounding which has often been lacking in the background of the decision-makers of the past.

Peter Lewis served as chairperson of a British Library Working Party which examined the various classification and indexing systems currently in use in the British Library. The main conclusions relating to in-house needs and to services provided for other libraries in Great Britain are discussed in Lewis's paper, while the performances of Bliss, DDC, LCC and UDC are evaluated as to meeting the needs. Although Lewis was not able to be present, his paper was distributed to the participants at the beginning of the conference. During the time scheduled for Lewis's paper, the conferees participated in small group discussions relating to his paper. Following the discussions, transoceanic telephonic communication was established with Lewis. For one-half hour, Lewis responded to discussion, comments, and questions from groups.

Hans Wellisch discusses the debt which the Universal Decimal Classification owes to DDC as well as UDC's reforms and revisions. He notes the work being done toward a Basic Medium Edition in English and the work toward a new class 4. In addition, he speaks of the work being performed on a Broad System of Ordering intended not to supersede existing indexing languages but to serve as a switching language.

Unfortunately, the manuscript of John Rather's presentation was not received for publication. As Chief of the Technical Processes Research Office, Processing Department, Library of Congress, Rather gave a preliminary report on investigations made at the Library of Congress which attempted to evaluate the relative efficiency of subject searching in an automated system using

Library of Congress classification notation, Dewey Decimal classification numbers and Library of Congress subject headings.

Derek Austin departs from a discussion of classification per se to present the PRECIS system. Austin summarizes his paper as follows:

> During the 1960s, the Classification Research Group in England investigated the construction of a faceted, highly articulated classification scheme to serve the dual purposes of (i) library organization, and (ii) the retrieval of relevant items from machine-held files. This research is briefly described, and is seen as evidence that a single classification scheme cannot serve these different purposes.

> Nevertheless, it was found that the results of the CRG research could be applied to verbal data. In 1969, the *British National Bibliography* began a research project in this field. This led to the development of PRECIS, the indexing system now used by *BNB* and a number of other agencies.

> PRECIS is briefly described from three viewpoints:
> (a) syntax: that is, the writing of coded input strings of terms, and the structure of index entries
> (b) semantics: the creation of a machine-held thesaurus which serves as the source of *see* and *see also* references
> (c) management, including indexer performance.

Paule Rolland-Thomas looks ahead to the future of subject retrieval as she reports on views expressed by library and other classificationists. Her paper provides the vision for the future.

The conference concluded with a panel of reactors to the papers and discussion. Betty M.E. Croft, Catalog Librarian at the University of Illinois at Urbana-Champaign, brought her twenty-five years of experience with DDC in one of the nation's largest university libraries into focus as chairperson of the panel. Other members were Grace F. Bulaong, Head of the Cataloging Department, Metropolitan Toronto Central Library, Toronto, Canada; Erma Jean Morgan, Deputy Librarian–Technical Services, King County Library System, Seattle, Washington; and Mary Ellen Soper, Assistant Professor, School of Librarianship, University of Washington, Seattle. The panel members brought a variety of experiences in several different types of libraries using both DDC and LCC schemes. The panel discussion is briefly summarized:

1. While it is agreed that catalogs and automated retrieval systems may be more important to the retrieval of subject information in the future than they have been in the past, the need still exists for some shelf browsing capabilities, especially in public library situations.
2. Many difficulties occur in the local library resulting from the issuing of new editions of classification schemes. Most libraries cannot afford to

reclassify. At the same time, the necessity for the use of cooperative agencies and networks pressures the local library to accept the decisions of the newest edition. The scattering of like or similar subjects causes hardships for library users. A challenge was issued to those charged with revision to find a moderate ground for change that would keep up with new knowledge while remembering the problems of libraries with diminishing budgets.

3. Considering how classification is used in the United States, there is no clear superiority in either DDC or LCC if only the schemes themselves are considered. Each has certain strengths and weaknesses. Reasons for selecting one scheme over the other or for deciding to reclassify from DDC to LCC often have come from factors other than those related to the schemes themselves. Administrative decisions relating to coverage, revision and availability, as well as political reasons such as prestige or following a fad, seem too often to have been deciding factors.

4. In studying the results of developments in classification research in other countries, it becomes apparent that classification is not fully utilized in the United States. Only the surface of its potential contribution has been scratched. The need for browsing capability on the shelf has contributed to the way classification has developed in the United States. The confusion over the function of shelf arrangement and subject analysis needs to be clarified by further study and examination.

5. The needs of library users call us to consider seriously the role of the classification of knowledge as we look to the future.

No conference is the work of any one person; this conference was no exception. Beginning with initial conversations between Herbert Goldhor, Director, Graduate School of Library Science, University of Illinois at Urbana-Champaign, and Richard B. Sealock, Executive Director, Forest Press, during the summer of 1974, and continuing through the publication of this volume, two years of work on the part of a number of persons have taken place. Only a few of those persons can be mentioned here, but none of those who contributed and who are not mentioned here should feel excluded from our expression of gratitude.

Forest Press should be mentioned for both intellectual and financial support. Many helpful suggestions were received from Richard B. Sealock. Robert L. Talmadge, Director of Technical Services, University of Illinois Library at Urbana-Champaign, represented Forest Press on the Planning Committee and provided further liaison with the cosponsoring agency. Michael Gorman, Head, Bibliographic Standards Office, Bibliographic Services Division, the British Library, London, England, was serving as Visiting Lecturer at the University of Illinois Graduate School of Library Science and was able, as a member of the planning committee, to make many suggestions relating to the international scene. Herbert Goldhor also served on the committee, and other faculty and library staff members helped in many ways.

Edward C. Kalb and Sara Nelson, of the University of Illinois Conferences and Institutes Office, assisted in numerous ways that relieved the rest of us of responsibilities. It is difficult to recognize fully their contributions to the conference with just these few words of acknowledgment.

Arlynn Robertson and Linda Hoffman contributed to the technical editing of this volume.

Kathryn Luther Henderson
Chairperson, Planning Committee

March 1976

DAVID BATTY
Professor
Graduate School of Library Science
McGill University
Montreal, Canada

Library Classification: One Hundred Years After Dewey

We shall not cease from exploration
And the end of all our exploring
Will be to arrive where we started
And know the place for the first time.[1]

For one hundred years in claim and counterclaim we have developed what have seemed at times to be highly diverse and divergent lines of thought in the theory of library classification. However, I believe not only that these different developments have contributed to our present philosophy and model of classification, but also that their differences were more apparent than real—we have often been bewitched by the appearance into paying insufficient attention to the creature beneath. In a very real sense, the most sophisticated modern theory is less a new structure founded on the work of a century ago than it is simply a validation and realization of that work.

In order to describe what we have now I must review how we came to have it, since the study of classification is often a matter of hindsight, of determining the principles that are the key to good organization in existing classification schemes. For this reason, I shall propose a theoretical model that seems to lie at the heart of all fruitful classification and indexing developments of the last one hundred years. I shall also refer to several episodes in the history of classification and indexing, and draw from those episodes the elements of greatest significance to point out an overall pattern, even though these elements may have seemed of great significance neither to their authors nor to their audiences.

In the world of documentary classification we must deal with assemblies of ideas: of objects, the problems or operations that affect them, and their context in time and space. It is not enough to imagine hierarchies of simple units of knowledge; the notations or codes by which we represent these assemblies must themselves be simple enough to be flexible also—and indeed flexible enough to be simple. It matters little whether we use words or arbitrary symbols as our codes, as long as the basic elements of the codes are simple, are comprehensible, and permit development and change without inhibiting consistent practice. Within the components of the assemblies it is desirable to have recognizable families of related concepts in order to move easily to unfamiliar levels of detail. Again, it matters little for this argument whether these family relationships, generic or functional, are displayed in explicit hierarchies or revealed implicitly through reference instructions.

At the beginning of our history stands one of its greatest landmarks: Dewey's *Decimal Classification.* Dewey's achievement, on inspection, is almost incredible—perhaps not as extensive as Ranganathan's, but infinitely bolder in the context of his era. In Dewey's day the notion of a universal classification scheme was revolutionary. Librarians made their own schemes, according to the vagaries of local academic preference or uncomfortable architecture. They borrowed schemata from philosophy (thereby limiting themselves to unitary organization), and notation from anything from an inchoate mnemonic urge to a reflection of the names of benefactors of parts of their collections. Dewey himself claimed credit for several features of his scheme: its ability to locate books relatively on the shelves, thus overcoming the accidents and limitations of fixed location in different libraries; its easy and mnemonic decimal notation; and its relative index, which encouraged consistent application. He emphasized that the scheme was a classification for documents, although he did not claim this as quite the innovation that it really was. He never specifically claimed credit for one of the most innovative aspects of the documentary basis of the scheme: the combination of more than one kind of idea was allowed and encouraged, reflecting the multitopic nature of documents.

All of these features are related. Relative location would be impossible without a notation that did not expand as knowledge grows, without changing the symbols used to represent already established major groupings or classes. The index must have unique and explicable notation to point to. What Dewey called "close classification" is impossible without the combination of ideas not only in explicit enumeration within the scheme, but also implicit in the availability of components whose notation facilitates assembly by the classifier.

Dewey's decimal organization and decimal notation have been criticized for the constraints they place on the true structure and division of knowledge. This is particularly true of the decimal notation, although the two have often been confused by intellectually myopic librarians. In fact, the decimal notation rarely inhibits proper division; there are many classes that do not use all of the ten notational divisions available, and others that use them as major groupings in classes with more than ten members—the class 970 *North America* is an example of both cases. The expressive use of the decimal notation with its fractional division contains a powerful mnemonic effect. Although a user may not know the meaning of 621.384152 *FM radio systems,* he will know that it lies in the field of 621.384 *radio engineering,* or at least in 621.3 *electrical engineering.* Dewey's practice of using notation consistently to represent concepts, often in combination with others, offers the effect of scheduled mnemonics, exploited later by the Universal Decimal Classification and Ranganathan's Colon Classification.

My thesis, however, concerns the internal organization of subjects, and it is in this connection that Dewey often only half-knowingly, made his greatest contribution in the exploration of the consistent construction of multitopic assemblies. His methods are clearest in the simplest classes, such as *language, literature* and *history.* In 400 *language,* for example, he recognizes that books may be written about two aspects of language (what Ranganathan later called *facets* of language): (1) the general theoretical aspects of language like *structural systems (grammar),* and (2) the particular languages, like *English.* He listed the theoretical aspects first, in 410, and the languages after them in 420-499, to achieve an order on the shelves that proceeds from the general to the particular. But then he went on to admit the subdivision of collections on particular languages, by the theoretical aspects, so that 420 *English* might include, for example, *English grammar,* and he arranged for the characteristic notation for 410 to be used to subdivide the language—in this case 5 from 415 *structural systems (grammar)* to create 425. This simple example reveals a model that has scarcely changed for one hundred years: the recognition of the characteristic aspects of the subject, the separate listing of those aspects in general-to-specific order, the availability of the detail from general aspect to divide the specific aspects further, the consequent assembly order of specific aspects divided by general aspects, and the mnemonic effect of the consistent use of simple notation from the two aspects.

Dewey made early use of standard subdivisions; in particular, the 09 history subdivision formed geographical subdivisions for any class by introducing further notation from the 900 class with its wealth of geographical detail. Before the turn of the century, at least parts of the Decimal Classification offered recognizable and descriptive notational assemblies to designate entities or events, the problems affecting them or the operations they undertook, and their geographical and chronological context—but not always. Dewey's internal class organization was often limited and confused. Sometimes he listed the several aspects in a class in a proper general-to-specific order, but failed to make provision for their combination; sometimes we can discern by hindsight the existence of two or more characteristics in the initial division of a class, but Dewey listed the resulting subdivisions not in ordered groups, but in a confused and confusing order. It is interesting to note that many of those subjects were emergent disciplines in Dewey's day: sociology, education, psychology—their features were known but had no recognizable shape. It is also interesting to note that in later editions of the scheme, the clarity of Dewey's unconscious organization was such that reorganization was relatively simple and mostly successful. However, Dewey was limited, as were all classificationists after him, by his contemporary climate of thought. Dewey could not think of a better organization for *law* or *education,* because he had no theoretical model against which to match the concepts he observed in those disciplines, and by which to organize them. That theoretical model began to emerge as a result of the study of successful elements of the Decimal Classification, and also in the pragmatic development of its inherent synthetic principles in the Universal Decimal Classification (UDC).

The 1895 Brussels conference sought ways to organize collections and bibliographies full of material in a variety of nonbook forms and about increasingly complex topics. The solution was to develop Dewey's Decimal Classification as a universal scheme that emerged as the Universal Decimal Classification in recognizable structure in 1906 and in name and detail in 1928-33. Much has been made of the extensive array of auxiliaries provided in the scheme; auxiliaries of addition and extension, of language and form, and of place, time and race. However, the main contribution in these areas is the use of nondecimal punctuation marks to signal the use of decimal notation already available in Dewey's scheme. This notational signaling allowed what had been done in limited areas in Dewey's scheme to be done in UDC universally without specific instruction. Whereas Dewey sometimes divided a subject by place without his usual indicator 09, but otherwise left it to the classifier to add 09, etc., on his own initiative, UDC created a general auxiliary for place by using Dewey's detail for 940-999 (now the *Area Tables*) and enclosing the number in parentheses to be used anywhere. Whereas Dewey almost always limited chronological subdivision to places specified in *history,* UDC created a general auxiliary for time, and enclosed dates, periods and notation for other chronological phenomena like periodicity in quotation marks, and allowed them to be used with any number in the scheme.

UDC's two principal contributions were the special auxiliaries and the use of a relational sign (initially the colon) to link any two notational elements. The special auxiliary is a specially notated list, usually of general aspects, theoretical topics, operations or problems with a class, whose members may be used to extend or modify any specific topic in that class. It represents a realization of the model already described as displayed in some of Dewey's classes. The notation of a "short dash" or "point zero" sets the special auxiliary off from the specific topics in the class and allows free assembly of the components.

The relational sign offers the same potential, but over the entire range of the classification schedules. There are no listed notational elements; the classifier may use the colon (and later also square brackets) to extend any class number by any other class number. Thus, both 633.491:632.3 and 632.3:633.491 may mean *parasitic diseases of potatoes.* However, only the former notation uses the thing/problem assembly order usually compelled by a special auxiliary; the classifier must therefore have an accurate perception of the character of the elements to be assembled, especially if more than two elements are involved. UDC itself recognized the dangers inherent in the use of this auxiliary and took away much of the value of the relational sign by the instruction to use *both* assemblies (an adroit maneuver called "reversing about the colon"). This practice effectively limited the relational sign to assemblies of only two components, and prevented the exploration of the problems of assembly of more than two components. In UDC, complex assemblies used the comparatively unadventurous common auxiliaries to specify the obvious and superficial contextual detail. It was left to Ranganathan to explore the intricacies of assembly order of several aspects internal to a subject.

During the nineteenth century the problems of the assembly of the component aspects of a complex subject were the concern also of indexers using natural language. They were, for instance, the predominant concern of Kaiser in his *Systematic Indexing* of 1911, which dealt with questions left unanswered by Cutter in his 1876 rules for the dictionary catalog. Cutter was mainly preoccupied with subject/place and with thing/kind-of-thing assembly, and with word order in phrase headings; he proposed a quasi-grammatical logic based on the structure of English syntax. Such a feeling was appropriate to an age that sought both the common origin of tongues and a syntax common to all tongues based on an assumption of consistent human cultural behavior. Fenollosa, in *Art of the Chinese Written Character as a Medium for Poetry* (1910), suggested the natural order of events in the world as the key to a universal syntax, unaware of dissimilarities as great as those between Hopi Indian culture and our own such that they have a different concept of time itself and the linear sequence of cause and effect, related to the absence of a verb structure recognizable in our terms. It was left to Edward Sapir and Benjamin Lee Whorf to explore the complex interaction of language and thought that makes us doubt the simplistic assumption of universal grammar except in the more abstract terms of Bloomfield and Chomsky.

Cutter's reliance on natural-language order worked well in noun/noun or adjective/noun assemblies, where in English grammar ' the modifying term stands first—thus producing consistently specific headings. Unfortunately, in an alphabetical index the same principle scatters members of the same group (represented by the second word) to wherever the first words are found. The classifying of any group that traditionally or usefully should stand together thus raises a conflict in the indexer's mind to the point of encouraging a mild professional catatonia that has prevented the development of a coherent body of principle to the present time. The only guide to practice is the Library of Congress subject catalog, affected more by the necessities of logistics and administrative consistency than by the epistemology of the information explosion. The problem grew worse with the increasing occurrence of entity/activity combinations; the conflict was now between adjectival noun/verbal noun and participle/noun, e.g., *serials cataloging* and *cataloging serials.* Kaiser's solution was the use of the formula concrete/process—an explicit instruction reflecting the entity/activity assembly order already observed in some classes of the Decimal Classification and the Universal Decimal Classification. Kaiser's suggestion was simple enough, but radical in the contemporary tradition of alphabetico-specific indexing based on natural-language order.

In the same decade a classification scheme was published that stands out as the strangest and most ironic experiment of all: Brown's *Subject Classification.* Of all classificationists, Brown, either instinctively or accidentally, was the most innovative and visionary, and also most imprisoned by his contemporary climate of thought. Dewey's scheme, the Universal Decimal Classification, Cutter's Expansive Classification and the emerging Library of Congress Classification were all organized around the disciplines then, as now, accepted as the main divisions of knowledge. All works in the field of medicine are grouped together, as are all works on economics, history, or art, but the specific subject "bubonic plague" will find a place in all those classes for its several different aspects. Brown proposed a scheme based on concretes like *bubonic plague,* that would collect at those concretes all their aspects and problems, like the medical aspect, the historical aspect, the economic aspect, and so on. This organization principle extended the entity/general aspect assembly order to include even the discipline name, as being of the greatest generality. There is a distinct logic in this arrangement denied by the discipline-based schemes; that is, in a discipline-based scheme we may organize a class as:

> zoology
> > (theoretical aspects)
> > embryology
> > (animals)
> > horses

and assemble the components in the retroactive order *horses-embryology*—but we do it within *zoology*. Brown's principle would look higher up the chain of general topics and include in its logical place as a general term:

> *horses-embryology*
> *horses-zoology.*

In Brown's classification scheme all general aspects of all subjects, including the names of disciplines, are included in a single auxiliary table whose members may be used to subdivide any specific concrete. Of course, in Brown's day a classification had to have notational order, and Brown was compelled to organize a sequence of main classes in order to organize his concretes, and also in order to list the disciplines when they stood wholly as themselves and not as aspects of a concrete. The result was a rather simple and limited hierarchical classification in which concretes appeared only once, under what Brown considered their original, basic discipline; all other disciplines where they might otherwise have recurred were left empty of everything except activities and problems peculiar to them. The result was to inhibit the growth of the subject classification in the logical direction of its philosophy, and instead clumsily convert it in development and application (mostly in Britain) into a simple, homespun, discipline-based scheme. Had it not been for the inhibiting effect of contemporary assumptions about classification, Brown might well have anticipated the later work of the British Classification Research Group by fifty years. But like Dewey, he had no theoretical model with which to measure and organize; his work provided the phenomena that others could analyze and build on.

Courtesy and stature demand notice of the Library of Congress classification and also of the work of Henry Evelyn Bliss in his books *The Organisation of Knowledge and the System of the Sciences* and the *Organisation of Knowledge in Libraries* and, of course, the expression of his theories in his work, *A Bibliographic Classification.*[2] The Library of Congress Classification is a large and powerful scheme, but its structure and detailed

organization owe more to the administrative policy of subject departmentaliza-
tion in the Library of Congress and to the book collection that it is designed
to organize physically, than to a body of principle designed to respond to the
epistemological complexities of the world of information today. Almost by
definition the Library of Congress Classification (LCC) is a return to the
pre-1876 world of in-house classification schemes affected by the physical and
political pressures of a single institution, and used by any other library at its
own risk. This is in no way to deny the position and power of the LCC
scheme; indeed, it may be pertinent to note here that in a generation or so it
may be the only scheme still used for shelf classification. If that happens, it
will be because of the authoritative position of the Library of Congress and its
contribution to catalog information in general libraries, rather than to any
internal excellence. As knowledge and information grow quantitatively and
change qualitatively, there is less need and even less opportunity for the
detailed physical organization of library material on shelves. Even the Library
of Congress scheme may ultimately be—and probably should be—replaced by a
general classificatory grouping with simple, repetitive mnemonic notation to
prevent the need for the gross movement of readers around the library;
subject access to material will be by detailed computerized indexes available in
on-line or printed form. In that future, classification will truly be a
fundamental study, since its essence has always been that of an organizing
principle to assemble or relate the component elements of complex topics; the
manifestation of that principle in a single, enumerated hierarchy with a
notation is almost secondary.

For Bliss, however, the manifestation was paramount. In spite of a
historical and philosophical study lasting almost a lifetime, Bliss did not
include in his classification scheme many features beyond a developmental
order of main classes (lost in a large library), an array of auxiliary schedules as
extensive as those of UDC, and a notation whose overriding quality of brevity
obscured almost every other advantage of the scheme. As with Dewey's
Decimal Classification, the seeds of development and good and flexible order
are there, and they may yet be brought out by the work of revision currently
in hand at North London Polytechnic, although the revision may be so drastic
as to suggest less a facelift than the transmigration of souls.

Of all classifiers, only Shiyali Ramanarita Ranganathan has been able to
respond pragmatically to classification problems and later to analyze his own
work to produce a new body of principle. Of all his achievements this may be
the greatest. During the 1920s Ranganathan forsook mathematics for
librarianship and, encouraged by the teaching of Berwick Sayers, rejected all
existing schemes for their logical and developmental inadequacies, and began
to design his own scheme. He used the entity/activity assembly pattern
common to Dewey's and Kaiser's methods, and the notion of explicit and

detailed auxiliaries from the Universal Decimal Classification. He especially emphasized the relational device of the colon, which he strengthened by using it to link even the component aspects with subjects, and he added two features of his own: a new and more economical way of listing the aspects within subjects, and a consistent order of assembly (and therefore order of the subdivision of complex topics) that simplified access to the scheme or to collections and indexes using it.

Ranganathan realized the true potential of Dewey's recognition of two aspects of a subject, and their assembly to describe complex topics. Dewey nearly always specified the assembly by instruction and within a complete notational framework, as when he extended 420 *English language* to make 425 *English syntax* by adding the 5 meaning *syntax* from the 415 *syntax general theoretical aspects of language* under 410. The Universal Decimal Classification had made it more explicit by the use of the colon—to make 420:425, and by going further still in using a special auxiliary to make 420-5, omitting the "41" since the division took place within the class 4. Ranganathan confirmed, extended and generalized this practice. He developed the aspects of subjects separately, calling them the facets of the subjects. Instead of including the more general facets as enumerated subdivisions of the more specific, as Dewey and the Universal Decimal Classification often did, he gave instructions always to combine the individual notation of topics from different facets by a colon. Thus, within the main class T *education,* the first facet contains educational institutions, and *universities* has the number 4. A document on university education is given the notation T4. Educational problems and methods belong in another facet, called by Ranganathan the energy facet and prefaced by a colon, where *curriculum* has the number 2. We may combine these two components (or isolates, as Ranganathan called them) to give T4:2. If we have a general work on curricula we may therefore assign it the class number T:2. Thus the colon becomes a constant indicator of the problem or energy facet.

After his first edition, Ranganathan extended the scheme as problems emerged in practical classification, although he sought always to obey the fundamental principles of logical classification, and also to be consistent with logical practices that emerged as the scheme developed. For example, he noted that sometimes members of different levels in a generic hierarchy might need to be used together in assembly, as in *buildings* and *parts of buildings.* He consequently recognized two separate facets (or levels of facet) in order to provide for that assembly. He also noted that some operations need agents to perform them, and so an additional facet of agent would be necessary for combination with operations. By the 1940s there were enough different kinds of facets for Ranganathan to identify definite categories, and to propose a consistent scheme of indicators to introduce them at any time. To introduce extra levels of the facet of entities (which he called personality) he used a comma; for the facet indicating the material of which an entity might be made he used a semicolon; for the facets listing activities or problems or operations (the energy facet) he used the colon, as he had done from the beginning; and for the facets of geographical and chronological specification he used the period, with different notational symbols with each. This overall categorization of facets gave the formula PMEST (personality, material, energy, space, time), which manifested that same order of increasing generality of the aspects assembled together that we have observed since Dewey and Kaiser—a principle which Ranganathan called decreasing concreteness.

Not all subjects use all kinds of facets, and some have more than one level in a single kind of facet; indeed, some have pervasive or overriding facets called system or special facets like *schools of thought* in *philosophy* or *soil-less farming* in *agriculture*. All subject classes are equipped with an explicit formula showing what facets they contain, and in what order isolates from the facets may be assembled. The notation of the main classes is alphabetic, usually a single letter (but sometimes two) and the notation of the facets is numerical in fractional division. Ranganathan also provided for the combination of elements from different subjects. The Universal Decimal Classification had already allowed this through the relational device of the colon, but did not indicate why or how such combination took place, except on an *ad hoc* basis. Ranganathan identified several kinds of phase relationships; these were to indicate influence, difference, comparison and orientation, as well as a general relationship. He provided a special notation to indicate each kind, and later even provided for phase relationships at different levels of subject division. He also developed an elaborate provision for specifying the form of the document.

Ranganathan's habit was to extend his own theory by a critical examination of the pragmatic answers that he had provided as consistently as possible within the theoretical framework developed to that point. By the 1950s he had identified and named many of the principal phenomena of multidimensional classification and had provided a working model of a new type of general classification scheme. Dewey's Decimal Classification and the Library of Congress Classification are usually termed enumerative because they attempt to enumerate specifically all the topics covered by the scheme. The Universal Decimal Classification is often called a synthetic classification because it synthesizes or assembles notation from a general list to represent complex topics not specifically enumerated in the scheme. All schemes that assemble notation for this purpose fall into this category, but Colon Classification and many schemes after it form a special subclass of synthetic schemes called faceted classification schemes, because they assemble elements from separately listed facets within each class; there is no (or very little) precoordinated assembly with a single notation. Because the facets themselves have a hierarchical order represented by the order of assembly and contain little hierarchies of isolates in generic groupings, Ranganathan perceived a single chain of increasingly intense subdivision in any assembly of notations, since the faceted classification scheme is only a kit of parts representing an *n*-dimensional classification. One of his most practical contributions to indexing besides the *Colon Classification* itself is his method of indexing by chain procedure—including alphabetical subject entries for levels indicated by the chain implicit in the class number, whether or not the collection includes any material at that level, in order to facilitate entry into the system for an inquiry at any level.

The recommendations of the 1948 Royal Society Conference and the interest of English librarians like Bernard Palmer, A. J. Wells, D. J. Foskett, and Jack Mills led to the establishment in 1950 of the British Classification Research Group (CRG). This group discussed and promulgated Ranganathan's theories, and in doing so translated them for the western world from the more elaborate and philosophical terms of Ranganathan himself. The members of CRG worked out special classification schemes of this new faceted type and in doing so provided a model that is still used today, even after CRG itself has moved on. The definitive expression of their theories is found in the 1957 *Proceedings of the International Study Conference on Classification for Information Retrieval,* otherwise known as the Dorking Conference, and in Brian Vickery's *Faceted Classification,* written in 1960 to guide librarians in constructing classification schemes. A. J. Wells became editor of the new *British National Bibliography* (BNB), and confirmed the new theory in the public library sector—as the other members of CRG had for special libraries—by insisting on good facet order in applying Dewey Decimal Classification notation to the books in the BNB. He also advocated such order in extending the notation where it fell short in Decimal Classification, and in using chain procedure to construct the index to the *Bibliography's* classified main listing.

A typical special-faceted classification of the type developed by the members of CRG has a core schedule for a single discipline or interdisciplinary area, in which the constituent facets are arranged in increasingly specific order and assembled retroactively in order of the increasing generality of the component terms, so as to represent complex topics. Unlike Ranganathan's scheme the facets are not rigidly assigned to categories, although the PMEST formula is reflected in the developing spectrum they cover. The notation is often alphabetic, because it offers a greater number of symbols and thus shorter notation for any given isolate, and the use of capital letters for the facets and of lowercase letters and sometimes numbers for the detail within them obviates the need for facet indicators. Any isolates may be used in combination; the only rule for assembly is that they be assembled in reverse order of the notation, to achieve a proper order of decreasing concreteness. In addition to the core schedule, there may be a fringe schedule which lists areas supportive of the core, although not belonging to it, such as the relationship of *computer science* or *education* to *library science*. The fringe schedules are not usually worked out in great detail, and are not used in combination as often as the core schedule.

The significance of the early work of the CRG (apart from introducing Ranganathan's ideas to the western world) was to develop a simple model for faceted classification that acknowledged the principle of decreasing concreteness for organizing the assembly of components without imposing a limiting categorization. One evidence of this acknowledgment appears outside pure classification in the work of E. J. Coates, a CRG member who had already worked on the BNB and devised a faceted classification for music for the *British Catalogue of Music*. Coates founded the *British Technology Index* and used CRG principles to organize natural-language subject headings of considerable complexity. In one sense Coates was heir to Kaiser, since his basic formula (*thing/material/action/agent*) reflects Kaiser's concrete/process formula, but in another and very real sense Coates's work was closer to the Ranganathan/CRG tradition. Coates's subject-heading formula followed an order of decreasing concreteness, and his automatic construction of references among the natural-language terms in headings relies on the assumption that the decreasingly concrete terms are logical steps in a chain. A significant departure from previous index-language construction came in his abandonment of a controlled vocabulary derived in advance from a study of the literature. Coates relied on his formula and reference structure to control subject statements as they occurred, but the growing index became its own authority file for the vocabulary. Until this development, the classic method had been to (1) analyze a sample set of documents in the field, (2) determine the concepts and their relationships, and (3) determine the best terms to represent them (clearly a necessary operation for classification, with its need to organize even similar terms in an orderly array). For almost the first time, the tools of faceted classification development were used in natural-language indexing and resulted in some new perceptions.

During this period another CRG member, Jason Farradane, proposed a system of relational operators that would link terms in index statements without regard for the existence of those terms in any formal arrangements other than the document in hand. Whereas Ranganathan and the CRG had concentrated on assigning terms to facets so that the relationships among terms were implicit in the already announced relationship of the facets, Farradane concentrated on the categories of relationship. His system of operators is complex and almost mystical in its derivation from theories of perception and cognition, but handled empirically and admittedly somewhat unfairly, it offers a good working system. It has contributed significantly to the philosophy of the CRG work by Derek Austin on a new general faceted classification, and of course to the new indexing system called PRECIS arising from that work.

We should note that throughout the 1960s, work on the automatic generation of index languages attempted to generate classifications or quasi-classifications using statistical analysis of the text of documents or their abstracts. However, in spite of elaborate recalculations, recomparisons, and rematchings of terms against the numbers of documents using them, statistical significance has so far failed to be accepted as semantic significance. Probably the best seminal work was done by Doyle, with applications by Sally Dennis; currently the most interesting work is that done by the Needhams, by Borko and by Salton. Nevertheless, the results still lack the necessary intellectual rigor.

I have said almost nothing about the thesauri used in post-coordinate indexing. From the early days of what we might call "free-form" post-coordinate indexing, the field moved toward ever-tighter control over vocabulary and relationships, until with categories, links and roles, infixes, etc., classificatory structure began to emerge. MESH (*Medical Subject Headings*) added a systematic index that is a broad classification—and two thesauri (*Thesaurus of Engineering and Scientific Terms,* developed by the Engineers Joint Council, and *Thesaurus of ERIC Descriptors*) have a similar apparatus. The prototype ERIC thesaurus devised by Barhydt at Case Western Reserve University had a frankly faceted structure, although the final thesaurus was to be an alphabetically ordered vocabulary; the systematic structure was to aid recognition of new terms and their relationships and development of the reference structure. Possibly the best example of the overt combination of faceted classification and alphabetical thesaurus came with the fourth edition of the English Electric Company's faceted classification for engineering and technology called *Thesaurofacet,* in which each side might act as a main index language, depending on system requirements, with the other acting as a complementary index.

Also in the late 1960s began one of the most significant developments in the history of classification and indexing and the third major landmark of the past one hundred years: the work on a general faceted classification funded by NATO and carried out principally by Derek Austin on behalf of the British Classification Research Group. Since Derek Austin's paper elsewhere in this volume describes in detail the development of PRECIS, I shall offer only an outline to support my thesis.

After considerable discussion in the 1960s, CRG agreed to simplify the faceted approach even more than they had in the 1950s. From Ranganathan's five fundamental but separate categories they moved to a spectrum organized according to the principle of decreasing concreteness. Now they resolved even these shades of distinction into two areas: entities and attributes. With these two categories of meaning they permitted the development of generic groupings by the principle of integrative levels, taken from Joseph Needham, in which collections of similar phenomena appear as an integrated unit at a higher level. The entity and attribute categories do not have a distinct order of priority, although it is typical for an index description to begin with an entity; they are put together by the use of connecting symbols called operators selected from a fairly generous list, in an order whose logic is determined by the semantics of the words in the contexts of the statement. The notational symbols of the operators automatically pull the string of terms (each preceded by its operator) into a useful order. The categories of entity and attribute may have a notation if necessary, or they may remain in natural-language form. PRECIS is an alphabetical indexing system that has grown out of that classificatory basis. To the vocabulary/operator structure is added a presentation format in which the string of terms is presented with each term successively in a lead position, qualified by any more general terms, and with any remaining terms left as a display to complete the "precis" of the article as described by all the indexing terms. To the intellectual elements of the new general faceted classification, PRECIS has added a necessary element, never previously explored, of a physical layout of display to aid the comprehensibility of the index statement.

The intellectual elements of this new classification and of PRECIS warrant close scrutiny. The operators, like Farradane's, and unlike Ranganathan's, are independent of the categories or facets to which terms may belong, but they reflect the meanings of those categories of terms dimly discernible in Dewey and developed to a highly sophisticated level by Ranganathan. The categories of entity and attribute seem to be direct descendants of the categories clearly discernible in some classes of Dewey's scheme, and explicitly stated by both Kaiser and Brown. In fact, however, they are an ultimate reduction of the highly sophisticated development by Ranganathan of those early, unformed categories. In the growth of many disciplines we may see a progression from empirical observation, through pragmatic application, to analysis and planned development. Dewey had an almost instinctive perception of the fundamental means to organize classes, although he was limited by the primitive state of the library art to simple, two-part structures. Against the context of his time, however, his seminal contribution seems tremendous. The towering baroque achievement of Ranganathan is at once the full and detailed realization of what Dewey and the UDC attempted, and also the new thematic foundation of a later age of classic simplicity.

If this musical metaphor seems lavish, or if you misunderstand my use of the term *baroque,* let me stress that Ranganathan was not so much the beginning of a new age as the final realization of the potential of the previous one. Ranganathan worked out in detail all the meaning and implication of the intent and attempts of Dewey, Kaiser, Brown, and UDC. He is the Bach of classification; all the contrapuntal experiments of his predecessors pointed to his invention, and in that flowering lay the seed of the next development. With the 1960s comes the age of synthesis, in which the previously apparently incompatible traditions of systematic and alphabetic indexing, and pre- and post-coordinate systems are seen to have a common underlying intellectual structure.

The information explosion of the twentieth century has brought not only a quantitative increase in knowledge, but also a qualitative change. Knowledge no longer has the development mechanization or even the same structure it had a century ago. Knowledge now grows by conscious synthesis in inter- and multidisciplinary areas. The essential problems of bibliographic organization—that books contain a variety of subjects and their aspects—are aggravated beyond the point where they may be ignored. Simple hierarchical systems suitable for marking and parking material on shelves will soon outgrow both their usefulness and their viability. General subject groupings, with simple synthesis and an even simpler mnemonic synthetic notation may be the last overt manifestation of the shelf classification. Nevertheless, it would be a mistake to see those shelf classifications only as listing mechanisms; their makers described them explicitly also as a means of naming and locating subjects, and tracing relationships among subjects.

Browsing in the future may be easier and more efficient in printed catalogs, or with a computer terminal display, using indexing systems based on our better understanding of the real nature of classification. The world of information has its own dimensions of space and time: we generate knowledge in the vertical hierarchies of accepted disciplines, but we use it in horizontal assemblies of relevant fact and method; we receive knowledge in known patterns from the past, but we must use it always to answer as yet unidentified questions in the future. In such a world, the heritage of systematic classification may be the best way we can rely on to trace our steps in *terra incognita.*

REFERENCES

1. Eliot, T. S. "Little Gidding." In *Four Quartets.* New York, Harcourt, Brace and Co., 1943, p. 39.

2. Bliss, Henry E. *The Organisation of Knowledge and the System of the Sciences.* New York, H. Holt and Co., 1929; _____. *The Organisation of Knowledge in Libraries and the Subject-approach to Books.* New York, H. W. Wilson, 1933; _____. *A Bibliographic Classification.* 4 vols. New York, H. W. Wilson, 1940-1953.

JOHN P. COMAROMI
Associate Professor
School of Librarianship
Western Michigan University
Kalamazoo, Michigan

The Historical Development
of The Dewey Decimal
Classification System

Melvil Dewey was born on December 10, 1851—on the tenth day of the tenth month.* To this fact I attribute the reason why Dewey conceived his idea of using Arabic numerals decimally to mark the subjects of books. I call this, happily, the "birthday theory." At this early hour you may not embrace this theory. Perhaps you will find more to your liking the "digital-clock-on-the-bar theory." Parched by a long prayer meeting, Dewey repaired to a local tavern to restore his depleted spirits. While staring over his beer at the digital clock on the bar, he conceived his decimal plan. Fortunately, he had stared at the clock after one o'clock, but before ten, and when the hour did not change. This theory has two known flaws: Dewey did not drink, and digital clocks were not then found on bars—or anywhere. I sense your reluctance to embrace this theory as well. Nevertheless, there are only two or three views regarding Dewey's conception that are better than the "birthday theory" or the "digital-clock-on-the-bar theory." None has been proposed that is worse, however, so I withdraw both.

---

*Roman calendar, of course.

Before proposing what I think actually happened, let me first set the historical situation and then review several other possible sources of Dewey's idea. In the early 1870s Dewey was casting about for a career. After rejecting several possible ones, he settled upon librarianship. He had faith that libraries would become vitally important to the education of many Americans. He suspected, however, that since libraries were not central to the process of organized education, they would not receive a large share of the educational budget. He knew that the best ways in which to husband the resources available were through standardization and centralization. Then, in a survey that he made of libraries in the Northeast, it became apparent to him that the common method of shelf arrangement—the fixed system in which a book was assigned a number which fixed it in space—was uneconomical. In other words, in cataloging a work, each library assigned a locational number particular to that library and subject to change when the library grew out of its original place; of course, the same work was cataloged many, many times. To prevent such unwise use of time and money, Dewey conceived his plan wherein the subject of a book, which does not change, would be indicated by arabic numerals used decimally, to the third digit if necessary, assuring easy expansion of any subject and enabling a book to be located relative to the rest of the collection. Its position was not absolute. Thus, renumbering an item would not be necessary when the library grew beyond its physical limits. Each digit at the "ones" level represented a class; each digit at the "tens" level represented a subclass; and each digit at the "hundreds" level represented a further level of subdivision.

It may appear that Dewey devised his scheme, or invented the decimal plan, to facilitate and economize shelf arrangement—not quite so. What he actually did was to devise a method for a subject catalog, and the books of the library stood on the shelves in the same order as they were found in the subject catalog. His scheme had this dual purpose from the beginning. The dual purpose, in fact, helps to explain the split personality that Dewey Decimal Classification (DDC) users have had to live with for nearly a century. DDC has attempted to provide currency and detail for the classified catalog, and at the same time has attempted to provide stability and short numbers for shelf arrangement.

Where did Dewey get his idea? Several proposals have been made. The first that I wish to discuss has been made by John Maass.[1] While Maass was putting the final touches to his work on the Centennial Exhibition held in Philadelphia in 1876, semi-serendipity intervened. He noticed a similarity between Dewey's notation and that of the decimal notation used to arrange the exhibits at the Centennial Exhibition, learned that the system used at the exhibition was proposed before Dewey conceived his idea, suggested that Dewey saw the proposal, and contends that Dewey was inspired by what he saw to conceive his decimal plan. This is possible, but not probable. The notation of the system used at the exhibition, devised by William Phipps Blake—a man of many parts—had Roman numerals I through X for the departments (classes), within each of which were ten subdivisions numbered 1-10, 11-20, etc. Each of these in turn had 100 subdivisions numbered 1-100, 101-200, etc. It was most certainly a decimal system, but its notation was not the sort that Dewey used, nor used in the manner to which we have become accustomed; that is, a string of arabic numerals beyond a decimal point. Note that in Blake's system the final class could have had the number X 100 1000. (It could also have had just 1000.) Now since 1000 could belong only to 100, and 100 only to 10 and 10 only to X, the notation was both hierarchical and expressive of the content of a class. I do not see, however, how Dewey, whose final class mark was 999, could have been led by Blake's notation to make the mental leap to decimal subdivision by nines, the zero being the general number. And it is the uniform subdivision by nine that makes Dewey's notation the elegant conception that it was: hierarchically expressive, universally understood, and short—at any rate, shorter than X 100 1000. Consequently, I think that Blake's notation was an unlikely link in Dewey's chain of thought, even if Dewey had seen Blake's proposal, which is putative.

The second possible source was the one indicated by Dewey himself in the preface to the first edition of DDC. In it he stated:

> In his varied reading, correspondence, and conversation on the subject, the author has doubtless received suggestions and gained ideas which it is now impossible for him to acknowledge. Perhaps the most fruitful source of ideas was the *Nuovo Sistema di Catalogo Bibliografico Generale* of Natale Battezzati, of Milan. Certainly he is indebted to this system adopted by the Italian publishers in 1871, though he has copied nothing from it. The plan of the St. Louis Public School Library and that of the Apprentices' Library of New York, which in some respects resemble his own, were not seen till all the essential features were decided upon, though not given to the public. In filling the nine classes of the scheme the inverted Baconian arrangement of the St. Louis Library has been followed.[2]

And perhaps the most fruitful source was not Battezzati's scheme, whether it was adopted by the Italian publishers in 1871 or not.[3] I suspect that Battezzati's contribution regarding the DDC was to play the role of a red herring. Nothing in his *Nuovo Sistema,* or in what the Italian publishers adopted, could have provided even one mental molecule in the chain of Dewey's thought. What Battezzati urged upon his fellow booksellers was a system wherein several catalog cards would accompany a new work, these to be used for various bookseller catalogs—a sort of *Books in Print* on cards. The cards for the subject catalog would be color-coded: white for religion, yellow for law, green for the sciences and arts, red for belles-lettres, and blue for history. The structure of the classification that Battezzati used was pure Brunet, the notation a mixture of Roman and arabic numerals and lowercase letters. For instance, V lla indicated *history–bibliography;* IV 6a indicated *belles-lettres–philology.* Battezzati's suggestion was actually a step in the process that has advanced as far as our current Cataloging-In-Publication. What Dewey was indebted to Battezzati for was the idea of title-slips, slips of paper possessing catalog copy for the work in hand and to be found with the book when it arrived at a library. He was not indebted to Battezzati for any aspect of the DDC.

If there were an identifiable outside source or sources of Dewey's idea (indeed, he could have done it solo) I believe it to have been in either or both of the men referred to after Battezzati in the above acknowledgment: William Torrey Harris of the St. Louis Public School Library and Jacob Schwartz of the Apprentices' Library of New York. From Harris, Dewey drew the structure of the DDC—more on this matter later. As Harris employed arabic numerals 1-100 to mark his classes and major subclasses, Dewey may have drawn his decimal idea from him. That is doubtful, however, for *history* was 79, and *British history* 93. What Dewey did not see in Harris's notation was the use of arabic numerals to subdivide a subject by nine. This, however, he did see in Schwartz's *Catalogue of the New York Apprentices' Library.* Schwartz had used capital letters for his classes and 0-9 for the subdivisions of each, 0 being used for the general number of each class, 1-9 for subdivisions.

I suggest that Dewey saw Schwartz's catalog before he conceived his own decimal idea, probably during his survey of library practice or during his perusal of library catalogs. Dewey said that he had not seen Schwartz's work, as indicated in the above quotation. Schwartz did not believe Dewey, and a decade later attacked him unmercifully for this very reason. I have been told that Harris, or his relatives, did not believe Dewey either, but I have not seen hard proof of this. Nevertheless, I am inclined toward disbelief.

These, then, are three proposals regarding the source of Dewey's idea. Until his secret diary is found and translated, we will each have to choose the proposal most congenial to our several natures.

On May 8, 1873, Dewey submitted his plan to the Library Committee of Amherst College, and it was accepted. Dewey was to produce 200 catalogs arranged by his system for use by the students and faculty of the college, the first fifty being for editorial proof. Having a notation and a means of subdivision, but no system, Dewey then cast about for one. He did not have to look far; he already had in mind the system he wanted to use. On the day after his plan was accepted, he wrote Harris for a copy of the catalog of the St. Louis Public School Library, a description of which Dewey had seen in

Harris's article in *Journal of Speculative Philosophy,*[4] and the structure of which he eventually used for the DDC.

For longer than they should have, scholars reported that Harris merely inverted the Baconian triad of history, poesy, and philosophy—which Bacon had considered the three departments of learning that had developed from the three faculties of man's mind, namely memory, imagination, and reason—and then expanded his scheme upon the resulting structure. That is an accurate statement of the sequence of events, but it does not explain why Harris did what he did. In the introduction to his catalog, Harris wrote that Bacon was on to a good thing, but not for the reasons given by Bacon. To Harris, the three categories did not represent departments of learning at all, but rather they represented the three forms that literature can take upon a subject. (You might prefer the term *mode* instead of *form.*) Harris then analyzed the three modes, or forms, into classes which were for the most part fields of study. The classes and subclasses were assigned arabic numerals through 100 apparently on the basis of literary warrant and without regard for hierarchical expression: 79 for *history,* 93 for *British history.* The overall order of his scheme reflected Harris's Hegelian definition of the world as seen through man's eyes. As this view provides the skeleton of Dewey's scheme, let me summarize it. First there are the three modes of dealing with a subject: the scientific, in which conscious system prevails; the artistic, in which unconscious system prevails; and the historical, in which system, if any can be said to exist, results from a concatenation of time and place. Within these three modes the contents of books—their subject-matter—determine the structure of the classification. The three modes unfold in the following way to produce the total Hegelian view.[5]

Science unfolds into philosophy, the source of system for all other fields and the most general field of study. Theology, the science of the absolute, and the ultimate field of study of philosophy, comes next. (Religion, which is not scientific but is tributary to theology, is included in theology.) As man achieves his most spiritual role within his society and in relation to the state, the social and political sciences are logically the next fields of study. The political sciences are jurisprudence (in which society puts constraints upon the individual), and politics (in which the individual reacts against the constraints of law, thereby producing perhaps an instance for an alteration of the practical will). The social sciences are political economy (whereby in combination man gains ascendancy over nature and uses it for his ends), and education (by which man is initiated into the society's *modus operandi*). Placed at the end of the social and political sciences is philology since it is the result of self-conscious thought, a society's best record of itself, and the connecting link between the spiritual and the natural.

The natural sciences now follow, and these are followed by the useful arts. The first unfold the laws of nature; the next apply them to social uses. The point of transition between the two fields is medicine—part science, part art, and all expensive. This brings to an end the subjects whose major mode of treatment is the scientific.

The second major mode is the artistic. Art unfolds into the fine arts: architecture, sculpture, drawing and painting, engraving, lithography, photography, collections of pictures, and music. These are followed by poetry, prose fiction, and the last of the artistic forms, literary miscellany. Although this ends the subjects whose major mode of treatment is the artistic, the number of works actually are neither few nor brief.

The final mode is the historical—history. History is comprised of geography and travels, civil history, and biography and correspondence. Heraldry and genealogy fall here. Harris did append to his catalog a class for works which treated subjects falling in several classes. Within this Appendix, which is what he called it, Harris placed collections, cyclopedias, and periodicals—several of the items that fell in Dewey's own generalia class. You no doubt can perceive the structure of the DDC falling within Harris's world view, and hence we see the apparently strange position of language and the reason for the distance between the social sciences and history, the 300s and the 900s. I suspect that the philosophical underpinning of the DDC has contributed considerably to its success. I suspect also that no private detective can be hired to confirm my suspicion.

Comprised of a preface of eight pages, tables of twelve pages, and an index of eighteen pages, the first edition of DDC appeared in 1876. Dewey set the number of copies at 1,000—a far cry from the 200 that he had been allowed to produce. The figure is, I think, not inaccurate. Dewey had run an extra "edition" beyond what he had been allowed, and it was published by Ginn and Heath. There were standard subdivisions at the general numbers for the classes. "Divide like" was used for geographical subdivisions, although the process itself was not yet called that. The index was called the "Subject Index" and indexed terms in the tables and often subjects outside the tables. For instance, North Carolina appeared in the index, although not in the tables. Even though it was not called "relative," the index was already behaving in that manner—and that was to add to the success of the DDC. For instance, one found *moths* at 595 and 646; *maternity* at 136 and 618; *tobacco* at 615, 178, and 633—yet not one of these terms appeared anywhere in the tables. Dewey said of the index in his preface: "Most names of countries, towns, animals, plants, minerals, diseases, &c., have been omitted, the aim being to furnish an Index of Subjects on which books are written, and not a Gazetteer or a Dictionary of all the nouns in the language."[6] From that day on the index was on a collision course to that distant time when it would no longer be possible to provide an "Index of Subjects on which books are written" because there would be too many subjects.

In addition to the DDC's intellectual cohesion, simple notation, stability, and helpful index, there were events and conditions that contributed substantially to its success in the next decade: (1) it was elaborately described in the U.S. Bureau of Education's *Public Libraries in the United States of America*[7] and discussed at the 1876 Philadelphia Conference of Librarians; (2) it was one of the few systems available to the public and was the only one advertised in the *Library Journal;* (3) as one of the editors of the *Library Journal* (and because of his increasingly important position in American librarianship), Dewey was able to further the progress of the DDC—for instance, marking DDC numbers on the title-slips mentioned above; and (4) lastly, although not the least of all the reasons, Dewey had the opportunity to expand the DDC.

During the years preceding the publication of the second edition, Dewey developed his scheme first at Wellesley and then at Columbia College with the assistance of Walter Stanley Biscoe and other scholars. (I must say a few words about Biscoe: he was Dewey's henchman from their days at Amherst until Dewey's death in 1931, and he was the theoretician of the DDC for most of this period. Many important classificatory decisions were made by him.) The second edition appeared in 1885. Its introduction was much fuller, having expanded from eight to twenty-four pages, with approximately thirty additional pages of explanations. There were a great many relocations and much reusing of numbers. To prevent the suspicion that succeeding editions would contain equally unsettling amounts of change, Dewey wrote: "Librarians making the necessary changes for the revised edition need not fear that a series of editions have begun each of which will call for such changes."[8] He kept his word. Although there would be great expansion upon the numbers of the second edition in the years ahead, there would be very few changes that would result in changed meanings of numbers. This policy is called integrity of numbers or stability of numbers. It was to be the guiding principle of the DDC for three-quarters of a century.

In the second edition—I will not catalog the changes of subsequent editions—standard subdivisions, then called form divisions, were applied to subdivisions of classes. "Divide like" had become a standard procedure and part of the classifier's language. *The Relativ Index* was named this for the first time, and so spelled—no final "e." Simplified spelling began in this edition. It was to grow steadily worse as subsequent editors increased its use in the mistaken assumption that it was what Dewey desired. In fact, Dewey did desire it, but he also desired international use of the DDC, and the increasingly atrocious simplified spelling was a decided impediment to this goal. Notes were many and useful. The decimal point appeared. It had not been used in the first edition. (A period had been used above the base line to indicate that the next digit indicated either size or accession number within that class or both. For instance, 973.4.18 would represent the eighteenth work on the quarto shelf for American History. It seems that Joseph Larned of the Young Men's Association Library of Buffalo was the person responsible for the convention of the decimal after the third digit.) There were now geographical and period subdivisions. There were tables at the end of the volume: one listed subjects divided geographically, one was a list of numbers of the various languages, and the last was a list of the subject divisions of languages. Here was the first auxiliary table, although it was not so called. The index had grown from 2,000 to 10,000 entries. Topics subdivided in the tables were in bold type. Dewey wrote of the index, "This Subject Index is the most important feature of the system."[9] He may even have believed that. Certainly, though, librarians inexpert in a field could place a book reasonably well with the assistance of the index. It was a godsend to the librarian who did not know everything.

The second edition was to the first as the chicken is to the egg. The egg is indispensable and holds the promise of a chicken. The first edition was promising; the second edition was the promise fulfilled. I do not think I overstate the case when I say that the second edition of the DDC was the premier achievement in the development of American library classification.

During the years of development of the DDC up until 1951—the date of publication of the fifteenth edition—there was a steady acceptance of the DDC at home and abroad. By *development* I mean only that the DDC expanded upon its second edition structure. There was little structural change; it simply grew. New editions came when old ones had been sold or when there was enough new material to justify bringing out a new edition. During the period of growth, certain events took place and certain people became involved; both were important to the development of the DDC and I wish now to turn to a discussion of them.

To begin, in the late 1880s May Seymour became editor of the DDC. Dewey and W.S. Biscoe had been responsible for editing it through the first three editions. During Seymour's editorship, from the late 1880s through 1921 (the fourth through the eleventh editions) the DDC doubled in size. From 1921 through 1938, during the editorship of her understudy Dorkas Fellows, (the twelfth through the fourteenth editions) the DDC again doubled in size. I mention the growth in size because I wish to call attention to the achievement in classification of these two relatively unsung women. Still, as formidable as their achievement was in classification, each also found time to accomplish major undertakings. Seymour was Dewey's right-hand woman for more than three decades, and was the major figure in the first ALA list of books for libraries; Fellows compiled one of the best sets of cataloging rules.

At Lake Placid Club, where for many years the editorial work was done, Seymour was known as the "specialist in omniscience," Fellows as the "walking encyclopedia"—both were fitting characterizations.

In 1896 growth of an international branch from the main trunk of the DDC began. At that time Paul Otlet conceived a plan to compile a universal bibliography to be arranged by a decimal system, preferably a somewhat modified DDC. He asked for and gained Dewey's permission to translate the DDC into French, making a few changes in religion, the social sciences, and technology. This was the beginning of an occasionally fruitful but usually frustrating relationship between the DDC and the family of decimal classifications fathered by Dewey but adopted and fostered by Otlet. The major members of the family have been the *Classification décimale* and the *Universal Decimal Classification* (UDC), an English translation of the French translation. The UDC is discussed elsewhere in this volume. Nevertheless, I do want to point out here that the French and American editions had drifted apart on the meaning of some numbers and that Seymour and Fellows were directed to reach concordance between the editions through the third digit. They never quite achieved this, but a good many small yet useful modifications in the DDC took place because of the attempt to reach concordance.

At about the same time as Otlet began his work, an important event did not take place. In 1899 Charles Martel of the Library of Congress (LC) approached Dewey and asked whether the DDC could be revised within a year so that it could be used as the classification scheme for the Library of Congress. The necessary revision included updating the sciences and technology classes, moving the social sciences nearer to history, and moving language nearer to literature. (J.C.M. Hanson, then head of the catalog department of LC, had just come from the University of Wisconsin where Cutter's *Expansive Classification* was used, and he wanted a classification the structure of which was much like Cutter's.) Dewey's promise of little change in the meaning of numbers that he had made in the second edition, his agreement to the French translation of the DDC and, more importantly, Martel's demand of great change in too short a period—one year—made the suggestion unacceptable to Dewey. I think that Hanson and Martel forced Dewey to refuse.

In memory of May Seymour, who had died in 1921, and as he himself was nearing the end of his life, Dewey signed all copyrights of the DDC in 1924 over to the Lake Placid Club Education Foundation, fully expecting the foundation to continue publishing the DDC. In 1933 Forest Press was incorporated, its primary role being to see that the DDC was published. The foundation also set up an internal committee to oversee development. Until his death in 1931, Dewey dominated anything connected with the DDC. After his death his second wife, Emily, was in charge of the committee, but she was clearly incapable of dealing with classification matters, and Dorkas Fellows determined the course of the DDC through her. It was at this time that the American Library Association again attempted to formalize an arrangement whereby librarians could have some input into the development and continuation of the DDC. The ALA quite simply wanted to see to it that the interests of the profession were made known to the foundation. (I say "again" for there had been during World War I an ALA committee called the Decimal Classification Advisory Committee, whose job it was to see that the interests of the profession were met. There were excellent people on the advisory committee, such as Clement Andrews of the John Crerar Library and Dorkas Fellows, to name only two. The advisory committee eventually ceased to function primarily because it was not making much of an impact on the DDC's course of development.)

The new committee's name made a three-line entry on a catalog card: American Library Association Committee on Cooperation with the Lake Placid Club Education Foundation Committee on the Decimal Classification. This committee was soon replaced by the Decimal Classification Committee, which was comprised of three members each from ALA and from the foundation, and was chaired by Milton Ferguson, director of the Brooklyn Public Library and a former president of ALA. The committee's purpose was to oversee the development of the DDC, and in one form or another it has done so to the present day. It is now called the Decimal Classification Editorial Policy Committee.

In 1938 Dorkas Fellows died, but not before she had done much of the work of expanding the fourteenth edition. Replacing her was Constantin Mazney, a cataloger from the University of Michigan. Myron Getchell, the man who was Fellows's choice to replace her and who had fully expected to gain the position, remained on in a subordinate capacity in order that the "apostolic succession"—the experiential link to the past—not be broken. Mazney and Getchell finished the work on the fourteenth edition, which was published in 1942 and was nearly 2,000 pages long. For the most part it was a giant second edition. Many still consider it the best edition ever. Just after it was published, Mazney was fired for a variety of reasons—mainly inefficiency. Getchell, considered by those who appointed the editor to be timid and ineffectual, was passed over for a second time. He then resigned, and "apostolic succession" was broken. There was no longer anyone at the editorial level who knew the old ways, or the reasons for them.

During most of the 1930s and 1940s there was an unremitting but fruitless search for an editor: Fellows had come to the end of her career; Mazney had proven incapable; and Getchell was unacceptable. The major reason why someone could not be found was that the foundation was unwilling to pay a wage commensurate with the talent and education requisite for a successful editorship. What then transpired has led to an unhappy period for library classification.

In the late 1920s, Dewey, his son Godfrey, and Dorkas Fellows had concluded that there should be three editions, or three levels, in the DDC family: (1) a bibliographic edition to handle documentation, (2) a library edition for shelf arrangement of libraries of medium size (or larger if the bibliographic edition was not used for this purpose in the larger libraries), and (3) an abridged edition for the smaller libraries and for library schools. Ten years later the Decimal Classification Committee decided that the fifteenth edition would be the library edition defined above, and by osmosis it came to be called the "standard edition." It was to have all of its classes expanded and then cut back to four, or five, or six digits, whatever was appropriate for a given class for numbering books for shelf arrangement 'for libraries of a medium size. The main reason for the tremendous expansion in the fourteenth edition was that it was the first step in preparing for the library, or standard, edition.

Although no one could be found for the editorship, someone now had to be found to ensure that the editorial office made progress toward the fifteenth edition. What appeared then to be an appropriate course of action was taken: a director of the editorial office was appointed—Esther Potter of the Brooklyn Public Library (a close friend of Milton Ferguson, chairman of the Decimal Classification Committee). Her experience was not in classification, and consequently it was not believed that she had the ability to be editor, although she was given the charge to find one if she could. She was also given the charge to find out what librarians desired in the way of a "standard edition," the official view, given above, already being known. This she set out to do and many dollars later concluded that librarians wanted an up-to-date scheme with short numbers. (Note that this was not what the original library edition was to have been—short numbers, yes, but on the old structure.) She attempted to provide this but proved incapable of doing so. Then, in order to bring the fifteenth edition out as soon as possible—Potter's travels and the editorial staff's work having consumed the available funds—Milton Ferguson was sent to Washington to finish the edition. He did so—and finished just about everything else in the process.

The fifteenth edition appeared in 1951 and was an almost unmitigated disaster. It was not the edition it was intended to be. The libraries for which it was intended could not use it—in fact, two-thirds of all users could not use it alone, and recourse to an earlier edition was necessary. Although it was 700 pages in length, it was actually only one-tenth to one-fifth the conceptual size of the fourteenth edition; that is, it had only one-tenth to one-fifth as many entries. Ferguson had literally eviscerated the DDC. It was far too abbreviated;

there was no provision for building numbers; the meanings of many heavily used numbers had been changed. The index had been compiled by someone from another part of the government, and did not work well—which would have been the case no matter who had made it, for the tables had been denuded of up to 90 percent of their contents. A revised fifteenth edition was hurried into print, but about all it managed to do was use up a good deal of what little money and goodwill were left.

Did anything good come out of it? Yes: the atrocious simplified spelling had been almost shed; the format was elegant for the first time; a great deal of deadwood had been eliminated; and a few areas, such as sociology, had been improved. But this little good did not begin to compensate for the great evil done. The worst effect was that Forest Press could not finance the sixteenth edition, although I admit that defections to the Library of Congress Classification and a loss of belief in the usefulness of the DDC for shelf arrangement may have been the worst effects.

At this crucial point in the history of the DDC the Library of Congress was approached through the American Library Association in the hopes that the library would assist in financing the next edition, for without substantial assistance the DDC would founder long before the sixteenth edition could be prepared. The library agreed to help. The arrangement to produce the sixteenth edition, in which costs were shared by LC and Forest Press, began in January 1954. In the bargain that was made, the library gained the power to appoint the editor. Its first appointee to the editorship was David Haykin, the first person to direct the assigning of DDC numbers to LC cards and a subject heading specialist at LC.

At this time another ALA committee, the Special Advisory Committee on the Decimal Classification, was formed to assist the editor and the Editorial Policy Committee in producing the sixteenth edition. It was actually constituted at the request of Godfrey Dewey, who was a member of the governing board of the Lake Placid Club Education Foundation and who thought that the editor and the Editorial Policy Committee could use all the expertise that could be marshaled. Unsaid was his desire to see that another fifteenth edition did not occur.

At all times a majority of the advisory committee's members was of the integrity-of-numbers camp. This group desired a return to the line of development of the first fourteen editions and a return to the meanings of the numbers of the fourteenth edition, from which the fifteenth edition had often strayed. On the other hand, David Haykin was of the keeping-pace-with-knowledge camp. Members of this group, which included most of his staff and a minority of the advisory committee, desired to have the structure of the DDC reflect the current view of knowledge. Whereas the conservative integrity-of-numbers camp would have new subjects placed in the old structure, the progressive keeping-pace-with-knowledge camp would redo the old structure and provide one better fit to accommodate new and old subjects. Haykin assumed that the progressive steps taken in the fifteenth edition were to continue. The advisory committee assumed that the line of the first fourteen editions was to continue in the sixteenth. If the advisory committee were taken seriously—most of them are not—a showdown between Haykin and the committee was inevitable. The stature of the committee's appointees and, more importantly, the sheer force of its chairman Janet Dickson gave its opinions the weight necessary for an honest hearing. Its opinion was that Haykin was changing too much and he had to stop. The showdown occurred in 1956.

When the smoke cleared, Haykin had resigned to return to another post in the Library of Congress. Thus, it was assured that the sixteenth edition would be primarily a return to the line of development of the first fourteen editions. To replace Haykin, LC appointed Benjamin Custer, head of technical services of the Detroit Public Library, who had demonstrated the requisite general ability and who possessed a conciliatory ability in the degree necessary to bring the sixteenth edition to a successful conclusion and all concerned to a smiling state. This he and Julia Pressey, head of the section that assigned DDC numbers to LC cards, did supremely well.

The sixteenth edition was published in 1958 and it vies with the fourteenth in being generally successful and widely respected. It was, in fact, a phenomenal success and much nearer to the idea of the library, or standard, edition discussed earlier. Although physically larger than the fourteenth edition, it had about one-half the number of entries. It was attractive, easy to use and, as Frances Hinton, the current chairman of the Editorial Policy Committee, said of it, it fit like an old slipper. Furthermore, the fifteenth edition had been no competition, the fourteenth was no longer available, and librarianship was riding an ascending spoke of the wheel of fortune. Custer did manage to insert a good deal of new material in the sixteenth edition, and he did some restructuring as well in *chemistry* at 546 and 547, the sort of thing that had not been allowed in the first fourteen editions. The sixteenth had more of the past in it than it did the present, but I think we should look upon it as the last of the old DDC line and the first of the new modern line. At the time, of course, it was perceived as being a return to what was known and accepted, which indeed it was—in part. The view of the conservative librarian—when it is not necessary to change, it is necessary not to change—had prevailed, and such librarians were happy that the various subjects of their collections were not dispersed by a new view of knowledge.

Since the following paper will deal with the seventeenth and eighteenth editions, I do not wish to proceed much further. I am constrained, however, to add two more paragraphs which belong to the thread of this discussion.

By the time the seventeenth edition was published in 1965, a stunning reversal of fundamental policy had taken place. No longer was integrity of numbers the guiding principle; keeping pace with knowledge was. Custer was by nature a progressive as far as classification was concerned. It would have been folly, however, for him to do anything other than what he was instructed to do for the sixteenth edition—that is, to return to the line of the first fourteen editions. The success of the sixteenth edition, on the other hand, added the dimension of success to his stature, and he was able to convince the Editorial Policy Committee that the future is longer than the past and that the DDC's structure should change when reason sees the need for change. This policy has continued to the present; the phoenix schedules and the new index are results of it.

The seventeenth edition was not, predictably, a successful edition. There had been too much change, and librarians who had applauded the sixteenth edition were bitterly disappointed. The idea of classifying by discipline, in which a subject is classed in the discipline in which it is used for study, caused no little difficulty in classfying. The new index, a radical departure from previous practice, received a hostile reception. The index was like a pair of magic shoes that carried the classifier much farther than a normal pair of shoes, but which pinched every step of the way. It proved so unacceptable, in fact, that at great cost to Forest Press, a revised index modeled on the old lines was prepared and distributed free to purchasers of the original index. In fairness it should be said that the original index did not have the time spent on it that it should have had, and that the index to the eighteenth edition is a better example of what the new index can do. On the credit side were many good internal improvements, the development of auxiliary tables, and the continued, now more obvious, movement toward making the DDC a modern library classification—which it is now becoming, to *most* people's satisfaction.

REFERENCES

1. Maass, John. "Who Invented Dewey's Classification?" *Wilson Library Bulletin* 47:335-42, Dec. 1972.

2. Dewey, Melvil. *Classification and Subject Index for Cataloguing and Arranging the Books and Pamphlets of a Library*. Amherst, Mass., Case, Lockwood and Brainard Co., 1876, p. 10.

3. The discussion in the following two paragraphs owes much to ideas suggested to the author by John Metcalfe and to Enzo Bottasso's "Genesi e Intenti della Classificazione Decimale," in *La Biblioteca Pubblica*. Torino, Italy, Associazione Piemontese dei Bibliotecari, 1973, pp. 177-207.

4. Harris, William T. "Book Classification," *Journal of Speculative Philosophy* 4(2):114-29, 1870.

5. Leidecker, Kurt. "The Debt of Melvil Dewey to William Torrey Harris," *Library Quarterly* 15:139-42, April 1945; and Graziano, Eugene E. "Hegel's Philosophy as a Basis for the Dewey Classification Schedule," *Libri* 9:45-52, 1959.

6. Dewey, *op. cit.*, p. 6.

7. _____. "Catalogues and Cataloguing; A Decimal Classification and Subject Index." *In* U.S. Bureau of Education. *Public Libraries in the United States of America. Special Report.* Pt. I. Washington, D.C., U.S.G.P.O., 1876, pp. 623-48.

8. _____. *Decimal Classification and Relativ Index for Arranging, Cataloging, and Indexing Public and Private Libraries.* 2d ed. Boston, Library Bureau, 1885, p. 46.

9. *Ibid.*, p. 32.

MARGARET E. COCKSHUTT

Associate Professor
Faculty of Library Science
University of Toronto, Canada

Dewey Today:
An Analysis of Recent Editions

Despite the title of this paper, I do not intend to make a detailed analysis of the subject content of recent editions of the *Dewey Decimal Classification* (DDC). Instead, I shall concentrate on certain classificatory changes within the system, and try to show how these changes seem to spring in part from changes in the editorial development of editions 16-18 of DDC,[1] and in the administrative and editorial frameworks within which the editions appear.

In my own research on classification systems, I have become increasingly fascinated by the ways in which the classification systems themselves are determined, shaped and changed by the people who devise and revise them. As has been said many times, the first fourteen editions followed in a largely unbroken line, with some relocations, but basically with expansions. Then came the abortive fifteenth edition.[2] That this edition was recognized as a disaster became obvious with the appearance of the revised fifteenth edition in the following year.[3] This was followed by the contractual arrangement between the Lake Placid Club Education Foundation (LPCEF) and the Library of Congress (LC) that LC should be responsible for the editorial work on future editions, for the length of the contracts. On January 4, 1954, LC began the editorial work, with David Haykin as editor. Benjamin Custer succeeded him as editor in 1956.

DDC-16 seemed to continue the straight-line pattern of DDC-1-14—but did it really? Lucile Morsch, chairman of the Decimal Classification Editorial

Policy Committee (DCEPC) wrote in the foreword to the edition: "Responsibility for editorial policy rests with the Decimal Classification Editorial Policy Committee, a joint committee of the Lake Placid Club Education Foundation, the American Library Association, and the Library of Congress."[4] While various advisory committees had previously existed, the formal professional responsibility by the editor, an LC staff member, and the advisory function of the DCEPC for editorial policy influenced the intellectual and classificatory changes in DDC-16.

In his introduction, Custer recognized that:

There is no avoiding the fact that, historically, the DC is based upon a Protestant Anglo-Saxon culture. ... Yet the editors have considered that they had a prime responsibility for furnishing a satisfactory and useful classification for the libraries of the United States, and solution to the problem of a classification universally acceptable has not yet been found. In spite of this, the present edition has made a start toward providing more useful expansions of topics in which libraries of cultures other than Protestant, Anglo-Saxon, and Western are likely to excel.[5]

Problems of the lengthy notation were recognized, "particularly in those areas where whole new disciplines of science have sprung up since the original pattern was establisht." In addition, the degree of expansion for all subjects was linked without explicit reference to E. Wyndham Hulme's principle of literary warrant: "the editors ... have been guided by the principle that the existence in American libraries of more than twenty titles which would fall in a given number raises a presumption in favor of subdivision."[6]

The admission that DDC was not a perfect classification system, that it did indeed reveal national, religious and cultural biases, and that it could be revised according to principles introduced an entirely new aspect for editorial policy and evolutionary development. Yet, the old conflicting DDC principles of the "traditional policy of integrity of numbers" and "the philosophy of keeping pace with knowledge"[7] continued, as they continue still.

While facet analysis and faceted classifications were being widely discussed even in North America by 1958, after the founding in 1952 of the Classification Research Group (CRG) in Great Britain, there is little direct evidence of their impact on the DDC-16—yet the seeds are there. They were there, of course, in Melvil Dewey's identification of literature being divided by language, literary form, time period and form division in the 800s; in his organization of the 400 class by language, and then by the linguistic problem. He recognized "facets," although of course he could not anticipate Ranganathan's terminology.

DDC-16 permitted a few new facets in a way which had not been evident in earlier editions, through Dewey's "divide like" mechanism. For example, 616.1-616.998 *specific diseases,* could be divided like 616.07-616.092, largely by what we might now term the "energy" or "action" facet; 331.382-331.3898 *child and youth labor* could be divided by the major industries in 620-698; and the former one-page *form divisions*[8] had burgeoned to five pages.

Why the very word "facet" should be frightening or suspect to American librarians, I do not know. As we have seen, the concept was known to Dewey and was practiced unknowingly by the use of the "divide like" technique by every classifier. A citation order was used which was inherent, for example, in some of the directional notes in the 800 class (e.g., 821.002-.09 *form divisions, and types of poetry,* from which the classifier was directed to a model in 811.002-.09, where he found additional notes). Nevertheless, the same citation order by directional notes was omitted completely in other parts of the 800 class (e.g., 823 *English fiction,* where he found permission for division only by a time period).

By the seventeenth edition, the editor was firmly stating the aims of a classification system and recognizing the existence of other systems, even of the suspect Colon Classification:

> the development of an integrated plan . . . will provide systematically for the tens and hundreds of thousands of subjects on which books are and may be written in this age of multiversity and specialization. . . . It requires the intense efforts of specialists in librarianship, in subject classification, and in the countless disciplines of which the world of knowledge is composed. . . . For this reason, librarians have generally found it advantageous to follow, with local adaptations where necessary to meet local needs, one or another of the commonly used book classification systems, among the best known of which are Bliss's Bibliographic Classification, Ranganathan's Colon Classification, Dewey's Decimal Classification, Cutter's Expansive Classification, the Library of Congress Classification, Brown's Subject Classification, and the Universal Decimal Classification.[9]

Due to the apparent timidity of the editor, the DCEPC or the Forest Press, the dread word *facet* is cautiously and seldom used: "Only the word 'facet' is of recent origin; Dewey understood the concept." Custer stated:

> Division of a given subject in DC by more than one principle, or characteristic, is as old as the first edition. . . . It is true that editions prior to the present one did not always recognize and make provision for division by more than one principle, even when the literature would seem to have warranted it; and when they did make such provision, they did not always clearly differentiate among the various principles.

Examples of Application of Several Facets

BASIC SUBJECT		PRIMARY FACET	
617.1	Wounds and injuries	Add to each subdivision *;	
.14	*Wounds	001-008	Standard subdivisions
.15	Fractures	01-09	General aspects
.16	*Dislocations		Divide like 617.01-617.09

SECONDARY FACET		TERTIARY FACET	
617	Surgery	616.075 Diagnoses	
.01	Complications and sequelae	.0755	Clinical diagnosis
.02	Special texts	.0758	Microscopy in diagnosis
.07	Surgical pathology		
.073	Surgical nursing		
.075	Diagnoses		
	Divide like 616.075		

**Table 1. Classification of "Clinical Diagnosis in the
Surgical Treatment of Wounds."**

Source: Dewey, Melvil. *Dewey Decimal Classification and Relative Index.* 17th ed. rev. Lake
Placid Club, N.Y., Forest Press, 1952, Vol. 2, pp. 679-700.

    To clarify these issues and further to emphasize subject integrity, this edition makes many new provisions for division by more than one principle.[10]

    Probably the most obvious new facet was the Area Table by which the place facet (with *area* broadly defined to include *socioeconomic regions and groups* and *persons*)[11] was detached from the 900 class from which it had previously been derived by "divide like." Less obvious facets occurred, with or without specific editorial mention. One such example, not mentioned by the editor, occurred in the 610s (see Table 1).

    Table 1 shows examples from the schedules to illustrate the various principles or characteristics of division and the resultant problems. It is possible to achieve a precise notation for the complex concept *clinical diagnosis in the surgical treatment of wounds:* 617.160755. The citation order in which the facets are to be combined is clearly stated in the directions at each step. The use of a facet indicator—the retention of the "0"—is clearly indicated in the example, e.g., *emergency surgery* 026, which accompanies the "divide like" instructions for 01-09 General Aspects. The facets are not clear facets; thus, in 617 *complications* and *special texts* jostle coordinately with *surgical pathology,* and the hierarchical relationships are confused in the subordination of *surgical nursing* (a less preferred option) and *diagnoses* to

	Women
331.4	Women
▶	331.42-.43 Specific elements
.42	Wages
.43	Married women
.48	In specific occupations
.481	Service and professional
	Divide like 011-999
.482-.489	Other
	Divide like 620-690

Table 2. Table for 331.4.

Source: Dewey, Melvil., *Dewey Decimal Classification and Relative Index*. 17th ed. Vol. 1.
Lake Placid Club, N.Y., Forest Press, 1965-67, p. 296.

surgical pathology. The action *clinical diagnosis* and the agent *microscopy in diagnosis* are confusing coordinates, subordinate to *diagnoses*. Nevertheless, the seventeenth edition made a valiant effort in regard to facets.

When the same topic is examined in DDC-18, it is apparent that some of the facets have been sorted out, at least by the use of umbrella headings, e.g., 02 *special topics* and 05-09 *other general aspects* in the facet under 617 *surgery and related topics,* but that the confusion under 617.07 *surgical pathology* and under the extension of 616.075 *diagnoses and prognoses* remains.[12]

Another example of a different type, cited by the editor in his discussion of facets, occurred in DDC-17 at 331.3-.6 *special classes of workers.*[13] The special classes were grouped as *specific age groups, women, substandard wage earners,* and *other groups.* The foci or concepts within the primary facets were normally divided by a secondary facet of occupation, by dividing like 620-690 or 001-999 as appropriate. However 331.62 *immigrants* had a secondary geographic facet by the use of the area notations for the place of origin, plus "0" as a facet indicator, plus a tertiary geographic facet using the area notations for the place reached. In contrast, 331.63 *native-born nonindigenous ethnic groups* achieved an ethnic facet by dividing like 420-490, plus the "0" facet indicator, plus a geographic facet using the area notations for the place reached. Within these four groups the citation order for synthesizing the facets was usually clearly stated, and a table of precedence for the groups at the beginning of the section enabled the classifier to avoid cross-classification for a topic such as "youthful convicts who are married women" (see Table 2).

The basic subject group of 331.4 *women,* however, revealed the inability to identify facets which would be relevant to the whole section of 331.3-.6. It should be noted that there was a group for *women* but not for *men,* so that a basic or facet division by sex was not possible. Because the facets and their synthesis had not been seriously considered as a problem, how did the classifier cope with topics like "salaries of married women lawyers"? This problem has been solved in DDC-18 by a directional note which requires the use of 331.43 without synthesis, so that the facts of sex and marital status become the deciding factors, rather than the wages, salaries, professions and occupations.[14] With some justification, some members of the DCEPC hurled charges of a sexist bias at the DDC on April 26, 1974;[15] there was subsequently found to be little evidence of sexism, however, and both the editor and the DCEPC will undoubtedly be watchful in examining the subdivisions and terminology of future draft schedules.

The clear facet groups in 331.3 and 331.5-.6 in DDC-17 made the deficiencies of 331.4 only too clear in their lack of subject and hierarchical integrity, which were the much-vaunted principles of DDC-17. While true facet analysis—the ability to synthesize concepts and notation—and a specified citation order may seem academically remote from the needs of working classifiers, their absence throughout much of the DDC intellectual structure makes the subject anomalies, faulty hierarchies, and resulting cross-classification militate against sound consistent classification for the users' needs in shelf groupings and detailed specific classified catalogs, bibliographies and files designed for information retrieval.

Many examples of facets from the schedules and tables of DDC-17 might be cited. However, another interesting idea advanced by the editor showed the extent of influence on him of the exponents of faceted classification, spearheaded by the Classification Research Group (CRG). In his discussion of the possible use of DDC in detailed classified files, by the full use of the permitted synthesis, the editor discussed the need for the "0" as the facet indicator, and for the avoidance of cross-classification by various precedence formulae and citation orders. He concluded with the advice: "Class the subject by (1) kinds, (2) parts, (3) materials, (4) properties, (5) processes within it, (6) operations upon it, (7) agents."[16] Anyone who is familiar with the work of the CRG will recognize this as a CRG modification and expansion of Ranganathan's famous PMEST facet formula. This is almost an exact quotation from a statement on citation order in the *Universal Decimal Classification* (UDC) by Jack Mills, one of the early and most influential members of the CRG.[17] The wording is expanded and examples are added in DDC-18, but the CRG's citation order continued unchanged.

The CRG and faceted-school infiltrators went virtually unnoticed by U.S. librarians. Among the many reviews of DDC-17 I have examined, two critics directly commented on the new faceted influence; one was a British librarian and one was a Canadian.[18] Other reviewers went on to praise the Area Table, damn the index, approve the attempts to remove the Protestant Anglo-Saxon bias, and essentially deplore the attempt to return to "subject integrity."[19] The objections were not to subject and hierarchical integrity *per se*, but to the relocation of topics by which the integrity must be achieved, and thus to the possible re-use of numbers before the end of the 25-year starvation period which existed at that time. Looking back ten years later on the reviews, I believe that the criticism was not of the principle of subject integrity, nor even of the principle of "keeping pace with knowledge." Rather, it sprang from the hard, pragmatic realization that all the centralized and commercial services, from LC on down, would use the relocations, reassigned numbers and full notational extent of the synthesis resulting from the obvious and hidden facets, and thus that libraries faced devastating problems in their open-stack collections.

The desire by librarians for notations shorter than those provided in the LC bibliographic services, coupled with the inability of unsupervised technicians (and possibly of librarians) to cut the notation at meaningful points in the notational string, led LC in 1967 to record in all the LC bibliographic apparatus, centrally assigned DDC numbers in segments by the use of prime marks. If libraries could not cope with the precise notational synthesis which specialized libraries needed for their information retrieval, the Decimal Classification Division (DCD) of LC had to do the work for them. Within individual libraries, in the battle between economy (in time, and therefore in money) and specific subject analysis and retrieval, economy won.

The facets and their frightening results which had lurked implicitly in DDC-17 were glaringly obvious in DDC-18. One curious anomaly is that the word *facet*, which had appeared so cautiously in the editor's introduction to DDC-17, seemed to disappear completely from the pages of DDC-18. It is not in the preface, the editor's introduction, the glossary, nor in the Index to Preface, Editor's Introduction, and Glossary.[20] However, the number of faceted auxiliary tables increased from two to seven. As a result, completely faceted synthesis was practiced by librarians with apparent ease in applying Table 4, "Subdivisions of Individual Languages," to asterisked topics in 420-499; and it was attempted with considerably more difficulty by the application of the complex Table 3, "Subdivisions of Individual Literatures," to asterisked topics in 810-890.[21]

The faceted auxiliary tables for "Racial, Ethnic, National Groups" (Table 5) and "Persons" (Table 7)[22] were particularly welcomed by librarians. Their use obviated the need for difficult and often inappropriate synthesis by dividing like 420-499, 001-999, or 920.1-928.9, or for the forced acceptance of an imprecise notation because there was no opportunity for synthesis.

These tables have proved so popular that there have been numerous requests to the editor that their use be permitted with any appropriate number in the schedules. Such a synthesis has long been permitted for geographic areas by the use of standard subdivision -09 plus the area number, where the area number may not be added directly. The same kinds of facet indicators are needed for tables 5 and 7, and the editor and the DCEPC struggled for several meetings, between April 26, 1973 and April 26, 1974, to find suitable facet indicators as leads-in with the shortest possible resulting notation. After several unsuccessful attempts, the DCEPC recommended to the Forest Press Committee (FPC) the use of the -088 s.s. for Table 7 and -089 s.s. for Table 5.[23] Screams of anguish over lengthy notation may perhaps be tempered to mild whimpers or even faint expressions of pleasure when the synthesis is desired for one's own local needs.

Other less noticeable facets appeared in the schedules of DDC-18 by combinations of notations from several tables, separated by the "0" facet indicator, as at 301.4511 *aggregates of general, mixt, North American origins;*[24] or from combinations of schedules and tables which might even be derived in multiple stages. For example, consider the precise topic specification, as well as the intellectual gamesmanship of 636.59201-.59208 *turkeys–general principles,* which permits synthesis from 636.01-.08 *animal husbandry–general principles* or of 636.089 *veterinary sciences–veterinary medicine,* which permits additional synthesis from 610-619 *medical sciences– medicine.*[25] Fortunately for the sanity of classifiers and particularly of library school students, the "divide like" instruction gave way to the simple "add to" instruction. With crystal clarity in most cases, the editor's directional note at each stage specifies not only the base number to which the addition is made, but also "the numbers following" from which the succeeding facet notations are derived. Other facets emerged in revised sections of the schedules, as they received routine editorial scrutiny.

It would be possible to continue the search through DDC-18 for facets, indicators, citation orders, and other devices to gladden the mind of the theoretician. It is more important to see where we have come from with Dewey since 1873-76, to see where we are now with DDC-18, published in 1971, and to assess the means by which we have come.

Figure 1 illustrates a theoretical chain of influence. Dewey's first edition was conceived in 1873 and published anonymously in 1876.[26] In 1895, the Institut International de Bibliographie (IIB) adopted DDC-5 (1894) as the basis for its proposed UDC, with Dewey's consent. However, the two systems apparently went separate ways. UDC in its turn was the intellectual inspiration of S. R. Ranganathan, who from 1925 was busily improving on the potentialities of the UDC. After experiments in the University of Madras Library, Ranganathan began to publish his *Colon Classification* in 1933. His

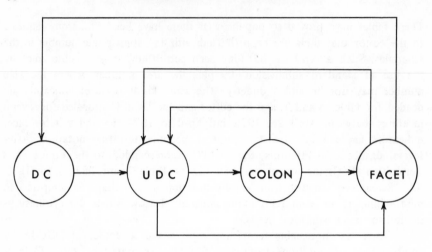

Figure 1. Theoretical Chain of Influence
Source: Cockshutt, Margaret E. "Professional Involvement in the Evolution of the Dewey Decimal Classification" (EPC Exhibit 71-63). Washington, D.C., 1974, p. 4.

sixth edition appeared in 1960, and the seventh is appearing posthumously, in parts, under the aegis of Ranganathan's disciples.

In his six editions, frightening to North American pragmatists in their rapid and continual adoption, rejection, and violent change of concepts, notation and classificatory devices, Ranganathan showed the practical and basic importance of both facet analysis and the identification and listing of the fundamental component parts of each subject. He further demonstrated the subsequent grouping of the parts into facets or groups, with each facet possessing only one common characteristic, and the method of synthesizing concepts from facets by a stated citation order, in order to avoid cross-classification.

The incredible Ranganathan jargon—which appears to be in the English language, but which is really in "Ranganathanese"—was new; the simple conceptual facets were long known to Dewey, at least in the 400 and 800 classes, and through him to the developers of UDC. Undaunted by economic pressures, and without the desire for a constant shelf address for a document. Ranganathan continued his theoretical and applied research, always experimenting and changing. In turn, his theories and devices, such as his "phases" and the formerly named "octave device," circled back to influence the UDC, and moved forward to influence the CRG. Now, somewhat hesitantly in DDC-17 and openly in UDC and DDC-18, the direct impact of the CRG's

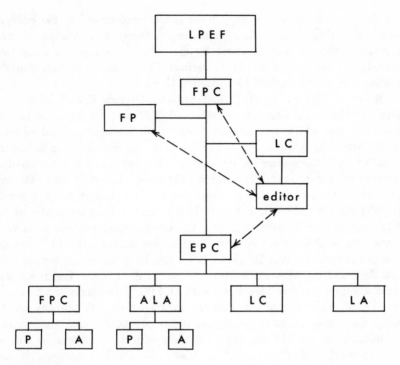

P = Permanent
A = Appointed on nomination
— — — — = formal and informal communication

Figure 2. Tripartite Structure
Source: Cockshutt, Margaret E. "Professional Involvement in the Evolution of
the Dewey Decimal Classification" (EPC Exhibit 71-63). Washington, D.C.,
1974, p. 8.

faceted experiments can be seen. What began as a chain of influence is now a
series of three intersecting loops. The complex present structural control of
the system is illustrated in Figure 2.

How did this happen? Without doubt Melvil Dewey was the dominant
influence on the DDC until his death. By the time DDC-16 appeared, control
of the DDC was in the hands of the LPCEF (now the LPEF) and its nonprofit
subsidiary, the Forest Press, founded by Dewey in 1922 and incorporated in
1933. The LPCEF had signed its contract with LC for the editorial work to
begin in 1954; and beginning with DDC-16 we have the editorial work done
by LC's professional staff, under the editorial supervision of a professional

librarian. Thus, there was a truly professional involvement in the editorial process, and there was a firm basis for professional evaluation of new classification theories and practices by the editor. Practical assessment was increased by the merger of LC's Decimal Classification Section and the editorial office in the Decimal Classification Division.

In 1937 Godfrey Dewey established the Decimal Classification Committee, on which were represented both the LPCEF and the American Library Association, and which was concerned with both management and editorial policies. After the disastrous DDC-15, the ALA also established a short-lived Special Advisory Committee on the Decimal Classification, which consisted of a group of senior and conservative librarians. In 1952 the Decimal Classification Committee was renamed the Decimal Classification Editorial Policy Committee (DCEPC), and in 1955 it became a joint committee of the LPCEF and the ALA, with additional permanent representatives from what are now the ALA's Cataloging and Classification Section, the FPC and LC (while it continues to edit DDC). In 1973, the 1968 agreement between the Forest Press and the ALA was amended to permit the Library Association also to have a voting member appointed to the DCEPC.[27] Gradually the functions of the DCEPC have changed, so that it now advises the FPC directly on the development and editorial implementation of DDC, and makes recommendations to the FPC on matters needing editorial consideration and on the acceptance of draft schedules of which the DCEPC approves. It also advises the editor informally on ideas presented as trial balloons, more serious formal proposals, and various stages of draft schedules.

The present DCEPC is a committee of ten people: three appointed on the nomination of the ALA, three on the nomination of the FPC, one on the nomination of the Library Association, and three permanent members to represent the three official participating organizations. Or we can mix by nationality: one Englishman, one Canadian, eight persons from the United States. Or we can sort by professional contribution: three library school faculty members, three catalogers, four administrators. Or I might venture personally to group by classificatory ideologies: two (sometimes three) theorists, eight (sometimes seven) pragmatists. All are strong-minded, so that the discussion is professional and vigorous.

The DCEPC meetings are also attended by the executive director, editor and assistant editor of the Forest Press (all as nonvoting participants), and recently, on invitation, by the staff of the DCD in rotation as observers.

As I have perceived the meetings since 1970, the various combinations of the DCEPC and others in attendance are healthy and valuable for the development of DDC. It is essential that the DDC be intellectually and structurally sound, and the input of new ideas by the theorists and the editor should ensure that the DDC editorial staff and the DCEPC are aware of current research and trends in classification theory. It is also essential that the DDC be practical in its application and that it fit into current library administrative goals and practices; the catalogers and administrators help to ensure this. The DCD staff should be aware that the proposals are discussed thoughtfully and carefully from all angles, and that the draft schedule criticisms are based on rational arguments rather than on arbitrary whims; the presence of the DCD staff as observers should facilitate this awareness. It is essential that the tripartite bodies are officially informed, through their members and through documents, of the policy recommendations and of the reasons for which they are made.

Why do these growths and changes in the editorial process, administrative development, and professional involvement matter? They matter because the varying needs of users in libraries of all sizes and types must be represented: users who want broad shelf groupings and location addresses, those who want a detailed specific information retrieval system, skilled original-classifiers, technicians working with derived copy, library school students trying to learn the theoretical base and the practical mastery for use in their new profession, and so on.

Contact between "the profession," i.e., the users, and the editor takes place through various formal agreements between the DCD and the *British National Bibliography*, the *Australian National Bibliography*, and *Canadiana*, as well as informally (see Figure 3). There have been various field surveys, questionnaires, draft reviews by subject experts, and official and informal visits by various officials of LPEF, the FPC, the Forest Press, and the editor on this continent and abroad. That DDC is now regarded as a truly international classification, can best be conveyed in the statement now adopted by both the DCEPC and the FPC:

> The Decimal Classification is an American classification, international in standing and application. In preparing an edition it is desirable to allow positively for the needs, both in detail and in order, of countries outside the U.S. Where there is a conflict between these needs and those of the U.S. the editor should give his preference to the needs of the U.S. but must make provision for an alternative use by libraries outside the U.S. in a manner appropriate to the particular problem.[28]

So the editions march on, in English, in French, and in a host of other translations and adaptations. As DDC-18 went to press, plans for DDC-19 began. As Paul Dunkin wrote: "In the making of an edition of Dewey there are many things: emotions, logic, traditions, economics, a Committee—what not?"[29] Or, as Heraclitus wrote about 500 B.C., with a sense both of *déjà vu* and of wonder at something new: "Upon those that step into the same rivers, different and different waters flow down."[30]

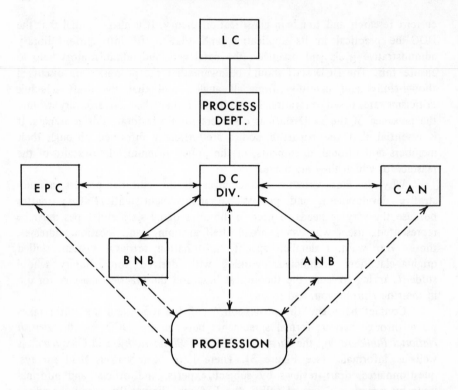

Figure 3. Informal International Involvement (Impressionistic)
Source: Cockshutt, Margaret E. "Professional Involvement in the Evolution of
the Dewey Decimal Classification" (EPC Exhibit 71-63). Washington, D.C.,
1974, p. 13.

REFERENCES

1. Dewey, Melvil. *Dewey Decimal Classification and Relativ Index.* 16th
ed. 2 vols. Lake Placid Club, N.Y., Forest Press, 1958; _____. *Dewey
Decimal Classification and Relative Index.* 17th ed. 2 vols. Lake Placid Club,
N.Y., Forest Press, 1965-67; and _____. *Dewey Decimal Classifi-
cation and Relative Index.* 18th ed. 3 vols. Lake Placid Club, N.Y., Forest
Press, 1971.

2. _____. *Decimal Classification.* 15th ed. Lake Placid Club,
N.Y., Forest Press, 1951.

3. _____. *Dewey Decimal Classification and Relative Index.* 15th
ed. rev. Lake Placid Club, N.Y., Forest Press, 1952.

4. Morsch, Lucile M. "Foreword." *In* Dewey, *Dewey Decimal Classification . . .,*16th ed., *op. cit.,* vol. 1, p. 1.

5. Custer, Benjamin A. "Editors Introduction." *In* Dewey, *Dewey Decimal Classification . . .,* 16th ed., *op. cit.,* vol. 1, pp. 15-16.

6. *Ibid.,* pp. 18-19.

7. Morsch, *op. cit.,* p. 2.

8. Dewey, *Dewey Decimal Classification . . .,* 16th ed., *op. cit.,* vol. 1, pp. 89-93.

9. _____, *Dewey Decimal Classification . . .,* 17th ed., *op. cit.,* vol. 1, p. 6.

10. *Ibid.,* p. 45.

11. *Ibid.,* vol. 2, pp. 1265-66.

12. _____, *Dewey Decimal Classification . . .,* 18th ed., *op. cit.,* vol. 2, pp. 1073-93.

13. _____, *Dewey Decimal Classification . . .,* 17th ed., *op. cit.,* vol. 1, pp. 295-96.

14. _____, *Dewey Decimal Classification . . .,* 18th ed., *op. cit.,* vol. 2, pp. 647.

15. Decimal Classification Editorial Policy Committee. "Minutes of EPC Meeting No. 70, April 25-26, 1974." No. 71-3. Washington, D.C., Editorial Policy Committee, 1974, p. 12.

16. Dewey, *Dewey Decimal Classification . . .,* 17th ed., *op. cit.,* vol. 1, pp. 25-26.

17. British Standards Institution. *Guide to the Universal Decimal Classification (UDC).* London, British Standards Institution, 1963, p. 14. (FID No. 345.)

18. Tait, James A. "Dewey Joins the Jet Age," *Library Review* 20:220-24, Winter 1965; and Cockshutt, Margaret E. "[Review of] *Dewey Decimal Classification and Relative Index,* 17th ed.," *Ontario Library Review* 50:80-82, June 1966.

19. Dewey, *Dewey Decimal Classification . . .,* 17th ed., *op. cit.,* vol. 1, p. 45.

20. _____, *Dewey Decimal Classification . . .,* 18th ed., *op. cit.,* vol. 1, pp. 7-65, *passim.*

21. *Ibid.,* pp. 375-94.

22. *Ibid.,* pp. 398-406, 420-39.

23. Decimal Classification Editorial Policy Committee, "Minutes . . .," *op. cit.,* p. 7.

24. Dewey, *Dewey Decimal Classification . . .,* 18th ed., *op. cit.,* vol. 2, p. 614.

25. *Ibid.,* pp. 1034-1109, *passim.*

26. _____. *A Classification and Subject Index for Cataloguing and Arranging the Books and Pamphlets of a Library.* Amherst, Mass., 1876.

27. Decimal Classification Editorial Policy Committee. "Minutes of Meeting No. 69, November 1-2, 1973." No. 70-3. Washington, D.C., Editorial Policy Committee, 1973, p. 1.

28. Library Association. Dewey Decimal Classification, Sub-committee. "British Recommendation for Policy on International Use" (Editorial Policy Committee Exhibit No. 68-10b). Washington, D.C., Editorial Policy Committee, 1973, p. 3.

29. Dunkin, Paul S. "New Wine in an Old Bottle," *Library Journal* 90:4050, Oct. 1, 1965.

30. "Heraclitus of Ephasus," *Collier's Encyclopedia*. Vol. 12, 1970, p. 55.

MARY ELLEN MICHAEL
Consultant
Forest Press
Lake Placid, New York

Summary of a Survey
of the Use of the
Dewey Decimal Classification
in the United States and Canada

Within the last ten years, three studies have been performed dealing with the use of Dewey Decimal Classification (DDC) outside the North American continent.[1] To date, there has not been a similar survey aimed at assessing the situation in the United States and Canada. In response to this need, Forest Press, publisher of the DDC schedules, has sponsored a survey to measure the use of the DDC by libraries and processing centers in these two countries. This paper highlights some of the findings of this survey. The full report has been published by Forest Press.[2]

There were four major objectives of the survey: (1) to determine the extent of use of the DDC by U.S. and Canadian libraries of different sizes and types, (2) to obtain information about the application of the DDC to library collections, (3) to determine the problem areas in the application of the DDC for collections in these two countries, and (4) to ascertain to what extent the DDC is taught in library schools and what problems are encountered in teaching it.

The survey was divided into three phases to meet the above objectives. First, a questionnaire was mailed to a ten-percent sample of all types of libraries—school, public, junior college, college, university, and system libraries. This questionnaire was also designed for processing centers, both commercial and nonprofit. Secondly, follow-up visits were made to processing centers and large libraries (those holding 500,000 volumes or more) that had responded to the mail questionnaire. More detailed interviews were conducted with the classifiers at these large DDC-oriented libraries concerning their experiences and problems with the scheme. The third phase consisted of another mail questionnaire sent to instructors in cataloging and classification in all accredited and unaccredited library schools in the United States and Canada. The results of this latter questionnaire are not included in this summary, however. Table 1 lists the libraries and processing centers which completed the questionnaire.

The U.S. Postal Service was unable to forward twenty-five of the eighty-four questionnaires to commercial processing centers because they had gone out of business or had no forwarding address. An additional five centers responded that they process books only and do no classifying. Since it was decided to include all larger libraries (500,000 volumes or more) and all commercial processing centers in the survey, the responses of these libraries weight the questionnaire results. Libraries using the Library of Congress Classification (LCC) were eligible to answer several questions.

Table 2 compares type of library to classification scheme used. To give a true picture of the use of DDC and LCC in the United States and Canada, a 10 percent sample is given to reflect the total population. In the survey, all libraries over 500,000 volumes were studied. Table 2 lists a 10 percent sample from this group.

School and public libraries comprise 69 percent of DDC users. Junior colleges and colleges are more evenly divided between the use of the two classification schemes. LCC is used in universities more frequently than is DDC, while DDC is used more heavily in school, public, and library system libraries and processing centers. (Some noncommercial processing centers are also school, public, or academic libraries.)

While Table 2 lists libraries and processing centers that fall in the 10 percent sample, Table 3 details only those libraries of 500,000 volumes or more. As mentioned earlier, all libraries in this size category were sent the questionnaire. Of these 242 libraries, 201 completed the questionnaire. Of the 201 libraries represented in Table 3, 18 are Canadian. Of these eighteen libraries, twelve university libraries use LCC and one library system also uses LCC. All five responding public libraries use DDC.

The majority (63 percent) of larger libraries in both countries use the Library of Congress Classification. Fifty-seven percent of these LCC libraries

	United States		Canada		Total	
	Number	Percentage	Number	Percentage	Number	Percentage
School	135	59.7	91	40.3	226	19.6
Public	473	94.6	27	5.4	500	43.4
Junior college	86	91.5	8	8.5	94	8.2
College	85	97.7	2	2.3	87	7.6
University	158	89.3	19	10.7	177	15.4
Library system	24	85.7	4	14.3	28	2.4
Processing center	33	82.5	7	17.5	40	3.5
Total	994	86.3	158	13.7	1152	100.0

Table 1. Distribution of Respondents by Type of Library.

	LCC Library		DDC Library	
	Number	Percentage	Number	Percentage
School	2	0.2	220	24.6
Public	4	0.4	432	48.4
Junior college	45	5.0	47	5.3
College	44	4.9	35	4.0
University	36	4.0	5	0.5
Library system	1	0.1	22	2.5
Processing center	1	0.1	9	1.0
Total	133	14.7	770	86.7

Table 2. Type of Library Compared to Classification Scheme Used.

	LCC Library		DDC Library	
	Number	Percentage	Number	Percentage
School	–	–	1	0.5
Public	7	3.5	50	24.9
Junior college	–	–	–	–
College	4	2.0	–	–
University	115	57.2	14	7.0
Library system	1	.5	4	2.0
Processing center	–	–	5	2.5
Total	127	63.2	74	36.9

Table 3. U.S. and Canadian Libraries of 500,000 Volumes or More and Classification Scheme Used.

are affiliated with universities. Public libraries in this size category are the heaviest users of the DDC scheme.

Only 4 percent of LCC libraries—as compared with 29.5 percent of DDC libraries—do all or most of their own original classifying (see Table 4). Almost 75 percent of LCC respondents do some original classifying, while approximately 45 percent of DDC libraries fall in the same range; 21.3 percent of LCC libraries and 26.9 percent of DDC libraries do little or no original classifying.

A substantial proportion of those libraries responding that they do all or most original classifying are smaller libraries that often do their own classifying without resorting to available cataloging services, and large libraries using editions of *Dewey Decimal Classification* other than the eighteenth. Although this latter group uses many of the numbers given on LC copy, the large libraries still check all numbers against their various practices. Many respondents construed this as original classifying.

Only libraries which use DDC for their main collection of books were eligible to answer the next section of the questionnaire. When asked what would constitute the optimum interval for publication of DDC editions, most of the respondents preferred that new editions be published every five years. The larger libraries of 500,000 volumes or more preferred a span of seven years between new editions. Large public libraries accepted new editions more readily than did large academic libraries; the costs entailed in this may account for the latters' reluctance to favor frequent editions. Moreover, academic librarians have wanted new editions to aid in classification of new subjects, not for the updated structure of knowledge.

DDC classifiers were asked to indicate their view of the purpose of classification. The greatest number of those answering (356, or 44.1 percent) view classification as educational-efficient, or the process of gathering together those works most used together in a functional grouping. The next largest group (38.2 percent) view classification as primarily subject analysis. Only 9.4 percent of the classifiers think that the main purpose of classification is as a locational device ("mark and park").

The majority (63.6 percent) of those classifiers represented in Table 5 preferred that a classification system maintain stability of numbers, while 31.9 percent thought that a classification system should keep pace with knowledge as reflected in the literature of a subject. Care must be taken here when making inferences. There may have been a false dichotomy posed. It is possible to advocate *both* keeping pace with knowledge and maintaining stability of numbers; new subjects can be located at existing numbers.

Respondents were asked to indicate their attitudes toward a selection of features of the DDC system. The features were pure notation, hierarchical notation, phoenix schedules, continuing revision, stability of numbers, index,

	LCC Library		DDC Library	
	Number	*Percentage*	*Number*	*Percentage*
All original	4	1.6	88	10.8
Most original	6	2.4	152	18.7
Some original	190	74.8	367	45.1
Little original	47	18.5	164	20.1
No original	7	2.8	43	5.3
Total	254	100.0	814	100.0

Table 4. To What Extent Does Your Library Do Original Classifying?

Preference	*Number*	*Percentage*
Keeping pace with knowledge that reflects current trends in the literature of a subject	255	31.9
Stability of number, i.e., finding places within the current structure for new subjects	508	63.6
No opinion	36	4.5
Total	799	100.0

Table 5. Keeping Pace With Knowledge vs. Stability of Numbers.

and mnemonics. The majority of those libraries expressing an opinion had a positive attitude toward the listed aspects. The index of DDC received the highest positive response (62 percent). It should be noted that as the question is worded, this must be interpreted to be an approval of the inclusion of an index with the scheme (as opposed to LCC's lack of a comprehensive index) rather than being a judgment of the quality of that index. As a method of change in the DDC system, continuing revision was looked upon more favorably than were the phoenix schedules.

Related to the question of preference of frequency of new editions are the questions of reclassification and stability of numbers versus keeping pace with knowledge. The most severe form of keeping pace with knowledge would be to redo the entire classification with each new edition. The next most drastic manner is the phoenix schedule. The strictest form of stability of numbers would be to alter nothing, providing locations for new subjects either at old numbers or previously unused numbers. The only change would occur with expansion, and even then there would be little change.

Number of digits to the right of the decimal	Libraries	
	Number	Percentage
one	7	2.2
two	58	18.1
three	175	54.4
four	42	13.1
five	22	6.9
six or more	27	8.4
Total	320	100.0

Table 6. Artificial Limit to Number of Digits to the Right of the Decimal Imposed by DDC Libraries.

Revision of the DDC, which most responding libraries favored implies either of the two fundamentally different courses described above: (1) finding a place for a new subject within the old DDC structure, leaving all existing subjects (whether current or not) where they are; or, (2) tearing down the old structure and providing new places for both existing and new subjects, including reuse by old or new subjects of numbers once having other meanings. While almost all university libraries visited in interviews were somewhat positive about continuing revision, five out of six favored stability of numbers as a preferred course as opposed to the phoenix concept. Large academic libraries desire little change.

Eighty-seven percent of respondents thought that more instructional notes in the schedules would be helpful. Eighty-four percent also favored greater detail in instructional notes. It appears from the data here and elsewhere that a good deal of work needs to be done to make the contents of the schedules more accessible to catalogers. Next to the phoenix schedules and, perhaps, reworking the index, helping the classifier to use the DDC more accurately should be the first priority for the upcoming nineteenth edition. More and better notes of all sorts are needed, especially those that explain alternate locations for material on a particular subject.

Libraries were requested to specify whether they impose an artificial limit on the number of digits to the right of the decimal point of the available DDC number. Such a policy is held by 43.3 percent (353) of the libraries. By size, the groups most commonly imposing an artificial limit are the larger libraries. Of these 353 libraries, 320 specified the artificial limit for number of digits to the right of the decimal (see Table 6). The majority (54.4 percent) of libraries with an artificial limit on number length limit their numbers to three digits to the right of the decimal.

The 48.7 percent (397) of the libraries which do not impose an artificial limit were asked exactly what factors determine how much a number is shortened. A variety of responses were given, the most common being that the length of the number used is determined by the extent of collection development, or foreseeable development, in each particular subject area; 61 percent of the respondents cited this consideration. Logical sense of number and previous practice were cited by 19 percent. In actuality, the classifier might rely on a combination of factors, but the tendency is to express but one facet on the questionnaire. A few librarians stated that the length of the number is determined by the size of the book spine.

Catalogers were asked to what extent they use segmentation of DDC numbers as found on the LC cards, in *Publishers' Weekly,* and through other services. Approximately 70 percent of the responding libraries use the segmentation provided in these services to some extent. Segmentation is valuable to the smaller libraries but much less so for the larger ones, which use it as a guide, but rarely as more than that. More care is apparently needed in determining breaking points, and perhaps guidelines for segmentation should be examined.

Classifiers were asked to indicate, by circling all applicable responses, what methods of treating biography are used in their libraries. The two most widely used ways of dealing with biography are B or 92 (used in 59 percent of the responding libraries), and 920 for collected biography (used by 62 percent of DDC libraries). Classifying biography under subject using standard subdivision -092 is used by 14 percent of the libraries, while 12 percent classify biography under subject without using standard subdivision -092. Evidently, DDC's preferred practice of classifying biography with the subject has not been widely adopted by libraries using DDC. Many libraries marked several choices, indicating that a mixture of several methods of handling biography in a single library is not an uncommon occurrence. The larger libraries indicated several ways of handling biography in the same library. As might be supposed, this is not true of the smaller libraries. The larger libraries have the highest percentages using DDC's preferred practice of classifying biography under subject, while very few of the smaller libraries classify under subject.

Most public service librarians in the larger libraries prefer to classify biography with the subject because it keeps the biographies in their divisions. Branch librarians are an exception to this rule, however. No matter how biographies are kept together, biographies of artists, athletes, musicians, etc., usually go with the subject, often without indication that the work is a biography. Several libraries class biographies by subject, but often do not use -.0924 because of the length of the number. The indication *B* on an LC card is always welcome, but occasionally suspect.

	Yes, class according to the prescribed methods of the 800s		No, depart from prescribed methods of the 800s	
	Number	Percentage	Number	Percentage
School	188	90.4	20	9.6
Public	385	90.0	43	10.0
Junior college	39	86.7	6	13.3
College	34	91.9	3	8.1
University	14	56.0	11	44.0
Library system	21	91.3	2	8.7
Processing center	13	92.9	1	7.1
Total	694	89.0	86	11.0

Table 7. Types of Libraries Which Do or Do Not Class Works of and about Literature According to the Prescribed Methods of the 800s.

Libraries were then asked whether DDC should continue to classify biography with the subject as the preferred method. The majority (56 percent) favored its continuation. (Note that the number favoring the continuation of DDC's preferred method of classing biography is quite a bit higher than the number actually using this method.)

Classifiers were asked whether they class literature according to the prescribed methods of the 800s; 89 percent answered affirmatively. This percentage holds approximately true for all types of libraries except those in universities, where only 56 percent class literature in the 800s—44 percent do not (see Table 7).

Literature and its criticism surely present the greatest difficulty for Dewey libraries of any type. Although most catalogers cut off before the period, thus losing some economy in not accepting LC numbers, their troubles have only begun. A cutter number has to be assigned and criticism indicated, if this assignment is even done. Most processing centers, since they are not providing call numbers for a single collection, do not use cutter numbers. For the most part, the initial of the author's surname or the first three letters of his surname suffice. One-fourth of the larger public libraries also operate in this manner, somewhat to the dissatisfaction of their public service librarians. Both sorts of libraries usually do nothing for fiction in English, other than an *F* or *Fic* or *SS col* for a collection of short stories or *SF* or *M*, etc. The indication of type of fiction is usually put on the book's spine by the branches or departments in public service. More often than not, academic libraries use regular methods for classifying fiction. It is with criticism that most problems for the public are found, for criticism and literature are often mixed indiscriminately or the criticism is put in an unlikely place.

| | Full Edition | | | | | | | Abridged Edition | | | |
	18th	17th	16th	15th rev.	15th	14th	other	10th	9th	8th	other
School	187	7	3	1				29	4		
Public	212	40	25		5	4	5	83	48	26	3
Junior college	36	3	3	1				5	1		
College	30	5	2								
University	20	3	3			1			1		
Library system	19	3	1					4			
Processing center	12							4			
Total	516	61	37	2	5	5	5	125	54	26	3

Table 8. Primary Edition Used by Type of Library.

Respondents were requested to list the primary edition in use in their library or processing center; Table 8 indicates the results. They could list one of the full and one of the abridged editions if they used both as their primary editions; otherwise, only one could be listed. Seventy-six libraries use two primary editions. Some of these libraries reported that they use the full edition for their adult collection and the abridged one for their juvenile holdings.

No colleges reported using any abridged edition of the DDC as their primary one. Only one university library uses an abridged edition for its juvenile collection. More public libraries reported using the abridged than did other types of libraries. Library systems and processing centers use only the most recent edition—the tenth abridged. Schools and junior college libraries list the tenth or ninth abridged as their primary editions. Only 11 percent of school libraries report using an abridged edition. One school librarian asserted, "the tenth edition is too abridged even for our elementary schools. We continue to use the bracketed numbers." However, the sample of school libraries in this survey was taken from the mailing list of those schools which receive DC& (Dewey Decimal Classification: Additions, Notes, Decisions). These libraries tend to use the full edition. Further study is being made of school libraries and primary edition used.

Most academic libraries did not accept each new edition as it came. Their nonacceptance had variety: one library went from the fourteenth edition to the sixteenth to the eighteenth editions, using a few numbers from the fifteenth and seventeenth. Another has remained with the sixteenth edition, having retained the author numbers of the fourteenth and abolished whatever fifteenth-edition numbers it had adopted.

Processing centers usually accept each edition as it is published, and they accept DDC numbers on LC cards as they come. The reason for such acceptance is simply that processing centers do not have to wrestle with a large working collection immediately beyond their doors. The decisions of processing centers affect a distant client. Thus, decisions regarding change are more easily made and defended.

The larger public libraries have, for the most part, begun to behave like processing centers and smaller public libraries in that they are moving toward uncritical acceptance of DDC-18 numbers, and they retain older numbers or older classes.

Another question put to classifiers concerned the need for in-service training materials to supplement current and future editions of DDC. The largest percentage (42.8 percent) of those responding would like to receive some type of in-service training material. Twenty-nine percent do not feel they need such materials and an equal number had no opinion. University libraries had the greatest proportion of those desiring in-service training materials (64 percent), while junior colleges are the next largest group (56.5 percent). One-half of the library systems and one-half of the processing centers would like to receive such materials. Colleges were the group least interested in such materials, with 46 percent stating that they have no need for them.

Catalogers are cynical about the sort of continuing education they have received, hence the many negative responses concerning in-service training. A significant number, however, see the need for training themselves and the clerical staff who are increasingly taking on cataloging responsibilities, especially at Ohio College Library Center terminals. Many respondents did see the need for explanations of the new aspects of a new edition. Several called for a new guide, one similar to the 1962 _Guide to the Use of the Dewey Decimal Classification._ One classifier commented: "Such a guide could introduce the DDC system to newcomers. Library school preparation is too general."

Libraries were queried concerning their need for discontinued numbers for retrospective material. The majority (51 percent) indicated that they do not need discontinued numbers for retrospective materials. One-fourth of the respondents said that their libraries do need these numbers, while another one-fourth do not know. Library size has little influence on whether discontinued numbers are needed. In only one category is there a majority response indicating the need for discontinued numbers—universities (58 percent). The college library category is the only other group with a sizable percentage (44 percent) needing discontinued numbers.

	Yes		No		Total
	Number	*Percentage*	*Number*	*Percentage*	
Less than 5,000	2	7.4	25	92.6	27
5,000 to 10,000	0	0.0	63	100.0	63
10,000 to 25,000	12	11.0	97	89.0	109
25,000 to 50,000	5	10.9	41	89.1	46
50,000 to 100,000	12	17.9	55	82.1	67
100,000 to 250,000	10	30.3	23	69.7	33
250,000 to 500,000	5	35.7	9	64.3	14
500,000 to 1 million	8	36.4	14	63.6	22
1 million or more	19	59.4	13	40.6	32
Total	73	17.7	340	82.3	413

Table 9. Size of Library Compared to Use of Locally Produced Expansions or Variation of Schedules.

The majority (51 percent) of respondents indicate satisfaction with the precedence notes for eliminating cross-classification in the DDC schedules. Only 11 percent are not satisfied with the notes, and 37 percent have no opinion. Respondents were then asked if they would like to have more precedence notes, such as:

155.42 – 155.45

Observe the following table of precedence,
e.g., preschool boys   155.423

Exceptional children
By class type, relationships
By age groups
By sex

Although the majority of libraries are satisfied with the present content of DDC's precedence notes, 38 percent of all respondents—or 65 percent of those voicing an opinion—would like more precedence notes included in the schedules.

A final question directed to libraries was: Does your library or processing center use locally produced expansions or variations of schedules? Approximately one-half of the 848 respondents completed this question. All types of libraries (except junior colleges) use locally produced expansions with almost one-half of the colleges, universities and processing centers reporting the heaviest use.

Table 9 gives the breakdown by size of library for use of locally produced schedules. All sizes of libraries (except the 5,000 to 10,000 volume category) use locally produced expansions or variations of schedules. Libraries of one million volumes or more report the highest use of local schedules.

Those libraries which have local schedules were requested to specify in what areas they are used. They listed a wide variety of subject areas. Some of the expansions reflect the local area, e.g., "Texas counties"; others cover general subject areas such as literature and history.

Most of the libraries visited were suffering from current or impending reductions in staff and/or book budgets. One-third of the libraries had already become part of a computer network; almost all of the rest expected to become part of a network within the next few years. The reductions and the possibility of networking have brought most of the cataloging staffs of the libraries visited to a reassessment of the roles of classification and cataloging. Although they would like to keep material together, many have given up the attempt to do so. The general, discipline approach at the shelf that was once possible is rapidly disappearing in the bulk of the classification; thus, the public catalog has become much more important in subject searching. General searches must now be done at the catalog. Most, if not all, library users other than librarians are not aware of this and are consequently poorly served. What is not realized is that the subject catalog was devised to allow specific subject searches, and now general searches by discipline are virtually impossible. The degree of disservice to the patron is greater in LCC libraries where the extent of change is not so obvious and is therefore far more insidious. With DDC, at least, the public service librarians can readily perceive a relocation of *British history* from 942 to 941, or of *computers* from 651.8 to 001.6. Recognition of change in DDC and ignorance of change in LCC, which is far greater than most librarians realize, contradicts the adage that the baby who cries gets the bottle. In this instance the baby who cries comes to be despised or, at best, is accused of being the only baby in the world who cries.

REFERENCES

1. Vann, Sarah K. *Field Survey of the Dewey Decimal Classification (DDC) Use Abroad.* Albany, N.Y., Forest Press, 1965; Davison, Keith. *Classification Practice in Britain.* London, Library Association, 1966; and Sweeny, Russell. "Dewey in Britain," *Catalogue & Index* 30:4-6, Summer 1973.

2. Comaromi, John P., Michael, Mary Ellen, and Bloom, Janet. *A Survey of the Use of the Dewey Decimal Classification in the United States and Canada.* Albany, N.Y., Forest Press, 1976.

JOEL C. DOWNING
Director, English Language and Copyright Services
Bibliographic Services Division
The British Library
London, England

Dewey Today:
The British and European Scene

At a point halfway through this institute and at the commence-
ment of the second evening session, I am appalled at the problem of making
my contribution intellectually stimulating as well as entertaining. I cannot
regard my paper as something other than a watershed. Earlier ones have
stressed the history of the Dewey Decimal Classification (DDC) and its place
in the North American scene, while I have been invited to survey somewhat
wider horizons (with apologies to the North American continent) in the shape
of British use and influence, with what I trust will be a suitable appendix on
the European scene.

My own direct involvement with DDC is relatively recent, although I have a
professional relationship which goes back to the twelfth edition. As assistant
editor of the *British National Bibliography* (BNB), I became relatively close
with Dewey, although again only in an indirect sense— as I was particularly
responsible for cataloging rather than classification. I became more involved
with DDC when, as Secretary of the Cataloguing and Indexing Group of the
(British) Library Association, I was asked in 1968 by the Research Committee
of the association to assist in the reconstitution of its Decimal Classification
Revision Subcommittee. Such a subcommittee had existed in earlier years, and
already had some contact with the editor of DDC and the Forest Press. It
would be impolitic of me to examine publicly the reasons for the lack of
growth in those earlier relations. What should be emphasized here, I think, is

the tremendous degree of good faith that has been established between DDC and British librarianship since then.

The first object of my paper is to describe the place of Dewey in Britain in the late 1960s, and then to relate the many acts of collaboration which have taken place since then. Finally, I shall discuss the possibilities of the establishment of a foothold by DDC in Europe.

It is my personal view that nearly all the comments and criticisms of Dewey which were generated in Britain during the 1950s and 1960s were fully justified. Unfortunately, during the period when DDC-16 was in preparation, little notice was taken in America of British representations, particularly as used by BNB. No one in the United States appreciated the significance of the regular production, in BNB, of a classified catalog organized by DDC. If the response had been more spontaneous we could have had a table of standard subdivisions in DDC-16 and much of the progress established with DDC-17 and DDC-18 would have been consolidated at an earlier date. Everyone would thus have gained from a continuous and intimate relationship between DDC and British librarianship well over ten years in advance of the present time. However, during the 1950s and 1960s, we in Britain did not appreciate why our American counterparts were unable to accept our suggestions immediately. We did not fully realize that Forest Press was operating a business enterprise which at the time was suffering financially. Quite justifiably, Forest Press was careful not to upset the market which had provided it up until that time with an established income. In addition, American librarians had little training in the theoretical principles which we in Great Britain had absorbed during the postwar classification renaissance. In fact confusion probably resulted from British ideas on the philosophy of the classified catalog—a tool of which, because of the existence of the services of the Library of Congress, U.S. librarians had little experience, and even less need.

When our committee began work in 1969, it immediately became clear that there was little we could do to assist in the preparation of the DDC-18, the schedules of which had already been prepared in draft. We were given the opportunity to comment on these draft schedules as they then existed, but there was no possibility of modifying them to any great extent. We therefore concentrated our attention on checking those schedules which would be the subject of considerable British interest, such as government, education, botany, zoology, geography, history and other subjects where terminology between English and American-English is always at variance.

This work was interrupted by the news that the editor Benjamin Custer and the executive director of the Forest Press, Richard Sealock, were to visit Britain early in 1969 and were anxious to meet the committee. For this occasion we decided to review our entire relationship with the editorial office in Washington and with the publishers at Forest Press. We listed a number of objectives to discuss in broad terms with the visitors; these were as follows:

1. The committee should encourage discussion and comments on DDC in Britain and act as a channel of communication between the United States and Britain on all aspects of DDC theory and practice.
2. It should receive and coordinate the comments of British librarians for dispatch to DDC.
3. The committee should formulate criticism on topics of British interest present in the schedules.
4. The committee should gather information on inconsistencies in the operation of the schedules and their structure.
5. It should advise DDC on matters of general policy insofar as they reflect British attitudes in the study of classification.
6. It should assist in the preparation of interpretative and instructional aids and manuals for British users.

In addition, we wished to learn more of the operational background of DDC, such as: how the Decimal Classification Division (DCD) of the Library of Congress was organized; what the overall policy was in relation to the sequence of editions; how the quantity of relocation in each edition was decided; and what machinery should be set up between British and American agencies to achieve closer cooperation. One of the immediate results of this visit was that we were asked to prepare an outline paper for presentation at the next meeting of the Editorial Policy Committee (EPC). Another suggestion, which was accepted, was that the British committee develop relations with library associations in the British Commonwealth, with whom we already had a strong bond through common systems of professional education.

The outline paper which was presented to EPC referred to the previous British subcommittee as acting as an advisory body on matters intrinsic to DDC, whereas the new committee had the intention of serving in the broadest sense as a channel of communication in both directions for all aspects of theory and practice. I might add here that we were already being asked for advice on the British market. We find that we can be of considerable assistance to publishers in this matter.

We claimed in our outline paper, dated September 1969, that: British public libraries were all using Dewey Decimal Classification and that a number of university and college libraries were moving in that direction; for historic and academic reasons British library schools paid considerable attention to DDC; and the largest service agency, the British National Bibliography, and a number of other agencies and services were concerned principally with DDC as a means of subject organization of knowledge and the classification of books.

In this way we stressed the significant user community in Great Britain, which now had a focal point in the form of a British committee.

The committee decided that there were both areas and directions of concern which we needed to emphasize. The areas consisted of the use, theory, education and future developments of DDC. The committee decided that it would concentrate specifically on British interests, but it was expected that these interests would have wider implications. There were two directions of concern: (1) toward DDC itself as represented by the Forest Press and the DDC division of the Library of Congress; and (2) toward users of DDC in Britain. We stressed the need for an effectual channel of communication with messages passing both ways. We pointed out that DDC could not expect support and assistance from us unless it was prepared to support us reciprocally.

Although these were simple statements, the overall situation was complex. Practicing librarians, library schools, and service agencies all had different needs, but it was agreed that the problems discussed should be resolved on the basis of a coherent view of the classification.

The statement was supported by an appendix indicating some of the technical problems which would serve to indicate the nature of British reaction to recent editions of DDC. I think it might be useful to note the principal ones here, at least in an abbreviated form. Those that concerned us seriously were problems relating to the order, detail, universality, and editorial control of the classification. Most of our comments fell under the heading "order." We were troubled by the continuing evidence of bad classification structure, such as the use of the subordinate numbers to express coordinate topics. We also commented on the placing of subordinate subjects in coordinate numbers. Many of the variants from the general to specific in the Dewey Decimal Classification are results of compromise made in order to minimize the quantity of re-used numbers. This is particularly noticeable in the general treatment of *transport,* which is placed at the head of class 380 *commérce,* while the different types of transport appear at 385-388. The introduction of centered headings in the seventeenth edition made up of "through" numbers allows for a concept to appear in its correct hierarchy, but the inability to use these numbers notationally reduces their value to absurdity. The British committee suggested that centered headings be regarded as alternative placings, but this was not accepted by the Editorial Policy Committee.

Comments were also made on the consistency of detail appearing in related schedules, and the need for consistency in the treatment of subjects of British interest. We did, however, welcome the increase in instructional notes and the general tidying up which was clearly evident in the schedules of the eighteenth edition.

Early in 1970, the Library Association received a joint invitation from the Forest Press and the Editorial Policy Committee to send a British representative to the meetings of the Editorial Policy Committee for an experimental period of three years. As chairman of the British committee I was nominated to attend, and I was called for my first meeting to Lake Placid in October 1970. After a visit to Lake Placid, no one can deny the extraordinary, intense energy of the man who did so much to establish librarianship as a profession in America and whose name has since become a household word throughout the library world.

It will be useful to repeat parts of the report I presented to EPC in 1970 when I stated that the majority of British libraries depended upon the Dewey Decimal Classification in a way no other group of libraries did, wherever they might be located. Because of the lack of centralized services in Britain during the first half of this century, libraries had adopted different editions of DDC and adapted them to suit their own convenience. It was natural that when a centralized service was created it was impossible to satisfy the particular classification requirements of any one group of libraries, even though they might use the same classification system and even the same edition of that system. In fact, the primary aim of *British National Bibliography,* established in 1950, was to produce, by the continuous cumulation of material prepared at weekly intervals, a reference tool which would be able to satisfy bibliographical and subject inquiries of considerable depth. The utilization of this information at any local point for the purpose of cataloging and classification was only a secondary objective and was certainly not part of the overall design of the bibliography. It would seem now, more than twenty-five years later, that the secondary objective is of at least equal importance to the first.

The establishment of British centralized bibliographical services after World War II coincided with the study, and introduction into Britain, of the ideas of Ranganathan. Whether or not the *British National Bibliography* had utilized the theories of Ranganathan to strengthen and support the natural choice of the fourteenth edition of DDC for its systematic display of material, the ideas of Ranganathan would have been imported into Britain and developed through the agency of the newly founded library schools. These developments could not be overlooked by anyone concerned with recording the place of the Dewey Decimal Classification in Britain. The full flush of enthusiasm for these new ideas in the United Kingdom and their slower penetration into the North American curriculum led, on both sides, to a lack of appreciation of each other's problems.

It had been recognized in Britain, since the inception of the Shared Cataloging Program of the Library of Congress, that bibliographical communication needed a standard international format. This was further emphasized by the rapid development of computerized services. The successful operation of these services required a closely defined base in both cataloging and classification. It was for this reason that the BNB decided to classify its entries from January 1971 on according to the practice advocated by the DDC editors and also to utilize the eighteenth edition for this purpose. This decision brought considerable advantages to British librarians in that for the first time since the publication of DDC-15, they knew from which specific source BNB chose its classification numbers.

The reaction of British libraries to DDC-18 has been watched by the British subcommittee with interest. We are particularly concerned with gauging subscribers' reactions toward the effort made to maintain a consistent editorial policy with respect to new numbers, relocations and phoenix schedules. Continuity of editorial policy must be apparent from one edition to the next. A regularly published statement of intent in this field is very necessary. The repetition of such a statement encourages present use and strengthens sales potential for the years to come. The permanence of DDC's editorial office is one certain advantage which DDC has over some other published schemes, and every opportunity should be taken to demonstrate the advantages so gained.

Some of us in Britain feel that librarians have too long been concerned with maintaining an inflexible set of disciplines for the organization and control of bibliographical information, whether in descriptive cataloging or classification. We suggest a wider appreciation of the philosophy that librarianship and information science are, in fact, the flexible controls over the ever-changing state of knowledge. So many of the problems facing catalogers and classifiers have arisen because librarians are not prepared to change their practices due to the inflexibility of their record. They must be persuaded that the only means by which they can keep their services in line with the demands of their users, and with the development of culture and society, is by incorporating the improvements that are constantly being introduced into their services. It is pointless to produce revised codes of cataloging and new editions of classifications, and to engage their implementation by centralized services if these developments do not receive greater usage at local service points. This message should be continually emphasized by those services occupying strategic positions of influence and persuasion.

It will be seen that the British committee has been concerned principally with the image presented by DDC to British subscribers. If one puts aside the different theoretical approaches to classification and the different subject presentation in catalogs which exist between Britain and the North American continent, one cannot ignore the frequent claims made in the past that the DDC has given little hospitality to the British scene—its institutions, its vocabulary, its ecology and natural resources—to say nothing of the needs of the European continent. We were therefore anxious to improve this image by making suggestions which we thought EPC should consider.

It might be useful here to summarize some of the other reactions to DDC which existed in Britain in the mid-1960s in order to give an idea of the very great progress which has been made subsequently. At a public meeting in 1967,[1] A.J. Wells, then editor of BNB, spoke of the considerable disquiet with which DDC-17 had been greeted on both sides of the Atlantic. He was worried by the strong suggestion that DDC-18, when it came along, would countermand much of DDC-17. The absorption of modern theories of classification into the intensively revised subject areas would mean that subsequent editions would eventually bear little relation to the then-present seventeenth edition. He went on to add that BNB had long been asking DDC for facilities for compound number building. When these facilities eventually were provided, it was found that American librarians had no appreciation of them, because of their different approach to subject retrieval. In Britain we would still need to provide supplementary schedules in many underdeveloped areas to support our detailed indexing procedure. All that we could do to satisfy our domestic critics would be to provide, somewhere in our entries, standard numbers drawn from the latest editions and presented in a prescribed form according to DDC editorial rules.

This latter suggestion developed from the many criticisms which were supplied in answers to a questionnaire circulated in Great Britain by the Library Association with the financial support of Forest Press. It seemed from the responses that BNB was tackling the impossible. Librarians required short numbers to express specific subjects of great complexity. They wanted to be able to retrieve subject material expertly and exactly by means of BNB indexes and classified sequences, but they were not prepared to use BNB's expansions in their catalogs, nor on their books, nor even long numbers authoritatively derived from DDC schedules.

At this point, you will undoubtedly be interested in hearing some of the conclusions of the report: *Classification Practice in Britain,*[2] which followed the analysis of the responses to the questionnaire just mentioned. Although the editor, Keith Davison, emphasized the value of the statistical analysis, his general conclusions are worth summarizing. It appeared in 1964 that there would be an increasing demand for specificity, particularly in classified catalogs, but also to some extent on the shelves. Specificity should not be obtained at the expense of simplicity of notation. Davison also claimed that users of DDC were generally satisfied with a great deal of the schedules. British librarians wished for increased specificity in the classification of European subjects. It was generally easier for a librarian to reduce long numbers than to carry out his own expansions. It seems that more libraries were prepared for major changes than was imagined and would be ready to cope with major reclassification if the result would lead to an obvious overall benefit. He tersely expressed as a final conclusion that the way lay open for anyone who could provide a brief simple classification, with brief simple notation, which would provide absolute specificity for all subjects. This was the perfectionist—but impossible—demand of many librarians. We at BNB and the DDC editorial staff in Washington both experience continual pressure from these extremities.

From the mid-1960s, BNB's philosophy with respect to bibliographical control was changing. It had been chosen in 1966 by LC to serve as the guinea pig for what became the National Program for Acquisition and Cataloging (NPAC). It was gaining international horizons and appreciated that the need for common practices lay beyond national limits. The development of the MARC project immediately after the success of NPAC further encouraged international standardization. It was against this background that we in BNB moved closer to DDC. Here was a meeting of two avenues—one originating with the BNB subscribers, requesting (even demanding) the production of "pure" DDC numbers, and the other stretching across the Atlantic Ocean toward LC, via NPAC and MARC.

Following a visit from Benjamin Custer, editor of DDC, to BNB in the spring of 1969, it became obvious that we could only achieve compatibility with his division in Washington by forming a more intimate relationship. Together we managed to contrive a system of information exchange which has served us well since then. Moreover, it allowed us more effectively to provide standard DDC-17 numbers as a supplement to our own modified DDC practice. Classifiers in the two organizations, have dispatched queries and comments to each other, although early in the exchange it appeared that they were writing notes to each other rather than classifying books. Now the documentation has been almost completely reduced, and a remarkable degree of compatibility is maintained. This was attained not only by means of verbal communication; the Forest Press readily agreed in 1972 to the exchange of staff between LC (DCD) and BNB and provided the wherewithal to make this possible. Those involved at levels other than management became acquainted and thus paved the way for a happy and easy relationship between the classifiers on each side of the Atlantic. To some extent our internal organizational problems were resolved by the decision that beginning in 1971, BNB would be computer-produced through the medium of British MARC tapes and computer-controlled typesetting machinery. We would break with the past and use standard DDC numbers taken from the latest edition. For a number of years it has been possible, therefore, for DCD to accept class numbers applied to British books and so help to increase its output. Naturally, there were disagreements at first and as I have indicated, these led to a considerable amount of feedback in both directions. An exchange of catalog cards with appropriate notes was all that was necessary. Even in 1970, DCD estimated it was able to use over 80 percent of the numbers assigned by BNB.

BNB also uses DDC numbers taken first from LC cards, and later from Cataloging in Publication material for American titles which appear on the British market. Nearly all of these numbers are accepted by BNB. LC information arriving too late for immediate use regularly highlights differences in classificatory attitudes, although it must be remembered that the number of instances is a very small percentage of the tens of thousands of items handled by both parties. Most of the differences occur when each team ignores a geographic application within its own society and culture, significant to the other team, but taken for granted by the home side. Sometimes the physical format is treated differently in descriptive cataloging practice and this justifiably leads to a variance in subject specificity.

At BNB we have no manual of classification practice other than the editor's introduction to DDC-18. We cannot pop our heads round the door and ask for his immediate advice. Inquiries by correspondence have only a retroactive value. It is unheard of for us to stop the machine to await the result of an inquiry. So we make our mistakes publicly in the "Weekly Lists" and correct them afterwards in our cumulations.

After the criticism BNB received from its subscribers during the first twenty years of its existence, it is surprising to learn that all did not take kindly to our "pure" Dewey numbers. It was claimed that they were not the same as their own "pure" Dewey numbers, and what was BNB going to do about it? The treatment of nonnarrative history is a case in point. In its original classification practice BNB had enshrined the British attitude toward history. History could be treated in nonnarrative form and still remain history. Geography and travel was used only for books concerned with contemporary description of people and places. We all suffered a traumatic shock when DDC-17, and later DDC-18, placed many works of historical nature in the 910s. As many letters from librarians on the classification of history reached BNB as had earlier reached us on the use of letter notation.

BNB's use of DDC-18 is a continuation of the compatible practice developed in using DDC-17. We classify strictly by the schedules and tables and not by privately revealed knowledge of editorial practice. Differences due to subject analysis are to some extent unavoidable. When the schedules provide options we construct numbers according to the editor's preference. Although options may be preferable in local library situations, it is not an easy matter for a national cataloging agency, working in an international format, to prefer particular options. There may, however, be very good reasons for doing so because of a particularly significant local demand. For example, this occurs in Britain with respect to the citation order in class 340.

Many British librarians would prefer to have the option to class under the jurisdiction used by the national agency, but international agreements in the use of compatible programs at present take no cognizance of such situations. A limited number of options throughout the entire schedules must, I think, be permitted in national machine-readable records in order to make the widest use of these records possible.

An interval of several years elapsed between the introduction in BNB of standard DDC numbers as a supplementary service and their use since 1971 for the arrangement of the classified sections of the "Weekly Lists" and "Cumulations." It was a good thing that we had this interval, because we had to provide a link missing from the sequence of our subject retrieval operations.

From 1951 until 1970 our subject index was an inversion of our classified display. A specific subject index entry was created for each class number, and, although we admitted synonyms as lead terms, there was no possibility of rotating the constituent elements of a subject index entry to provide alternative approaches. These approaches were met by searching the classified file from a superordinate number down to the number precisely expressing the subject in mind. This might, on many occasions, take us to hypothetical divisions beyond the most specific DDC number available. Such situations occurred, even after 1960, when BNB introduced so many of its own expansions to numbers by letter notation. Users were given one subject index entry, or a related synonymous entry, specific to their needs. If they did not approach from this point they then had to sharpen the focus of their search by working down the classified file.

This constitutional weakness in chain indexing had been regarded as unavoidable; however, those who were searching for new indexing techniques saw the possibility of overcoming the defects with the aid of the computer. Until 1970, BNB's subject index had been constructed from the DDC numbers applied to the entries in the classified catalog. The index entries resulting were as relative to DDC as its own Relative Index, even though we did not accept DDC terminology. Our subject index entries demonstrated the strength and the weakness of DDC as well as our ability to use the schedules effectively. Sometimes we contrived to overcome the weaknesses by "unethical" practices (at least to the followers of Ranganathan) of turning the chain: that is, of not expressing the constituent elements of a subject concept in exactly the same order they were stated in the class number. At other times we were embarrassed by the profligate use of digits in DDC numbers which expressed notational hierarchy and little else. Here index construction had to jump deftly from one sought term to the next, ignoring the no-man's land in between. After some experimentation, however, the index and the classified file worked handsomely together for twenty years.

Chain indexing in BNB was superseded in 1971 by the newly developed PRECIS[3] indexing system, which provides specific rotated subject entries from all sought terms. PRECIS does not rely on the composition of the class number for the structure of its entries. In contrast, the PRECIS analysis of a subject concept treated in a document guides the classifier in the selection of a DDC number for that document. Elsewhere in this volume, a paper by Derek Austin (principal developer of PRECIS) discusses this development further.

There are a number of factors relative to the use made of DDC in Britain which must continually be borne in mind. It is difficult to put them in order of importance and their order in the list is no indication of their relative significance:

1. the development of the UK MARC project in Britain, leading to the machine production of library catalogs through printout, phototypesetting, microform, and on-line services (you will notice that I do not include the card catalog as a continuing feature of our library landscape);
2. the restructuring of local government in Great Britain, which has led to the creation of quite large units capable of utilizing sophisticated computer services. These larger local library units find the task of reconciling the different intellectual systems they have inherited too great for their own individual attention and they are prepared to make far greater use of centralized services;
3. the creation of the British Library, which will surely lead to a greater degree of integration within British librarianship. Peter Lewis's paper (elsewhere in this volume) describes the work that has taken place to assess the Library's own needs within the sphere of classification and indexing. The exact relation between those needs, the requirements of the national bibliography and the users of the centralized services must be correlated.

I predict that future editions of DDC will continue to be essential to British librarianship as long as they are restructured in no greater detail than DDC-18 and as long as they intelligently anticipate the development of new subjects.

It must be remembered that Dewey's system *lives*, not at the Library of Congress, nor at BNB, nor at Forest Press, but in the libraries which are using it on their shelves and in their catalogs. And it lives there, not in a standard and authentic form, but in modifications of infinite variety. This is contrary to the best intentions of the policy of integrity of numbers, which has been maintained to aid consistency of use throughout successive editions. Nonetheless, a degree of integrity in numbers is necessary, but other very positive features should not be completely sacrificed on this altar. The possibility of increased standardization in use is enhanced by mechanization. DDC is produced in one of the world's largest libraries; yet it is not used there for subject retrieval. It is employed in many important bibliographical listings, but those publications are rarely associated with the ordered collection of books on the shelves of a library. DDC is created in abstraction, where there is no direct application to a collection of books. The first point at which the practical problems of application are appreciated is in the use made of the classification by individual libraries. Here, I claim, lies the cause of many of the defects which have been introduced into the classification in the past, and which we are trying to eradicate.

Let me now relate something of the British DDC Committee's endeavors. Its membership is drawn from public, academic and national libraries, as well as representatives of British library schools. On several occasions it has had the pleasure of the presence of a chairman of Forest Press, its executive director and the editor of the DDC. Such meetings have greatly increased our appreciation of each other's problems and have led to a mutuality of attitudes which can benefit the classification and librarianship all over the world.

The renewed relationship between DDC and the British Library Association was so successful during its initial experimental period from 1970 to 1973 that at its conclusion the Forest Press, with the full agreement of the American Library Association, decided to request the appointment of the British representative to the Editorial Policy Committee for a further period of six years, and to give that person the power to vote. In this way British librarianship is now part of the constitution of DDC and I trust that it will continue to be so represented in the future.

It is true that as it devotes energy and resources to broadening its horizons DDC may still look anxiously over its shoulder to American librarians. This is because its earlier policies have occasionally led to severe criticism, especially from the home market. The success of DDC-18 has removed a considerable degree of uncertainty, however, and there has been continued improvement in the sales since the appearance of DDC-16.

Undoubtedly for this reason, suggestions made by the British committee with respect to DDC-19 have been considered very generously. Perhaps the most significant degree of cooperation was shown in the request made by EPC that the British committee should prepare the editorial rule governing the objective for foreign use. The following draft, submitted by the Library Association committee, was approved by EPC and accepted by Forest Press:

> The Decimal Classification is an American classification of international standing and application. In preparing an edition it is desirable to allow positively for the needs, both in details and in order, of countries outside the U.S. Where there is conflict between these needs and those of the U.S. the Editor should give his preference to the needs of the

U.S., but must make provision for an alternative use by libraries outside the U.S. in a manner appropriate to the particular problem.

The Editorial Policy Committee had already accepted some critical comments from the British committee to restrict the use of centered headings (e.g., 385-388 *transportation*) and to reduce the number of options which occur throughout the schedules, most of which are relics of practice derived from earlier editions of DDC. Our efforts have ensured that the arbitrary selection of subject areas for total revision (i.e., phoenix schedules) should be replaced by a comprehensive review of the whole classification. The Forest Press boldly accepted the revolutionary suggestion that a prospective phoenix schedule for 780 *music* should be prepared in Britain, and it generously provided funds for the exercise. In 1974 the work was placed under the direction of Russell Sweeney of the Leeds Library School, with the British committee acting in a guiding capacity. The objective of our proposals has been to restructure the class as economically as possible, giving ample facility for synthesis and permitting scores and musical literature to be classified homogeneously. We have worked on the principle that the primary characteristic in musical literature is the composer, and that in this category such a characteristic takes precedence, in the organization of scores, over the natural order of executant, musical form and musical character.

One other important area of responsibility which was given to the British committee was the preparation of revised Area Tables for Great Britain, following the reorganization of our local government, which became effective during 1974 and 1975. All the new authorities and their immediate predecessors are included in these tables as well as all significant natural features, so that the British Isles are now treated in the same depth as the United States is treated in DDC-18. The Forest Press has made these tables available to all subscribers in Great Britain as a gratuitous supplementary service.[4]

In preparing these tables it was suggested by the British Committee, and accepted by our American colleagues (who, like all Americans, consider Britain and England as synonymous), that it was now necessary to distinguish between England and Wales on the one hand and the British Isles, Great Britain and the United Kingdom on the other. The notation -41 would represent the general areas of the British Isles and Great Britain, while -42 would be limited to England and Wales. This has meant that the number for Scotland is -411, collateral with Ireland at -415. Such a decision has implications in 914 and 940, to the extent that the Area Tables, geography and history schedules now present a consistent structure; consequently, a history of Britain classifies at 941, a history of England at 942, with the existing period divisions applying to each area according to treatment.

Responses from a number of libraries, to which the British committee submitted its proposals, were most encouraging. The revision gives us a much more rational presentation for local material than we have ever had before in DDC. What might have been a bold and possibly unwarrantable decision, if taken unilaterally by DDC, has the cooperative support of an official Library Association committee and so becomes more acceptable within our shores. It is because of the problems encountered in applying effective notation to the new authorities, and at the same time avoiding the use of excessively long numbers, that caused us to ask DDC to regard the Area Tables for Britain as deserving phoenix treatment.

The British committee pressed for some time for an amendment to the eighteenth edition phoenix schedules for 340 *law*. In the total revision of this schedule, the need to allow for a primary division by jurisdiction was ignored. Many reviewers commented on this defect and were supported by representations from the British committee. Subsequently, this point has been conceded and an option has been created at 342-348, making it possible to arrange legal material first by jurisdiction and then by problem.[5]

Similarly, representations have been made concerning the interpretation by DDC of civilization and history, referred to earlier. A reappraisal of these subjects has been made with the object of permitting a less rigid definition of the term *history*. This has enabled British libraries to resume their traditional practice of classifying non-chronological treatment of historical subjects with other historical works, without conflicting with the general intentions of DDC editorial policy. This was announced in *DC&*[6] and adopted by BNB and LC in January 1975, together with the new Area Tables for Great Britain.

As a commercial publication, DDC must continue to absorb as much comment as its market will bear. Now that 45 percent of its sales are to countries other than the United States and 26 percent fall within an area considered by the publishers as being subject to British influence, DDC is doing all it can to remove the impression that it represents a limited range of North American attitudes. It is seeking a new image while endeavoring not to hurt too greatly those who have supported it in the past. For this reason DDC has sought and welcomed the assistance and advice given by the British committee. It sees DDC's use in British libraries, the *British National Bibliography* and UK MARC as a positive recognition of its continued vigor. With the constant development of automated services, the exploration of all avenues leading toward national and international standardization is essential. The degree of cooperation existing among DDC, the Library Association and the British Library is an expression of hopes and intentions for the future, so much so that it is already being copied in Australia and Canada.

At this point it would be useful to summarize the use made of DDC in Britain. The Library Association conducted a second survey on behalf of

Forest Press in 1972; I will give a brief analysis of the returns. We had a 92.5 percent response rate to our questionnaire, which was distributed to over 1,000 libraries. Of those libraries, 48 percent were public, 32 percent college, and the remainder was made up of university, national and other libraries. The libraries using DDC represented 79 percent of the total number.* UDC claimed 7 percent, LC and Bliss 4 percent each. Of the 744 using DDC, 59 percent were public libraries, 35 percent were college libraries, while university and other libraries added up to 6 percent. The largest area of non-DDC use was in university libraries, which represented 6 percent of the total libraries responding.

At the time of the survey, nearly one-third of DDC libraries were using DDC-16 and nearly one-fourth were using DDC-18. The others used mainly DDC-17 and DDC-14. Even at that time more than 200 libraries were considering changing to DDC-18 and I am certain that many have done so since, particularly as they become involved increasingly with centralized services such as BNB and UK MARC. It is only fair to state that the Library Association does not hold a comprehensive list of special libraries; thus, from this survey the apparent use made of UDC in Britain will be misleading. The survey does, however, give a fairly accurate analysis of the attitude of general libraries to classification.

There is little evidence of the use of the abridged edition of DDC in the United Kingdom; considerable use has been made however, of the *Introduction to the Use of the Dewey Decimal Classification in British Schools,* the second edition of which was published in 1968. A newly revised edition is in preparation with the assistance of the British School Library Association. Our DDC committee has been involved as advisers to the Forest Press in this matter, and it is my firm opinion that the third edition will lead to a greater use of DDC in British schools. Regrettably, our schools are not as well endowed with libraries as are those in North America. There is the possibility of a market for the abridged edition when we have more secondary schools with established libraries under the charge of qualified librarians (as distinct from teachers or teacher-librarians).

All in all, there is evidence of a growing interest in DDC in Britain which stems from a number of associated factors: (1) the increased response to British needs in the subject content of the classification, (2) the improvements in structure and philosophy which have been increasingly evident from DDC-16 on, (3) the general tendency to standardization in

---

*It will be noticed that this figure differs appreciably from that reported by Lewis on p. 104 in this volume. It appears that there is no one authoritative list of British libraries, and that the British Library survey reported by Lewis was done by Aslib and included all special libraries which were institutional members.—Ed.

libraries, (4) the acceptance of standard-DDC numbers by BNB, and (5) the broadening interest in UK MARC, with the acceptance of computer-produced catalogs in microform and the potential of on-line services.

There appears to be little evidence in Britain of a flight from Dewey. If this came about, it would undoubtedly need to be initiated by the national bibliography. However, there is little likelihood of such an event when so much in the field of Universal Bibliographic Control[7] is modeled on what has happened in Britain in the last twenty-five years. As future security, there is the gradual internationalization of MARC, which is now established as the primary communication format for bibliographic data. We cannot afford a burden of additional systems on our already fully loaded communication format. Those systems already in the field—and capable of maintaining their lead—will stay in front.

The Decimal Classification will continue to serve to organize material on shelves in libraries; it will serve to exploit in bibliographies a wide range of general literature, certainly as long as traditionally published tools are required, but its place as an aid in subject indexing may decline in the face of competition from computer-generated indexing systems such as PRECIS.

It will be argued by some that DDC needs no more expansion or rationalization, and that it should achieve and maintain a status quo, thus relieving librarians of the necessity of upgrading their records and changing the class numbers on their books. May I ask those who represent this point of view whether they regard any current classification as being near perfection? Are they content to let the order of material on their open shelves represent outmoded attitudes toward knowledge? Would they still accept DDC-11 if they accept DDC at all?

While we cannot expect a total and instant rationalization of the Decimal Classification, we have seen positive progress toward improvement in the last three editions and we must expect, and demand, a continuation of those achievements in all succeeding editions. That the Decimal Classification has at last appreciated the existence of librarianship outside the North American continent must surely indicate that the profession in America is not unaware of its responsibilities to the world at large. Dewey belongs to all; it escaped from Amherst nearly a century ago. It has crossed oceans and penetrated continents, and cannot afford to be restrained as an isolationist within the heart of the Midwest. Those who avoid issues by ignoring problems are only storing up even greater difficulties for those who succeed them. We must therefore look for the continued growth and maintenance of the classification in spite of that local phenomenon, the flight from Dewey.

I cannot believe that any one of the currently used general systems of classification is so near perfection that it does not warrant improvements which must be mirrored in notational changes or dual provision. Those who recommend and accept systems because there is little or no evidence of published modification are deluding themselves. All one can hope is that the changes effected in any general system of classification are compatible, change to change, edition to edition. If not, users and classifiers lose faith. It is perhaps the saddest of ironies that DDC is the only general system of classification which examines itself publicly every few years. In doing so it demonstrates at once both its strengths and its weaknesses. Regrettably, criticism always focuses on the apparently worst defects in any system. The Forest Press must continue to take a positive attitude toward the need for maintenance and revision. DDC could die as quickly from a lack of tonic as it could from too great a dose of aperient.

We come now to the appendix—Europe. Here, the use of DDC is limited to selected libraries scattered widely throughout the continent. I have circulated a questionnaire to the seventy-five libraries that purchased the English edition of DDC-18. There could, of course, be more who purchased DDC-17 and DDC-16, but some limit had to be placed upon the exercise. The sample is not great enough to generalize. There are public, academic and special libraries that use DDC-18. Approximately one-half of those queried have replied. Of those the larger proportion use DDC-18 for their stock, and there is little evidence of the continued use of earlier editions. Those not using DDC-18 use either their own system or UDC.

The libraries using DDC-16 modify or supplement it to varying degrees. The modifications are introduced to satisfy local needs, especially in language, literature or history, and sometimes in public administration, law and topography. You will notice here the similarity to the British committee's early objectives. Naturally some libraries reduce the length of numbers. Among suggested improvements there is a plea for standard English; American terminology and spelling is sometimes very baffling—even to British librarians. A simpler introduction might help librarians for whom English is a second language. Less American bias in content is called for by a few libraries, with a plea for greater awareness of European needs in Area Tables, history schedules, and similar topics. Special libraries wish for greater detail in social sciences, education and psychology. Generally, such comments are limited to the social sciences and the humanities. It can be assumed that most libraries specializing in science or technology are using other classification systems.

Although we cannot expect a tremendous interest to be created for DDC in Europe generally, it must be remembered that Scandinavia and the Netherlands use English as their second language. Jointly they represent one-half of the European subscribers to DDC-18. The standardization of library services developing through MARC will very probably lead to some increase in the use of Dewey in these countries. In other areas the publication of a standard translation of DDC may well do much to encourage the use of the classification. This has been proven by the appearance of the French edition of DDC-18. We know of the considerable interest shown in France, which may lead to the development of a somewhat similar system of bibliographic control to that used in Britain.

French public libraries have been using the Dewey Decimal Classification for many years, although I expect that, like in Britain, there are a variety of interpretations. There is little evidence in France of interest in the original English DDC-18, but I am sure that the publication of the French translation will do much to encourage standardization of practice. This will receive further support when it is possible to extend the services of *Bibliographie de la France* to include DDC class numbers on the catalog cards which it has now begun to issue. It is to be hoped that such a service will commence in 1976, and we can foresee the French library profession taking its place among those responsible for the increasing internationalization of the Dewey Decimal Classification.

The production of a further Spanish translation of DDC will undoubtedly affect its development in libraries in South and Central America, but I have no information which would lead one to believe that what may happen in France will occur in Spain. Similarly, there seems to be little possibility of integrated development in Germanic areas, although a small number of technological libraries are showing increasing interest in MARC operations; for instance, Bochum (Germany) University Library extracts subject descriptors and Decimal Classification numbers from the LC and UK MARC tapes.

Despite the fact that the use made of DDC in Europe is small compared to use in Britain, one cannot fail to note that in some European countries, national bibliographies are arranged by or contain DDC numbers: Iceland, Italy, Norway, and Turkey. Each presents its entries in a different way. Norway makes its principal list under author with a classified index of entries. Italy and Turkey have arrangements according to DDC classes, the former using DDC-18 and giving considerable specificity in class numbers and order. The Turkish national bibliography, arranged in broad DDC classes, is subdivided alphabetically by author. Italy and Norway are among the largest supporters of DDC in Europe and we should note that each country uses DDC in its national bibliography.

While I do not think that a broad frontal approach by DDC toward libraries on the continent of Europe is possible, I do consider it essential that the DDC inform them continually of its development, both in policy and content. The sheer universality of DDC and its implementation in MARC projects in other continents make it essential for libraries in Europe to know something of its nature and its place in the field of Universal Bibliographic Control. It is possible that an enlightened policy maintained and developed by the DDC will lead to a fuller appreciation in the multilingual arena of Europe. One should not see this so much as a marketing policy, but as a contribution in the best interests of information and its place in society. However unusual its spelling practice may be, DDC today is part of the English language heritage and where our language is used, so will be the Dewey Decimal Classification. It is for this reason that the Forest Press has asked the British Library Association to hold, as part of the centennial celebrations during 1976, an international seminar on the Decimal Classification, to which representatives from European countries will be invited; the intention is to include those interested in the present or the prospective use of the classification in its various linguistic forms and editions. It is hoped that such an exchange of ideas will help to identify the problems which the Dewey Decimal Classification must face in the future—a challenge which I wish I was young enough to see fulfilled in its entirety.

REFERENCES

1. "Farewell to D.C. 17," *Catalogue & Index* 7:1, 12, July 1967.

2. Davison, Keith. *Classification Practice in Britain.* London, Library Association, 1966.

3. Austin, Derek. *PRECIS: A Manual of Concept Analysis and Subject Indexing.* London, BNB, 1974.

4. "Area Tables -41 and -42." In *DC&.* Vol. 3, Nos. 4/5, p. 6, April 1974. (Supplement to *Dewey Decimal Classification,* 18th ed. Albany, N.Y., Forest Press, 1971.) (Pamphlet)

5. *DC&.* Vol. 3, No. 3, pp. 4-5, April 1973.

6. *DC&.* Vol. 3, No. 7, April 1975.

7. Anderson, D. *Universal Bibliographic Control.* München, Verlag Dokumentation, 1974.

GORDON STEVENSON
Associate Professor
School of Library Science
State University of New York at Albany

The Library of Congress Classification Scheme and its Relationship to Dewey

It strikes me as an interesting circumstance that I have been given the opportunity to speak about the relationship between the Library of Congress classification (LCC) and the Dewey Decimal Classification (DDC) on November 11, a day which I will always think of as Armistice Day. There is no armistice for the respective advocates of these two great classification systems; or, if there is an armistice, there should not be one. The long-range implications of the issues surrounding the Dewey/LC debate are too crucial to pretend that differences of opinion over the merits of the two systems are trivial. LCC and DDC are very, very different. They are so different, and they are different in such ways, as to raise the most basic questions about the very purpose of general library classification, its structure, its uses, and its future in the United States. In a very real sense, these are competing systems. Decisions are made, human resources are allocated, and money is invested in one system or the other. This competition was neither asked for nor wanted by the Library of Congress nor the publishers of the Dewey system. But it does exist and has been a rather expensive proposition over the past ten to twenty years, if not longer.

At the moment, it seems obvious that Dewey has come out very poorly in the United States insofar as many academic librarians are concerned.

Despite its losses, however, a recent report covering the years 1967-71 indicates that of 1,160 accredited, four-year nonspecialized institutions of higher learning, the libraries of more than 400 have remained with Dewey.[1] Although the Dewey-to-LCC movement may have lost its momentum and may be near an end, it is not likely that it will be reversed unless there are drastic changes in the relationship between Dewey and the bibliographic needs of academic librarians. This relationship is changing—and has changed considerably during the past few years—as the Decimal Classification Division of the Library of Congress has increased its annual coverage of the English-language literature from 20-30,000 items to more than 100,000 items during the past year. However, at the present time I am less concerned with academic libraries than I am with public and school libraries. If, in view of this, I seem to spend a disproportionate amount of time commenting on academic libraries vis-à-vis Dewey, it is only because there is much we can learn from the academic librarian's approach to the problems of classification and reclassification.

With the tremendous push toward the development of state, regional, and national bibliographic networks, I am seriously concerned that LCC's firm place in existing and incipient network data bases (which are geared primarily to the needs of university libraries) will be used as a rationale for structuring public and school library networks to use LCC to the exclusion of DDC. This is probably the most important practical issue on which I will comment.

What I will try to do here has been done before, most recently by Maurice Tauber and Hilda Feinberg in an article published in the *Drexel Library Quarterly* in 1974.[2] That article seemed to pull together rather neatly most of the background information which has led many librarians to the inevitable conclusion that the LCC system is the one to which they should commit their money, their energies, and—most importantly—their networks of automated bibliographic data bases. Heretofore, the advocates of LCC have addressed themselves primarily to the interests of college and university libraries. Tauber and Feinberg, however, have found evidence which has convinced them that public libraries, large and small, will find it advantageous to adopt LCC. We also know that several librarians have urged school libraries to switch to LCC.

Granting certain assumptions, one might indeed conclude that LCC is the system we need to take us through the last quarter of the twentieth century. However, I shall argue from different assumptions and try to make a case for the opposite conclusion; that is, that LCC is not the one to which we should commit ourselves at this time.

If I have some melancholy thoughts about the Dewey-to-LCC movement, this is not to say that I would presume to tell the Library of Congress what system best serves its needs. This is not the issue at all. With its massive collections of materials and with stacks which, for all practical purposes, are closed to the public, the problems of the Library of Congress are quite different from problems encountered by the thousands of libraries (including many university libraries) that are the principal means of direct public access to books in the United States. My criticisms are not directed to the LCC system as such, but rather to the value of that system as a national classification scheme to serve the needs of centralized classification and national networks involving all types of libraries. This is a role which the creators of LCC never envisioned. If it is achieving that role, it is a historical accident, a development that is taking place without any analysis of the problem, without thought as to the function of a national system, and certainly without planning. The Library of Congress is in the best position to know what system it needs to organize its collections within the framework of its functions and services. I would only insist that what is good for the Library of Congress is not necessarily good for all libraries in the United States, nor even for all or most academic libraries in the United States. The assumption that whatever the Library of Congress does is *ipso facto,* good for all libraries has been the most pervasive "truth" invoked by the advocates of LCC.

Relationships and Comparisons

The point I will emphasize is that the wide adoption of LCC in the United States is going to have a profound impact on the future of general library classification for the next twenty years or more. I say this not because the Dewey system is "better" than LCC (although I believe this to be the case), but because of inherent weaknesses in the LCC system. In other words, it is not so much the fact that academic librarians have abandoned DDC which bothers me, as it is that they have adopted LCC. With their adoption of LCC, academic librarians have locked themselves into a system from which it will be nearly impossible to extricate themselves.

Since considerable literature on both systems is available, I will have more to say about the relationship between them than I will about the systems themselves. In addition, since the two systems have been compared extensively (usually in a way which demonstrates that LCC is superior), I will have more to say about the relationship of both systems to classification in general than I will about their structural differences. You will, I hope, pardon me if I slip into the pejorative rhetoric of those who have so vigorously advanced the cause of LCC and with equal vigor have apprised us of the folly of staying with DDC.

Obviously, what it is that makes the two systems different is important, although some librarians would argue with me on this point. Some librarians believe that the potential for subject retrieval by any general classification system is of such limited value that neither system, DDC nor LCC, need be evaluated by structural features as they relate to retrieval potential. This is implicit in one of the rationales propounded by Matthis and Taylor for the conversion to LCC: "Any reasonably comprehensive classification system developed and maintained by the considerable means of a federally supported agency, that is, the Library of Congress, is the logical classification system for general library use."[3]

Matthis and Taylor believe that if the situation were reversed (i.e., if the Library of Congress used DDC), then the DDC "might serve as the vehicle for a nationwide centralized cataloging and classification program."[4] Such statements, if you believe them, are calculated to remove the subject of classification from any discussion of reclassification, which is a tactical maneuver of such brilliance that it staggers the imagination. That these and many similar statements have gone unchallenged in the library literature suggests that, as crucial as I think structural differences may be, at this juncture it is much more important to try to understand why so many librarians place so little importance on structural differences. To say that there are no meaningful structural differences is to abandon general library classification as a nineteenth-century anachronism. If the advocates of LCC do indeed believe this, then they are in effect saying: "We don't know what we are doing with classification, but whatever it is we are doing, we can do it a lot more economically and efficiently if we go with LCC rather than with Dewey." I am suggesting that our perception of classification as a tool for subject access is more important for the future of classification than are the differences between LCC and Dewey. Classification systems can be changed for the better if we want to change them. The switch to LCC was not for the better; it was regressive—a step back into the nineteenth century.

These are the reasons why I think we should come to grips with the deeper implications of the circumstances surrounding the massive change in the United States from Dewey to LC classification, and with the literature which accompanied and encouraged that change. This may be the best way to approach the more specific and more practical problem of comparing and evaluating the two systems in terms of their relative usefulness in serving the needs of different types of libraries.

Classification, Libraries, and Librarians

The widely accepted conventional wisdom is that LCC is best for academic libraries and DDC is best for school and public libraries. I do not believe that this has been proven in any objective way. It has not been supported by hard research data. In any case, the more I think about the differences between Dewey and LCC, and the more I read of the literature on reclassification, the more inclined I am to believe that it is not so much a question of matching specific classification systems with specific types of libraries as it is a question of matching classification systems with different types of librarians. In other words, I do not think that in the end we are dealing with the problem of whether or not DDC, for example, is the best system for academic libraries, or whether or not LCC is the best system for school libraries. Regardless of the type of library in question (academic, school, or public), the choice of either system can be rationalized. If this is true, as I believe it is, then the librarian's understanding of, interpretation of, and expectations about the role of classification in subject control and access are far more significant than the current possibilities and limitations of any specific general classification system. The latter, which are essentially structural and in part mechanical features, can be changed—even though such changes are expensive to implement and are a considerable inconvenience at the input end of a system. The former, which are in fact attitudes, are more difficult to understand and change, because we are dealing with subjective evaluations, vested interests, philosophies of library service, and images and perceptions which are deeply ingrained in each librarian's attitude toward classification. In the United States, our expectations about the possibilities of classification have been somewhat circumscribed by certain historical events which took place many decades ago, but which still condition our attitudes about the uses of classification.

Bases for Comparison

Following are some aspects of classification which we would have to consider in some detail if we were to evaluate the relative merits of the two systems in terms of the needs of libraries today and in the future:

1. *Inner structural features* This refers to the classification itself, which is a list of concepts arranged in a systematic order so as to display subjects and the relationships between subjects in what our British colleagues call "a helpful order." This is what classification is all about, but various auxiliary devices are needed to make a system operational.
2. *Exterior structural features* The notation is the exterior feature and represents the inner structure. The notation may be a symbolic language revealing the inner structure (as in DDC), or it may simply provide a location tag (as in LCC). What we want from a classification system will determine what sort of notation we want.

3. *Ancillary features* These are structural features which, although obviously quite important, are not really integral to a system. These can be changed without actually affecting anything really basic about the system. This category includes indexes, the physical layout of the schedules on the printed page, updating services, guides, directions for input, etc. When any of these are inadequate or lacking, there is no reason why they cannot be improved or developed.

4. *Efficiency* To analyze and compare the efficiency of systems is clearly a most basic aspect of our problem. This is to ask: Does it work? How well does it work? Does it do what a classification system is supposed to do? These are difficult questions to answer, and surprisingly little research has been done with either LCC or DDC. This involves studying a system at the output phase, at the point where the user interacts with the system.

5. *Input* If systems create problems at the input stage, this may be caused by inner structural inadequacies—or it may simply mean that the classifier does not have the information needed to interpret the schedules.

6. *Automation* Another mechanical aspect of great importance is the extent to which the system can exploit the potentials of the computer. When we use the computer with a classification system, does it provide new approaches to subject access, or does it only replicate our manual systems? If it does the latter, then the computer is little more than a very efficient and extremely expensive typewriter.

7. *Historical aspects* An examination of the history of classification might not seem to be of much help in solving current problems. On the other hand, I believe that a thorough study of the history of classification in the United States would tell us much about the singular lack of imagination we have brought to recent classification problems.

8. *Flexibility* One would like to know to what extent a given system is flexible enough to adapt to the changing nature of knowledge, and also to what extent it permits flexibility in its application at the local level. How this flexibility is achieved is important. Of these various bases for comparison, the one which will be considered the least significant by many academic librarians, network propagandists, and administrators is the potential for flexibility at the local level. The trend to standardization and centralization assumes that the needs of classification and its uses are the same for all types of libraries and for all sizes of libraries; this proposition strikes me as patently absurd.

9. *Costs* The last thing I would consider is the cost of a system, not because I do not realize how crucial this factor is, but because I would want first to know exactly what I would be paying for. Also, I would try to find some way of estimating the costs (or at least the value) of the system at

the output stage. All cost estimates I have seen so far are costs which result at the input stage; estimating cost is a difficult problem. How can one translate the value of expressive notation to the reference librarian into hard cost data?

Interpretation of Differences

Any librarian contemplating changing from DDC to LCC should carefully consider each of the above points. Furthermore, in considering costs one should distinguish between the costs of descriptive cataloging (including subject description) and the costs of classification. It would seem to me that no one should be given the responsibility for choosing one system over the other until that person has a thorough grounding in classification theory and a detailed knowledge of the practical dimensions and structural features of both systems. I have met too many librarians who have switched to LCC only to discover that they do not know how to interpret the LCC geographical tables, that they do not understand LCC's use of preempted cutter numbers, or even the structural implications of a strictly ordinal notation of the type used in the LCC system.

The problem we have with these various aspects of classification when we use them as the basic for comparison and evaluation is that we do not all agree on their function or importance. For example, in examining and evaluating structural features, I would place great importance on expressive notation and synthetic features of the systems. But if, for whatever reasons, we believe that expressive notation and synthesis are of little value (or, indeed, may be negative features), it is clear that we have reached an impasse. Another structural feature is the use of logic in the construction of classes and subclasses. Some prominent librarians have praised LCC because it is *not* logical, and have criticized DDC because it *is* logical, claiming that nonlogical systems can adapt more easily to changes in the structure of knowledge.[5]

Another criterion used to evaluate a classification system is the extent to which it somehow manages to present a useful version of the world as it is (or at least a reasonable facsimile thereof). Even in such a seemingly noncontroversial set of subclasses such as those representing political or geographical areas, there are strong differences of opinion as to the need for currentness. The recent change in the political organization of England brought forth a supplement to the DDC schedules which provided a list of the new political units and a revised notation to represent these units. Not everyone was happy with this change in DDC, and many would have preferred that the system not be changed. It is at such times that one can sympathize with the editors of DDC (or, for that matter, with the editors of any general and widely used system). It is clear that if we ask different things from a classification system, we will use different criteria for comparison and evaluation.

Needed Research

Obviously, we are concerned about how some of these conflicting ideas can be resolved. Is there some objective way of evaluating and comparing DDC and LCC? We do not know because we have never tried to find out. We have been too busy comparing costs to ask what it is we are paying for or why we are paying for it. We did not really try to answer the hard questions—and they are hard questions, ones which would involve new types of behavioral research. The one dimension of each system which lends itself to research relatively easily is notation: To what extent do enumerative hierarchical and ordinal notations lend themselves to on-line subject searching? One reason we may not have done this research—what work has been done has been accomplished by John Rather at the Library of Congress—is that it would prove that the DDC notation does have a future in on-line systems, whereas LCC does not.

Other areas of needed research are these:

1. The librarian's use of classification in reference and other readers' services—the extent to which the librarian, in functioning as a mediator between a library user and a local collection, uses a classification system as a way of thinking about the collection. Does the system provide a search strategy?
2. What versatility do different systems have in generating different types of references (i.e., can both broad and narrow bibliographies be generated)?
3. How can different systems be used in constructing user profiles for SDI (Selective Dissemination of Information) services and current-awareness services?
4. What actually happens at the output end of the system when a library user searches the shelves? We have established traditions of catalog use studies, but there is no comparable tradition in classification use studies.

I believe that librarians who have examined DDC and LCC from the point of view of their library needs have not considered all or even most of these basic questions about classification. If this is the case, how can we account for the "death of Dewey" in college and university libraries? A post-mortem is in order, but to understand what happened and why it happened we need to turn briefly to topics which at first may seem unrelated to the issue at hand.

Understanding the Great Switch

If we were to examine the literature produced in the United States on general library classification during the past ten to twenty years, we would find that one of the major preoccupations of librarians was not classification at all, but reclassification. That we should have been so preoccupied with reclassification rather than classification is, I think, an interesting commentary on the general state of classification in the United States. If I wanted to be uncharitable to both systems, I would say that what we have seen is the spectacle of thousands of librarians spending millions of dollars to the end of reclassifying from one nineteenth-century system to another, perhaps even more antiquated, nineteenth-century system. But that sort of characterization, although there is something to be said for it, would not do justice to the extent to which each system has partially escaped its nineteenth-century roots. On the other hand, it seems obvious that most librarians, when they felt they had to make a choice as to which classification system to use, never seriously considered that there might be some alternative system, or that it might be more advisable to construct an entirely new scheme. We need to consider why this was the case. I do not believe that the DDC-to-LCC movement can be understood unless it is considered against the whole intellectual, professional, and educational climate within which it took place. The movement from Dewey to LCC was surely one of the most time-consuming projects undertaken by U.S. librarians during the past several decades. Such a vast undertaking invites a detailed analysis. Such an analysis has not yet been made, and I will do little more here than to suggest approaches which might be appropriate.

If a postmortem were made, I think it would tell us quite a lot about things other than classification—it would tell us something about how librarians go about solving some of their problems. The questions that such a study would ask would have very little to do with the checklist of classification features I have mentioned above. Rather, it would ask why change took place, how it was disseminated, and what factors were so compelling as to set us on a course of action that will alter the future of classification longer than any of us can imagine. There surely must have been compelling reasons for this change.

I am seriously going to suggest that the change from Dewey to LCC had very little to do with classification. We could compare DDC with LCC in the most minute detail, and in the end would still not understand what has happened nor why it has happened. What is needed in this case is not research in classification at all, but research in the chemistry of change and in the rhetoric and motivation for change. Precedents, and indeed tools and models, for the needed research are available in that broad group of sociological studies identified as studies in the diffusion of innovations. These classic studies in the process of change have a long history in the United States, dating back well into the 1930s. The techniques involved have been used in dozens of different fields, but not—as far as I know—in any aspect of librarianship.

In suggesting studies in the dynamics of change, I am aware that there are some differences between the types of problems dealt with by E.M. Rogers and other specialists in this field[6] and those with which we must deal. Diffusion studies emerged when the U.S. Department of Agriculture wanted to find out why some farmers in Iowa readily accepted new strains of hybrid corn, while other farmers either did not accept them or did so at relatively long intervals after they were introduced. Acceptance patterns were studied, and farmers fell into various groups, such as early adopters, late adopters, etc. These results were correlated with a number of variables to identify opinion leaders and other dimensions of change patterns. If this seems like a farfetched source for the study of change in classification, it at least has this in common with our problem: the corn was the same, the differences were among the adopters. Note also that the research was about change as it resulted from innovative ideas. All well and good, but in the case of classification change, it is obvious that the LC Classification was almost as old as the product it replaced. Furthermore, the institutional setting of classification use suggests other ways that diffusion research in classification would differ somewhat from more customary types of diffusion research.

Anyone interested in exploring this idea further would also want to consider some types of marketing research. We are talking about a change in behavior. Advertising research is obviously interested in why people adopt one brand of soap rather than another, why they switch brands, and how something called "brand identification" is achieved. Advertising researchers know that many factors which influence consumers in their decisions have very little to do with the quality of the product or whether the consumer really needs the product. (If you have not read much in advertising research, I would not encourage you to do so unless you are already rather cynical, or unless you are prepared for considerable disillusionment about those friendly folks that bring you your favorite television shows.) About fifteen years ago, Bardin H. Nelson wrote what has since became a classic statement of the assumptions on which advertising is based. He called his article "Seven Principles in Image Formation." Here is the first of his seven principles: "People are not 'exclusively' rational creatures."[7] This is the conclusion one could come to after delving into the literature on reclassification. How else can one respond to reasoning such as this:

> Inasmuch as there seems little possibility of developing a classificatory
> language which will satisfy the demands of the super-specialist as well as

of the general reference librarian, it would seem that we must opt for the most workable tool at present available to carry forward the mundane but needful task of moving books and records from catalog department to shelves and catalog.[8]

The needs of the super-specialists (whoever they may be) have never been the issue, and the dichotomy between specialists and reference librarians is a straw man in the context of general library classification. Even if the dichotomy were accepted as valid (which it is not), the conclusion "to opt for the most workable tool" does not logically result from the premise.

The author of the above statement has confused ends and means, and has done so in such a way that if you do not accept his conclusion, then you put yourself in the position of being opposed to the "mundane but needful task" of making materials available to your library users as quickly as possible. And what is one to make of this statement by Matthis and Taylor: "Essentially the argument has now moved beyond theoretical discussions of the 'best' classification system and settled upon the real issue—the promise and prospect of centralized cataloging and classification"?[9] Anyone with even a passing acquaintance with classification theory knows that the arguments cannot possibly have moved beyond theoretical discussions for the simple reason that such discussions have never taken place. From the very beginning, the issues were practical and focused principally on economic factors of technical processing. On those few occasions when the advocates of DDC have tried to talk about structural features of classification systems, they have been accused of talking "theory" or, what is worse, of raising esoteric questions of philosophy: "These questionings of philosophical assumptions, once raised, tend to vitiate the impetus given to the spirit of change." By raising such questions (which, of course, have nothing to do with theory or philosophy, but with structure, function, and use) one can thus initiate "a preposterous dialogue of 'pro' this system and 'con' that."[10] Indeed, such questions, once raised, could vitiate the spirit of change; but whether the resulting dialog would be preposterous would depend on whether you are buying a product or selling it.

Without much further comment, I will quote a few more of Nelson's principles, and those of you who have critically read the literature on reclassification will see the connections. Nelson's second principle states that "People respond to situations in ways which appear to them to protect their self-images."[11] I have an idea that in the world of academic librarianship, self-images loom large in the decision-making process. The fifth principle tells us: "If an image is marked by doubt, uncertainty, or insecurity, utilize additional means for creating further doubts. Present the new image in a form whereby it will dispel anxiety or doubts."[12] His sixth principle is widely used by network developers: "Place the desired image in the most favorable setting. If at all possible, clothe the new image in the already accepted values of the people."[13]

Does all of this strike you as somewhat peripheral to a consideration of the change from DDC to LCC? Perhaps. But you will admit that the image of DDC was changed, that it was badly damaged, and that this set the stage for serious setbacks in its credibility as a viable classification system.

Parenthetically, I might add that the types of research which I have proposed might also be useful in understanding other library-type games and diversions, such as dividing the catalog, working for faculty status, changing administrative structures, joining OCLC, or whatever movement is currently substituting for the real problems of improving library service. If I have underestimated the depth to which advocates of change have explored some of the basic issues, I can only say that they did not state their case very well in the library literature. The central issue is the purpose of classification.

Purpose

There are two extreme views on the purpose of classifying books. On the one hand, some librarians consider classification to be an important device in providing access to library collections. Some of them have described classification as a map which guides the user through the collection, a device for discovering not only what one wants but what one did not know existed. In this ideal version of the purpose of classification, it is in fact a dynamic device of great importance in the learning process and in the acquisition of new knowledge. The other extreme says essentially that classification is not much more than a simple parking device: we mark and we park. The user's basic guide to the collection is the alphabetical subject heading catalog, and this catalog serves as an index to the classification system which organizes the books on the shelves. Those librarians who subscribe to the mark-and-park school will probably prefer the LC Classification. On the other hand, those librarians who place more importance on classification as a direct subject access device will probably prefer the expressive notation and modest use of synthesis available in DDC, since these offer a search strategy for open-stack collections.

Implementation

In the United States the purpose of classifying material is accomplished almost solely by using classification to organize books on shelves. This is supplemented by Cutter's alphabetico-specific subject heading catalog in its straight A-Z form or in its divided form. These well-known facts need to be brought up in considering the future of classification in the United States. If, for the foreseeable future, classification is to function only as a system of shelving books, then we are dealing with one problem. However, with the use of the computer in organizing bibliographical data, we have a new tool which can be a very powerful search tool. In other words, the classified catalog, which for all practical purposes has been a dead issue in the United States since around 1900, may be in for a new lease on life. To me, one of the most exciting possibilities for the immediate future of the DDC is found in the extent to which we can use it for on-line subject searching. This issue has been completely ignored or misunderstood in all of the literature on reclassification which I have consulted. Tauber and Feinberg, in the report mentioned above, state that "LC can be programmed to do *all that we have required* of an enumerative scheme up to the present" (emphasis added).[14] "All that we have required"—but in terms which might be relevant to computer potential we have required nothing, since our shelflists have been used only for inventory control. We can now ask a lot more than that.

This is where the notation of LCC and DDC have very great significance in terms of potential computer application. To understand the possibilities and limitations of each, we need to consider the nature of nonexpressive, nonhierarchical notation of the sort used in LCC. In such a system, the only approach is to a specific subject class. With an expressive notation we can pull out blocks of material; if the computer is programmed properly we can enter the system at any level and all of its subdivisions. This almost self-evident potential of DDC is one that has yet to be fully explored. Dewey also has the potential for further refinements in subject searching if a system of facet indicators can be established. Consider, for example, the possibilities of searching local subdivisions in LCC and DDC. With DDC, a run of the computer could pull out all classes starting, for example, with the number 78, the class for music. If one wanted only books about music in England, then a second run (using the local subdivision number from the Area Tables) would pull out relevant titles. Or, rather, it could if a consistent facet indicator were developed for local subdivisions. This, as you know, is a problem now because a standard subdivision may be identified by one or more than one zero. I believe that the Dewey system can adopt some of the synthetic devices used in the Universal Decimal Classification and come up with a system of notation which can both serve as a notation for physically shelving books and at the same time exploit the class numbers with search devices which complement the alphabetico-specific structure of subject headings.

Since we are getting Dewey class numbers on MARC tapes, it is possible that even those libraries which use the LCC system to shelve their books will have an on-line searching device by using the Dewey class numbers.

Now, to what extent the LC Classification can provide such access seems to me to be so small as to be virtually beyond hope. The LCC notation was never designed to serve such a purpose and its ordinal notation would probably present insurmountable problems. On the other hand, I would not want to underestimate the imagination and resourcefulness of the Library of Congress staff, and I look forward with great interest to what search devices they will design. Be that as it may, the computer is the challenge which DDC must face. Structural changes will have to be made to go beyond its current potential in on-line searching (which, modest as it may seem, is far superior to what is available with the LCC notation). In placing so much stress on the current and future on-line capability of DDC, I do so within the framework of most libraries currently using the system (and most libraries which have recently switched to LCC). I am aware that information scientists have stated that both DDC and LCC are inappropriate for computer application in subject retrieval. From their point of view this may be the case. An on-line classified catalog using DDC may seem to offer limited possibilities when compared to highly sophisticated *special* information systems; but for most general library book collections, such access would be a monumental step forward. If I have any doubts about DDC's future in relationship to a revived form of the classified catalog, they are related less to the system itself than to those of us in the United States who know so little about the potential of any classified catalog, manual or automated.

There is a historical dimension to this issue of the classified catalog that is just interesting enough to comment on briefly. Dewey himself was an advocate of the classified catalog, and did not look with much enthusiasm on Cutter's dictionary catalog. In 1888 he said, "The dictionary catalog has been a popular fad and will die out."[15] So much for Dewey as a prophet. In the first edition of his classification system, he noted that it was conceived as a system for organizing entries in catalogs, but could also be used for organizing materials on shelves and in files. When he was librarian at the State Library of New York, his subject catalog was a classified catalog. It may also surprise you to learn that Charles Martel, one of the prime architects of the LCC system, was also a firm believer in the classified catalog. He did indeed accept the alphabetical subject-heading catalog, but believed that any true research library had to supplement this catalog with a classified catalog. It was Martel's idea that the shelf list could be amended with guide cards, cross-references, and added entries in such a way that it could serve both for inventory control and for classified subject access.[16] I do not know to what extent the use of such a catalog affected the evolution of LCC subject headings (although I understand that music librarians find that a shelf list is absolutely essential as a supplement to their subject-heading catalogs). In American library education, I doubt that we have sufficiently stressed the extent to which classified systems complement the sort of access provided by alphabetical systems. If this distinction is not clear to many librarians in the United States, it is probably because they assume without question that alphabetical systems are for structuring catalogs and classified systems are for shelving books. Although this attitude reflects current practice, its implications for subject cataloging must be reexamined.

The technical problems that the Dewey system will have to solve are the result of its dual function as a system for structuring catalogs and a system for shelving books. As we have been told many times, the book is a one-dimensional physical object, and it can be classified in one place and in one place only. But catalogs can provide multiple access points, and there is no reason why a classified catalog should be limited to a one-place system, be it a manual or an automated classified catalog. In the United States, Dewey is used as a system for shelving books, and this is a function which is not likely to change. In other countries, DDC is used for both shelving systems and systems for the classified catalog (note, for example, the use of DDC in the *British National Bibliography*). If one were dealing with the classified catalog without the restraints of a shelving system, one could indeed develop a highly sophisticated searching tool. But the most valuable feature of the Dewey system is that it not only *can* be used for both functions, but that it *is* being widely used for both functions. It seems that for the working librarian this is a tremendous advantage, for one can indeed begin to structure a conceptual map of one's library collection. If knowing one's collection is a prerequisite for good library service, then the Dewey system has to be evaluated in the light of how it helps us to gain some sort of conceptual control over these collections, whether we are working directly with books or references to books in catalogs.

To those committed to the LCC system, the potentials of the classified catalog may seem somewhat less exciting than they do to me. But consider for a moment one of the standard working tools of the librarian: *Library of Congress Catalog: Books: Subjects.* The present structure of this subject supplement to the *National Union Catalog* is an unfortunate byproduct of our predilection for alphabetically arranged subject headings. As useful as this tool may be, I believe that if it were issued as a classified catalog (even if limited to the simplest form of such a catalog—i.e., arranged in shelf list order by the LCC system), it could serve its current function of providing subject access, but at the same time could combine the advantages of the classified approach. Furthermore, it would then give thousands of users of the LCC system what they probably want very much: a guide to LC's shelf-listing practices. A colleague once told me that if a library adopts the LC Classification system, that library is to a certain extent a branch of the Library of Congress. There is a lot of truth in this statement, because the application of the LC

Classification schedules, with their extensive use of alphabetically arranged subclasses with a cutter number notation, is in large measure controlled by what is in the Library of Congress collection. Thus, to make use of LCC coincide with its use by the Library of Congress (which, I take it, is one of the main reasons for adopting the system), the librarian must assume that he or she is adding material to the shelf list of the Library of Congress with its millions of entries.

However, if the structure of LC's *Subject Catalog* were to be changed, I think it would not be unreasonable to propose that it be changed to the same form now used by the *British National Bibliography*. Not only would this be a step toward the standardization of national bibliographies, it would also be a service to the thousands of libraries in the United States and abroad which use DDC; this could be done in such a way that it would considerably improve the utility of *Books: Subjects* as an access tool. Those librarians now using the LC Classification would lose little, if anything, but those many, many thousands of librarians using DDC would gain tremendously.

Academic Librarians and Dewey

I am not optimistic that academic librarians who have adopted LCC will in the near future change their ways of thinking about the potentials of library classification. Nor, for that matter, will they recognize the fundamental fallacy of bibliographical networks which simply deliver data without offering the possibilities of on-line subject access based on classification. On the other hand, if those who guide the future of DDC can do a better job of showing librarians how to exploit the system (both as a shelving system and an on-line access tool), then it is not unlikely that librarians already committed to LCC will make use of the DDC class numbers now available in machine-readable form on MARC tapes. This is one of several reasons why all material going into the MARC system, including all foreign-language material, should be given Dewey class numbers. Those who believe that the future of on-line access lies with a new system of subject descriptors rather than with classification are not taking into account the deep resistance which will come from academic librarians if the Library of Congress attempts to structure a completely new system of subject headings. I believe that academic librarians will strenuously resist such a change for the same reason they adopted the LC Classification system (i.e., the costs of cataloging and classification) and for the same reason they resisted those rules in the *Anglo-American Cataloging Rules* which adhered to the Paris Principles for the structuring of headings for corporate bodies; this, as some of you now know, was an expensive concession to the status quo, and the Library of Congress is moving ahead with its new policies and with "desuperimposition."

The "great switch" has some implications for the Library of Congress and its relationship to its own classification system. The LC Classification no longer belongs exclusively to the Library of Congress, or if it does, it soon will not. The thousands of libraries which now use the system will want to have a say in its future development. Even if the Library of Congress wanted to abandon its own system (and it is not clear to me why they need it), it is hardly likely that the combined pressure of academic libraries would permit this to happen. Furthermore, if the system is to provide the economic advantages which have been claimed for it—these claims, of course, were never made by the Library of Congress, but by academic librarians from relatively small colleges—then librarians will need more from the Library of Congress than they are now getting. They will need access to the Library of Congress shelf list, a continually updated single index to the complete set of schedules (and at a reasonable cost within reach of small college libraries), guides to interpreting the schedules, an on-line authority file, and probably more tools which have been developed at the Library of Congress for the in-house use of catalogers and classifiers.

Public and School Libraries

Public and school libraries are in a position somewhat different from that of academic libraries. It is possible, however, that the general atmosphere created by the advocates of LCC is one which may have already begun to sow some seeds of doubt in the minds of librarians who direct school and public libraries. These librarians have a longstanding involvement with DDC and there are compelling reasons why I hope this does not change. The LCC system is completely inadequate for their service-oriented philosophies and open-stack collections. Most of the economic advantages claimed for a switch to LCC have probably been largely eliminated by LC's Decimal Classification Division's increased coverage of the current English-language book production. If there should be any savings in cost, I cannot imagine that they would be significant enough to justify what would be lost with a switch to LCC.

I am not sure to what extent, in the next few years, public and school librarians will find themselves in the same position in which academic users of DDC found themselves a few years ago—that is, under strong pressure from network developers to reclassify to conform to existing bibliographical data bases. This pressure will surely become stronger as we implement network developments advocated by the National Commission on Libraries and Information Science. In the first place, I believe the economic arguments are spurious and were designed to benefit the economic base of the networks, not to benefit the users of the networks. In the second place, any network that attempts to provide a national service is not conceivable unless it includes both LCC and DDC numbers. For one thing, the Dewey numbers give public and school librarians options for close or broad classification which are absolutely impossible within the structure of the LCC notational system. I would encourage public and school librarians to insist that their networks include the Dewey system.

Most public and school librarians do not need me to remind them of the advantages of DDC, but what follows may be of some interest to network developers (who should also apprise themselves of the fundamentals of classification) and library administrators who may be too far removed from the public service desk to understand the role of classification in public services.

Librarians working with relatively small collections, as compared to the collections of large university libraries, have a completely different relationship to their collections. The universe of knowledge with which they must deal is still one that can be grasped in its larger outlines and in considerable detail by an experienced and educated librarian. The large university libraries are best categorized as collections of special libraries which are administered by subject specialists. (This is consistent with the Library of Congress Classification which has been properly decribed as a collection of largely uncoordinated special classifications which lack unifying structural features.) Perhaps this is why DDC has always been appreciated by public and school librarians and, at one time, by many college and junior college librarians in the United States. The collections with which they deal are general in the sense that they cover wide areas of knowledge which represent many disciplines. As I have noted above, under such circumstances classification can be an indispensable tool for the efficient use of one's collection in providing public services. The notation provides a symbolic language which is quite easy to learn. It permits a type of interaction with the collection and with users of the collection which I do not think is possible in the case of LCC's notational structure.

In public and school libraries, one is more likely to find attempts to use a single classification system for different media. Unfortunately, we have little research on just how well DDC works with such diverse materials as sound recordings, slide collections, media kits, and other nonbook media. We know that some libraries have adopted DDC for these materials, and it would seem to be an ideal system for both students and faculty, not to mention public service librarians. Perhaps future editions of DDC should provide some information on how to use the system with these nonbook materials. The available DDC options of broad or close classification would seem to be significant in this case. As for LCC, it has been used by some librarians to classify sound recordings, but does not seem to have much of a future with nonbook media in general.

International Implications

What futures do the two systems have at the international level? DDC, of course, is already somewhat of an international system. The LCC system is not international, and there is no possibility that it will ever be widely used outside of the United States. It is too closely tied to the very specific needs of the Library of Congress, and more specifically to the needs of the Library of Congress as they were conceived between fifty and seventy-five years ago, when the purpose, the plan, and the structure of the system were developed. Thus, the very factor which has been advanced for its wide adoption in the United States is, I would argue, the chief reason it has no future in the international exchange of bibliographical data.

To what extent the Dewey system will be seriously considered as an international standard is not yet known. Although its future in this role may not seem promising (despite its tremendous worldwide dispersal), it should not be ruled out yet. If the Library of Congress continues to include DDC numbers on all items issued on MARC tapes as that data base continues to grow, then DDC will be a serious contender at the international level. Certainly, the decisions affecting the British Library will have a bearing on the issue, as will the wider dispersal of DDC in France.

Alternatives

I have been assuming that the only real choice available is between DDC and LCC. I suppose that right now this is the case. If one were seriously to suggest that what the Library of Congress needs is a new classification, one would be considered quite mad. Such is the way we have been educated to think about classification in the United States.

If, ten to fifteen years ago, academic librarians had asked for a new, modern classification system, they probably could have gotten one. But now, having spent millions of dollars converting to LCC and having convinced themselves that it is the best of all possible worlds, the option of a new system has been closed and will remain closed for a long time. The point I am making is this: if (for reasons which they accepted as valid) academic librarians found DDC inadequate, and if there were no ways it could be changed to make it adequate, then they should have switched to something better than LCC. If there were no better system, then either the LCC system should have been completely overhauled or a completely new scheme should have been constructed. Of course, I believe that at that time, DDC could have been changed to serve academic librarians.

If you have the impression that I am somewhat skeptical about the wide adoption of the LC Classification by academic librarians and that I find the literature on reclassification completely unconvincing, you could not be closer to the truth. I believe that it is not so much what DDC has lost as what librarians have lost.

I am not sure whether I have read a paper or given a sermon, but whatever I have done, these things needed to be said and these questions needed to be asked. If I have produced little or no scientific evidence with which to further the cause of DDC, then I am in good company, for the most vigorous advocates of LCC have given us little more than opinion surveys, cost studies (which I cannot accept), and "good news" from network organizers, for as Marshall McLuhan has said: "Advertising is good news." If there is anything that can keep the Dewey-to-LCC movement alive, it will be our lack of understanding of the potential of general classification in library service. However, if the movement has run its course, we can now turn our attention to the uses of classification rather than reclassification. If we do this, then the future of the Dewey Decimal Classification is assured.

REFERENCES

1. Mowery, Robert L. "The 'Trend to LC' in College and University Libraries," *Library Resources & Technical Services* 19:389-97, Fall 1975.

2. Tauber, Maurice F., and Feinberg, Hilda. "The Dewey Decimal and Library of Congress Classifications; An Overview," *Drexel Library Quarterly* 10:56-74, Oct. 1974.

3. Matthis, Raimund E., and Taylor, Desmond. *Adopting the Library of Congress Classification System.* New York, R.R. Bowker, 1971, p. 2.

4. *Ibid.*

5. Richmond, Phyllis A. "General Advantages and Disadvantages of Using the Library of Congress Classification." *In* Richard H. Schimmelpfeng and C. Donald Cook, eds. *The Use of the Library of Congress Classification.* Chicago, ALA, 1968, p. 209.

6. Rogers, Everett M. *Diffusion of Innovations.* New York, Free Press, 1962.

7. Nelson, Bardin H. "Seven Principles in Image Formation." *In* Lee Richardson, ed. *Dimensions of Communication.* New York, Appleton-Century-Crofts, 1969, p. 55.

8. Matthis, Raimund E. "Moderator's Comments." *In* Jean M. Perreault, ed. *Reclassification: Rationale and Problems* (Conference Proceedings from the School of Library and Information Services, University of Maryland, vol. 1). College Park, School of Library and Information Services, University of Maryland, 1968, p. 27.

9. Matthis and Taylor, *op. cit.,* p. 3.

10. Matthis, *op. cit.,* p. 27.

11. Nelson, *op. cit.*, p. 56.

12. *Ibid.*, p. 58.

13. *Ibid.*, p. 59.

14. Tauber and Feinberg, *op. cit.*, p. 69.

15. "Conference of Librarians, Catskills, Sept. 25-28, 1888 . . . Third Day—Thursday, September 27," *Library Journal* 13:315, Sept.-Oct. 1888.

16. LaMontagne, Leo E. *American Library Classification*. Hamden, Conn., Shoe String Press, 1961, p. 316.

PETER LEWIS
Librarian
University of Sussex
Brighton, England

Factors in the Selection of a Classification Scheme for a Large General Library

T his paper concerns the British Library; by now it is well known that the British Library consists of more than one large library. One of its components, the British Museum Library, is among the largest in the world; two others, the Science Reference Library in London, and the Lending Division in Yorkshire, both have collections sizable enough to raise problems regarding classification. In fact, however, the Lending Division has long since rejected classification as an operational tool in any other than peripheral uses, and is not a component which enters into the considerations I am making today.

In addition to these, there is the Bibliographical Services Division, which is evolving from the formerly separate entity, the *British National Bibliography* (BNB). This division is the most significant user of classification at the present time. Not only is the *British National Bibliography* primarily dependent on classification for its arrangement and articulation, but the classification data supplied by BNB is a substantial element of the centralized cataloging service which it gives to all kinds of libraries in Great Britain. One of the functions of the Bibliographical Services Division is to extend this service to cover the needs of in-house bibliographic processing within the British Library itself.

I am therefore dealing not so much with a large general library as with a large and complex national library system. Moreover, this is a system in which all the components have had a prior existence as independent organizations, sometimes with a long history of service and administration of their own. This aspect of the matter creates problems of rationalization which are perhaps unusual in terms of their scale, but which may not be dissimilar from those which arise wherever uniform bibliographic control is to be imposed on any two or more existing libraries which have long-established prior commitments and investments in their own different forms of control.

What makes the British Library a particularly interesting case for the classificationist, in my opinion, is that its principal prior commitment is the classification service which it provides for other libraries, through the *British National Bibliography* and its contributions to the MARC record. Contrast this with the Library of Congress, for example, where classification policies and developments have historically originated primarily to meet in-house requirements, and have only secondarily been determined by the needs of other libraries using the data. The British Library begins with a service to other libraries, and one of the main questions is whether that commitment can be extended to embrace its own, newly conceived in-house problems.

We know what consequences may spring from too close an adherence to the dictum that "what's good for General Motors is good for the country." Essentially, the British Library has to find an answer to the question: Can what is good for the country also be good for General Motors?

The Working Party

In 1972, a Working Party was established with the following terms of reference: "to examine the various classification and indexing systems currently in use in the various component parts of the British Library and to consider the possibilities of rationalisation, taking into account the need for standardisation nationally and internationally." The Working Party consisted of senior staff members with responsibilities for classification and indexing policies and for programs in each of the various component parts of the British Library (BL) together with two external members: Herbert Coblans—a distinguished authority on classification and indexing in the international sphere, and myself, who was honored with an invitation to act as chairman of the Working Party. The research department of Aslib acted as consultants on technical questions.

The Working Party delivered its final report to the British Library Board in June 1974; this is projected for publication in 1976, together with the texts of those supporting studies which the Working Party appended to the report. In this paper I am therefore anticipating publication of the report to some extent, but my intention is to draw attention to those findings and conclusions of the report which seem to be of interest to classificationists and library administrators concerned with the problems of rationalization in this field.

I must begin this task by making the essential disclaimer that, although the authority for my comments derives from knowledge gained as chairman of the Working Party, nothing in what follows should be regarded as representing the official viewpoint or policy of the British Library Board. For one thing, the selection and interpretation of the Working Party's findings are my own. In addition, the British Library has not yet given a public indication of its endorsement of any of the recommendations made in the report.

The Problem

The only objective of rationalization is to achieve optimum cost-effectiveness. The ideal state of rationalization is one in which all requirements are met by a single system, generating the necessary data from a single source. The ultimate solution for the British Library would therefore be to find a single classification scheme which would yield maximum efficiency with respect to the following needs:

1. *The arrangement of books in the British Museum Library*   The British Museum Library (BML) previously has used no classification for the arrangement of its stock. However, there are plans for it to move into a new, custom-designed building sometime in the late 1980s; when that happens, it will place on open access approximately one-quarter million volumes in the fields of humanities and social sciences. For these it needs a suitable classification. The great bulk of its vast collections will remain on closed access, but the availability of a class number for all acquisitions would enable it to exercise the greatest flexibility and economy in redetermining the contents of its open-access collections from time to time.

2. *The arrangement of books in the Science Reference Library*   At present, virtually all Science Reference Library (SRL) stock is on open access, and classified in accordance with a special classification developed within the library itself from an earlier Patent Office Library classification. It is presently housed at two separate main sites, but it will eventually occupy one wing of the new British Library building and will thus exist physically next to the British Museum Library, with quick and easy access by readers from one library to the other.

3. *The arrangement of bibliographic records in the subject catalogs of both BML and SRL*   At present, the principal catalogs are the published *British*

Museum Subject Index, which covers the fields of the British Museum Library, and at SRL, the card catalogs, arranged in accordance with SRL's own classification scheme. It must be remembered, of course, that BML shares with SRL the task of conserving the British copyright deposit intake, along subject-divided lines, and there is an expectation that the published *British Museum Subject Index* may be extended in scope to embrace SRL's work in its own fields of responsibility.

4. *The arrangement of records in the British National Bibliography*   Arising largely from this need, and of equal weight in the Working Party's terms of reference, are the two following requirements.

5. *National standardization*   BNB and British MARC act as sources of centralized cataloging and classification data for a large number of academic and public libraries throughout the United Kingdom and elsewhere. The classification data used to arrange BNB, and provided in MARC, should meet the needs of shelf arrangement and bibliographic records in the greatest possible number of other libraries within the national network.

6. *International Standards*   As the principal national library, the British Library is increasingly involved in the interchange of bibliographic information at the international level. Classification and other subject data are a significant aspect of this interchange, in regard to the cost-saving utilization by all exchange partners of the information flowing through the international networks.

Indexing and Information Retrieval

We began in the sphere of indexing and information retrieval. We examined comprehensively the European and North American literature reporting experimental work or summarizing the present state of the art on mechanized searching and retrieval by means of MARC tapes or by Dewey Decimal Classification (DDC), Library of Congress Classification (LCC), or Universal Decimal Classification (UDC). We also studied problems, such as profile construction, that are raised by the use of classification in these spheres. This is a large and difficult area, on which it would be possible to spend the remainder of this session. I will restrict myself to reporting our conclusions.

A satisfactory basis for a machine information retrieval system cannot be established without first identifying comprehensively the range of services which it is to supply, and then investigating the particular problems of each service. At the British Library, the potential demand for such services is very large and diffuse and, at this stage of development of BL's internal and external connections, the problems of coordination and integration seemed to us nearly insurmountable.

In addition, we felt that experimental work to date demonstrates that *verbal* mechanisms are superior to classificational notation mechanisms in achieving effective specific subject retrieval systems.

Undoubtedly this second conclusion was colored by the fact that PRECIS (the Preserved Context Indexing System) already incorporates a "verbal" machine-based indexing system that has been used for four years by the *British National Bibliography,* and recently by some library institutions, to create subject indexes for classified arrangements of document citations.

PRECIS was, in fact, the only available machine-based indexing system that appeared to have the potential to meet whatever future requirements might arise in this spere in the British Library. We saw it first as a means of dealing with the immediate problem of the *British Museum Subject Index,* the production of which, in its present form, involves expensive manual elements and has been increasingly delayed because of staffing difficulties. A preliminary investigation showed that it was possible to manipulate PRECIS strings to produce mechanically an acceptable subject heading system which could replace the *British Museum Subject Index* with gains to the user, more efficient indexing information, and without an increase in cost. Further testing was undertaken and (subject to its satisfactory conclusion) we recommended that the PRECIS subject heading system be adopted to provide subject access to the BML collection and elsewhere as required. We saw it as the only means of providing a unified subject index to the BL Reference Division collections, and ultimately PRECIS strings would be added to all the records in the data base of the BL Reference Division.

Classification and Interlibrary Relations

Turning now to classification policies for the British Library in general, and for the BNB in particular, I have already emphasized that these cannot be determined without reference to the external use of classification schemes, nationally and internationally. The BL is committed to making its bibliographic data base available to other libraries and will itself receive large quantities of bibliographic records from other libraries for its internal use. There is, therefore, a potentially large demand from the library community for the provision of standard classification notations on British Library records. There may also be significant savings in the use of classification marks available on foreign records. The current ferment of activity throughout the library world in these areas suggested that further investigation of developments at a later date, when clearer pictures emerged, would be required before a final decision was made. Looking at it now, eighteen months later, I do not think that the pictures have yet become any clearer.

For the picture as it appeared then, we collected and analyzed information on the comparative use of the published general classification schemes, in British libraries and in the national bibliographies of thirty-three countries. From our analysis, there is no question of the predominance of DDC in Great Britain. We established that DDC is used by 47 percent of all libraries,* and that it controls the arrangement of 75 percent of all library holdings. In contrast to this, UDC is used by 22 percent of British libraries, but controls the arrangement of only 5 percent of library holdings. As for LCC, particularly favored by British university libraries, it is used by 2 percent of all our libraries and controls the arrangement of 6 percent of library holdings.

Internationally, it appeared that DDC and UDC have each an equal number of users at the level of the national bibliography or national library agency. We estimated that the annual output of authoritative machine-readable records which carry DDC numbers was about 131,000; there was a similar quantity of machine-readable records with LCC numbers, but none carried UDC numbers. On this evidence, we made a firm recommendation that the biliographic records created in BL's Bibliographical Services Division should continue to carry both DDC and LCC classmarks, and that they should do so as long as these facilitated the supply of exchangeable MARC records, and the generation of classified catalogs and bibliographies in forms acceptable and useful to public and academic libraries.

In recent years, there has been some lobbying in Great Britain for the addition of UDC numbers to the MARC data base, but the evidence we obtained of national usage did not support it very strongly. We concluded that UDC should only be added to DDC and LCC numbers if the British Library found it desirable to do so for its own purposes—that is, to facilitate information exchanges with other national libraries in Europe or elsewhere, or to provide a basis for its own shelf arrangement.

Classification for Shelf Arrangement

We now come to what proved to be the most difficult part of our brief: the determination of classification policies for the two great libraries of the Reference Division—the British Museum Library and the Science Reference

---

*It will be noticed that this figure differs appreciably from that reported by Downing on p. 73 of this volume. It appears that there is no one authoritative list of British libraries, and that the British Library survey reported by Lewis was done by Aslib and included all special libraries which were institutional members.—Ed.

Library. These two libraries have developed quite separately, on separate sites, with quite different histories, and with different operating policies.

The British Museum Library's particular need was for a classification scheme appropriate for the open-access collection, covering all fields of humanities and social sciences. Since it has not been classified before, there is no burden of reclassification involved.

The Science Reference Library, by contrast, was a postwar creation with its nucleus in the nineteenth-century Patent Office Library, and although its book acquisition programs have been extended to embrace all copyright deposit items in all of its disciplinary fields, it still has the particular task of supplying the requirements of industrial research and the patents community—a task which it brought with it from its origins as the Patent Office Library and the National Reference Library for Science and Invention. Furthermore, it has put a large investment of professional energy over the last ten or more years into developing a special classification of its own from an earlier form used in the Patent Office. For convenience we may call this system the SRL scheme. Its collections are arranged by this scheme, and so are its subject catalogs.

The problem here, then, is that the Science Reference Library sees itself as continuing to act as a discrete, "mission-oriented" library with its own role, its own identifiable clientele, and its own classification scheme as one of the tools by which it serves that clientele; the fulfillment of this mission is seen by its staff to require little interaction with its future next-door neighbor, the British Museum Library. What is to be gained by reclassifying SRL for the sake of uniformity with the BML next door?

There are two answers to that question. One is the proposition that the use of a single classification is cheaper overall than the use of two or more—especially when the single classification is one generated from the third corner of the triangle, the Bibliographical Services Division, and is salable, so to speak, to other libraries in the country and overseas. One drawback of the SRL's own scheme is that it is not used by any other library, and that its addition to BL's data base would be merely an additional expense, yielding benefit to none but SRL itself.

The other answer to the question is that a single classification for both libraries of the Reference Division will provide flexibility and economy in demarcating the spheres of responsibility for each of the two libraries, as new disciplines and cross-disciplinary literatures emerge in the future. It will allow a uniformity of approach to the changing needs and interests of British Library users in general.

Neither of these answers takes account of the quality of particular classifications, however. If one classification scheme is as good as another, the argument for standardization is simply one of cost and administrative economy, and the value of classification as a professional method is in some ways diminished. If you regard classification as one of the most important elements in good library service to a particular clientele, you must give weight to the argument that what is gained financially and administratively in a change of classification may be lost in service to readers, if the new classification is less effective than the old one in meeting the needs of those users.

It was not for the Working Party to determine whether SRL was to continue its "mission-oriented" role indefinitely, or alternatively to change its identity into a kind of scientific twin of the BML. What we could do, and did, was to examine the case that its present classification was significantly more effective for the control of scientific literature as a whole than any of the general classification schemes, which, being suitable for the BML, might also be used by SRL as an alternative to its own scheme for shelf arrangement. A study was carried out for us by Aslib of four general classification schemes: DDC, UDC, LCC and the Bibliographic Classification (BC). The last of these four was, of course, familiarly known in its original form by the name of its inventor, Bliss. What we studied was the preliminary schedules of the new revised version developed by Mills and others in England as a faceted classification.

The four schemes were compared with each other and ranked in terms of seventeen criteria which in summary may be grouped as follows: (1) effectiveness as classifications, as evidenced, for instance, by provision of helpful collocation, level of specificity, up-to-dateness, notational qualities and searchability; (2) ease of use by a classifier; (3) availability of schedules; (4) frequency and extent of revision; (5) mechanisms established for maintenance and revision; and (6) extent of present use by libraries and bibliographic services. Judging by most of the criteria related to effectiveness as classifications, and with particular attention to the most recent thought on classification principles (as exemplified, among others, by the Classification Research Group), none of the four schemes was rated very high. We felt that LCC was the scheme that probably met fewest requirements, and BC possibly the most. However, BC has yet to be published in its revised form, and we were assessing it largely on the basis of its authors' claims; the judgment is thus very tentative. DDC and LCC were both rated high for criteria related to ease of use, availability of schedules, and extent of use by libraries as a whole. In addition, DDC was the only scheme of the four that scored high for the criteria related to frequency of revision, and to mechanisms for maintenance and revision.

The investigation closely examined all of these questions, and took account of previous studies, such as the ALA Resources and Technical Services Division Classification Committee's "Statement on Types of Classification Available to New Academic Libraries."[1] The detailed analysis is to be found in a technical memorandum prepared by Aslib for the Working Party, and this will be included among the appendices of the published report. At the risk of considerable oversimplification, I can attempt here only to summarize our findings on the four schemes as candidates for the role of arranging one-quarter million books on the open shelves of the British Museum Library:

BC—This was potentially the most progressive and satisfactory system for future needs. It is being developed in its revised form by British classificationists, and is thus distinctive and symbolic as a significant national contribution to modern classification, in advance of all others. However, against this must be balanced the unknown and untried performance characteristics of the new BC and the lack of any determinate policies with respect to all the other criteria related to availability of schedules, revision machinery, and use by other libraries.

LCC—This is a series of classification schemes used by a significant number of academic and other research libraries, whose general objectives and collections have more in common with the British Library than do those of the British Library with those of other libraries. LCC numbers are also available from the MARC record. Nevertheless, LCC rates low on most modern criteria related to effectiveness as a classification scheme and/or revision mechanism; it was particularly felt that the scheme offered the least possibility for a necessary British Library participation in long-term development and revision in accordance with British needs.

UDC—In many ways, UDC is the most important scheme in the interests of international standardization, particularly as it is widely used in Europe. On the other hand, it is generally considered seriously out of date and in need of drastic revision, and its future is uncertain. If the British Library adopts UDC, it will be necessary for it to become closely and positively involved in schedule development, and probably to make some financial investment in it. In addition, from the British Museum Library user's point of view, UDC has some disadvantages in its notation, which is designed primarily for the arrangement of document citations, and not for shelf arrangement.

DDC—This is the scheme that emerged as the most likely candidate for the British Museum Library, not so much from its positive merits as a classification (although it was thought to have no fewer positive merits than any of its rivals) as from the relative absence of drawbacks. Its practical advantages were seen to be: (1) it is more widely used in Great Britain than any other scheme; (2) its schedules and index are complete, widely available, and reasonably easy to use; (3) it is already being applied to British copyright materials, as well as to a substantial proportion of other BL acquisitions; (4) there are well-established procedures for its maintenance and revision; and (5) indications were given to us by British representation on the Editorial Policy Committee, and by recent policy statements from that body, that British and European requirements can be effectively input into the revision machinery in the future.

Classification of the SRL

From these conclusions relating to BML, we were left logically with only three possibilities to investigate with respect to the Science Reference Library. These were: (1) to retain the present SRL classification, (2) to replace the SRL scheme with UDC, or (3) to replace the SRL scheme with DDC. The debate on the relative merits of DDC, UDC and the SRL schemes tended to revolve around three factors: collocation, specificity, and class occupancy. A study carried out by Aslib compared the extent to which UDC/DDC and the SRL schemes collocated works on related topics, and judged that the schemes were roughly equal in this respect. On the other hand, another study by the staff of the Science Reference Library concluded that the SRL scheme provided significantly better collocation than DDC for searches in the field of technology.

Then Aslib undertook a comparison of the specificity of the SRL scheme, the medium edition of UDC, and DDC in three subject areas. Only 54-59 percent of SRL classes had corresponding classes in UDC, while the figures for DDC were 36-38 percent. However, it was felt that it would be wrong to conclude from these results that the medium edition of UDC was less specific than the SRL scheme. A more detailed analysis of the situation, based on the class *physical chemistry,* showed that whereas only 58 percent of the SRL classes could be located in UDC, only 32 percent of the UDC classes had counterparts in the SRL scheme. Thus, since the overlap between the classifications was much less than might have been expected, there were no clear grounds for concluding that one of the schemes was more specific than another.

At this point, the SRL staff introduced the concept of class occupancy, to be measured as the number of documents filed at a single classmark; they defined an overcrowded classmark as one at which more than twenty documents were filed. Two studies were made of class occupancy and overcrowding. These can be compared only in very general terms, because of the different document samples used, and at this level of comparison they appeared to produce conflicting results. The first study by SRL found that, for three selected subject areas, between 3 percent and 24 percent of the SRL collection (classified by the SRL scheme) fell within an overcrowded class. If DDC were to be used, it seemed that this percentage might rise to 56-85 percent. However, this study had unfortunately omitted the facilities for synthesis in DDC, and the second study carried out by the Systems Development Branch of BL analyzed the effects of lifting this limitation, thereby allowing DDC a greater degree of specificity. This second study analyzed a complete set (as much as could be obtained) of all *statistical mathematics* entries classified by the eighteenth edition of DDC in BNB and LC MARC tapes. The set of 911 records produced 225 unique classmarks. Only 2 percent of the DDC classmarks were found to be overcrowded, but 36 percent of the sample fell within an overcrowded class. A further study of the effect on the full sample of eliminating those items which would not meet the criteria of a postgraduate selection policy would be necessary to measure the realistic level of class occupancy which would result, but it is a safe assumption that such an elimination would reduce significantly the numbers of documents in overcrowded classes. Therefore, from an SRL viewpoint, and again at the risk of oversimplification, the arguments for and against the three schemes studied can be stated as follows:

UDC—The defects of UDC are the same for the Science Reference Library as they would be for the British Museum Library. Nevertheless, as an admittedly science-oriented general classification, UDC is by tradition the first choice for scientific and technical libraries of many kinds; some beneficial spinoff in the direction of these other libraries might be expected from its adoption by SRL and its consequent inclusion in the central bibliographic record. If it were adopted by SRL, there would be a strong case for it also to be adopted by BML. As with any other classification not already in use at SRL, there would be on the debit side the cost of reclassifying some or all of the present SRL stock.

DDC—Again, those merits of DDC indicated for BML requirements would apply also for the Science Reference Library. The adoption of DDC would have the additional advantage of reducing the current work load, since a proportion of SRL's intake would be received with DDC classmarks already assigned. DDC shares with UDC the advantage of being an acceptable classification in principle to form the basis of a unified approach to shelf arrangement within the two libraries of the Reference Division as a whole.

On the debit side, as compared with the SRL scheme, there are the costs of reclassifying to DDC some or all of the SRL stock and, in contrast with UDC and the SRL scheme, the relative absence of recognition of DDC by scientists and technologists as a classification particularly well suited to their needs.

SRL Scheme–The SRL scheme has been tailored to the library's requirements during its primary period of growth as the National Reference Library for Science and Invention. Being an "in-house" scheme, it is entirely under the control of SRL staff, and may be modified at need to reflect changing user requirements, changing acquisition policies or changes in the literature as they occur. The retention of the SRL scheme would avoid the immediate cost of reclassifying some or all of the present stock. In the long run, however, some effort would be required to keep it up to date, that is, to avoid the situation of accelerating obsolescence that befalls all "homemade" classification schemes when their originators depart, or that has arisen to a lesser extent with UDC. This effort would not be offset by cost savings in other ways, although it may be that these savings would be relatively small. Retention of the SRL scheme would also involve the addition of extra SRL classmarks to certain categories of material within the BL data base.

The picture which emerges from studies of the suitability of DDC, UDC, and the SRL scheme for the Science Reference Library collections was thus unclear. The evidence we gathered did not demonstrate a clear superiority of any one classification scheme over another in terms of collocation, specificity or class occupancy; any decisions for changing from the present SRL scheme will have to be made on other grounds.

Two main conclusions followed from the whole investigation of classification schemes. First, if the British Library's two references libraries are to be regarded as a pan-disciplinary collection with a single classification, the choice for shelf arrangement appears to lie between UDC and DDC. Of these, UDC has a wider international authority (in Europe at least), and a more widely participative process of schedule development; but, as far as the national library community is concerned, DDC predominates.

Secondly, if the British Library Reference Division is to be regarded as two separate collections with a fairly permanent demarcation between them, different classifications for the two collections can be considered. As there is no intention of carrying over the existing pressmark system into the new BML Reading Room, the best choice of existing schemes there would appear to be DDC. For SRL there is no obvious best choice. The advantages of retaining the in-house scheme must be weighed against the long-term, overall advantages of changing to DDC.

We made two further points about the Science Reference Library. The first was that considerable effort had gone into the creation and implementation of its special in-house classification scheme over the previous ten years. However persuasive the arguments of cost-effectiveness might be, the abandonment of the SRL scheme might well be seen by the specialist staff of the Science Reference Library as an unfavorable verdict on their contribution to the library's work. It is difficult to weigh this factor, but there is no doubt that it must in some way be inserted in the equation of the decision-making process.

The second point we made perhaps counterbalances the first: the Science Reference Library today puts the greatest emphasis on meeting the needs of those who visit it, and thus rates classification for shelf arrangement high among its professional methods. Looking into the future, we may expect that the SRL will develop rather more into a central component of the developing national and international networks of scientific information transfer, and that it will be better able to perform this function if its classification and indexing systems match those of other components in the network, and follow the lines of the development being pursued within UNISIST. This requirement is likely to outweigh shelf arrangement as an institutional priority, and to reduce the validity of such measures as "class occupancy" in the determination of classification policies.

We had little help from the published literature concerning the determination of unit costs. Most of the unit costs quoted were so dependent on the particular circumstances and environment in which they arose that no useful generalizations could be made. There was a considerable amount of internal information in various forms, and the report's appendices included analyses and inferences drawn from them. However, they must be regarded as very tentative, since they were derived from data concerning stock sizes and rates of growth that may already have been out of date at the time we examined them.

We had hoped to get more accurate measurements by means of planned diary surveys of operations in various parts of the British Library, but unfortunately these had to be suspended. From what was available to us, we were able to reach certain preliminary conclusions:

1. PRECIS, as well as being more effective, would be significantly cheaper than the present manual system for compiling the *British Museum Subject Index.*
2. A single classification system for the whole of the British Library would be cheaper to operate than two or more systems.
3. LC Classification probably costs less to apply than any other of the general schemes.
4. DDC appears to cost less to apply than the SRL scheme.

Beyond these, there were few positive statements to be made.

Postscript

Since this paper was presented, the British Library has published the Working Party's report,[2] with a preface by the Director-General of the Reference Division stating that BL "accepts the recommendations . . . in general." Specifically, DDC is accepted "insofar as a single scheme proves to be necessary . . . [and] will be adopted immediately for certain open access collections." At the Science Reference Library, however, adoption is to be postponed "until the future accommodation pattern becomes clearer" and in the interim "all current intake will . . . be classified also by DDC" so as to "minimise the work involved in transferring at a later stage to a DDC arrangement, if this proved to be the best decision for a unified collection." The costs of delaying the SRL decision, says the Director-General, "though not negligible, are capable of being accommodated."

REFERENCES

1. "Statement on Types of Classification Available to New Academic Libraries," *Library Resources & Technical Services* 9:104-11, Winter 1965.

2. British Library Working Party on Classification and Indexing. *Final Report* (BL Research & Development Reports No. 5233). Boston Spa, BL Lending Division, 1975.

HANS H. WELLISCH
Associate Professor
College of Library and Information Services
University of Maryland
College Park, Maryland

Dewey Decimal Classification, Universal Decimal Classification, and the Broad System of Ordering: The Evolution of Universal Ordering Systems

Of the three systems named in the title of this paper, the first is familiar to everyone, even outside the profession of librarianship; the second is much less well known; and the last one is probably still a total stranger. Actually, to say that the Universal Decimal Classification (UDC) is little known in the United States is an understatement. Except for a handful of people who actually use the system, the general notion among many librarians in this country seems to be that the UDC is a quaint, even outlandish system, a transmogrification of Dewey performed by some oddballs in the city of Brussels. American textbooks on classification still call it the "Brussels Extension." Such ignorance and neglect is even more deplorable as the UDC is essentially of genuine American descent, being the offspring of the Dewey Decimal Classification (DDC).

When we celebrate the Dewey centennial, we can at the same time look back on exactly eighty years of UDC. It was in 1895 that two Belgian lawyers, Paul Otlet and Henri La Fontaine, decided to adapt the DDC for their plan of the Institut International de Bibliographie (IIB) as a classification system for the worldwide repertory of all knowledge recorded not only in books, but also in articles, reports, and any other kind of documents.

Their choice was mainly influenced by the features that were then unique to the DDC: (1) the system dealt with concepts and ideas rather than with books, although it was primarily intended for the arrangement of books on shelves; (2) its purely numerical notation constituted a universally understood metalanguage, independent of any natural language; (3) the decimal principle seemed to allow for unlimited expansion for the accommodation of new subjects; and (4) the synthetic devices of number-building and form divisions allowed for the synthesis of specific subject codes with those for recurrent, common and general topics. It was this last feature which appealed most to Otlet and La Fontaine, and they soon developed it into the versatile and elaborate "Auxiliaries," each introduced by its own symbol, thus creating the first "faceted" classification scheme (although this term was then not used).

What was still lacking for their purpose of close classification of minute details was sufficient subdivision in the main tables, and they proceeded immediately to refine the basic scheme. All this was done with the full consent of Dewey himself, who promised his "cooperation and criticizm" for all additions made.[1] So rapid was the pace of adaptation and elaboration that only one year later, in 1896, the UDC tables already contained 40,000 headings, while the DDC (then in its fifth edition) had less than 7,500. Dewey had to admit regretfully that a critical evaluation of these expansions and cooperation in their further development was a task which, for lack of time, he could not take upon himself.

For the next three decades, the two systems developed independently, yet more or less in parallel, with the UDC becoming more and more detailed, but still without changes in the basic framework devised by Dewey. In 1924 it was officially agreed upon to "harmonize" the DDC and UDC, so that the expansions made in Europe would also become an integral part of the American scheme, thus allowing for greater indexing specificity for those who wanted or needed it. In his preface to the twelfth edition of DDC, Dewey stated that the project was "well underway," and he praised the features that were most characteristic of the UDC: the Common Auxiliaries, based on his own Form Divisions, and the synthetic device of putting a colon sign between two or more UDC codes to indicate their relationship (a device which had its origin in Dewey's use of the digit 0 as a number-building device). Dewey stated that "IIB has devized and uzes injenius simbols" and extolled "their vast practical advantajes," concluding that "obviusly these simbols allow subdivision of the same number in many different ways without confuzion."[2]

However, despite Dewey's enthusiasm for the UDC and his endeavors to amalgamate the two schemes, developments took a different turn. In the late 1930s, and especially after World War II, the DDC and UDC grew further apart. Ironically, the differences occurred not so much in the "Auxiliaries," the feature that made UDC seem so unlike DDC, but rather in the subdivisions of the main schedules, where minute detail could have been achieved without radical departures from the parent scheme. In retrospect, we can only deplore that this was allowed to happen, not only because it led to much duplication of effort (since both schemes inevitably had to accommodate new ideas, inventions and phenomena within their basically still-identical frameworks of ten main classes), but also because a unified scheme might have resulted long ago in a worldwide system for the identification and effective retrieval of recorded information independent of language and terminology barriers. Only now is such a worldwide system about to emerge in the shape of the Unesco-sponsored Broad System of Ordering (to which we shall return later), and it is gratifying to observe that it has its roots in the two great decimal systems.

Even though DDC and UDC could no longer be reconciled, we are now able to perceive that they continued to influence each other: there is an unmistakable trend in the DDC to become less enumerative and more synthetic, more faceted, especially since the seventeenth edition. The gradual transformation of the Form Divisions into the present Standard Subdivisions, and the creation of the various Tables undoubtedly owe much to the development and mode of application of the Auxiliaries in UDC (even though the principle of general applicability of the Tables throughout the whole system has not yet been fully and consistently applied. For example, the Persons Table is not applicable in class 300, (where it would be most appropriate) because the direct subdivisions for persons are retained according to the principle of "integrity of numbers." Conversely, where DDC was better developed or more elaborate than UDC, e.g., in the historical schedules for the two world wars, or in the history and geography subdivisions for the United States and some other countries, the UDC followed the DDC and adopted its schedules in their entirety rather than developing new ones.

The UDC Today

The UDC as it presents itself today is undoubtedly vastly different from its parent scheme, although it still retains nine of the ten main classes of

DDC. The differences lie not only in the very large number of minute subdivisions for almost every subject, but also in the allocation of relative place for several major subjects, especially regarding more recent developments in science and technology such as nuclear science, engineering and computers. Although it has lost some ground to thesauri and specially devised classification schemes, it is still extensively used in Western Europe (particularly in the United Kingdom, Germany, the Netherlands and Belgium), it is being used by the Soviet Union and other East European countries for all scientific and technical publications, and it is widely used in the Latin American countries. The number of libraries, indexing and abstracting services, and individual users has been estimated to be at least 100,000—perhaps more. Only in the United States has the UDC not met with appreciable success, despite the efforts of several large special libraries and of American and Canadian information scientists who were instrumental in demonstrating the potential of the UDC in computerized information retrieval.[3]

Despite its phenomenal growth and apparent success, during the past two decades the UDC has been the subject of severe criticism, both from outside observers (including some who had never been actual users of the scheme and were thus not well qualified to evaluate its merits and demerits) and from within. The minute subdivisions, once thought to be the strength and pride of the system, have been found to be excessive in number, leading to unwanted redundancy and consequently to retrieval failures; classes 5 and 6, devoted to the sciences and technology, are now hopelessly overcrowded (a fate they share with classes 500 and 600 in DDC); finally, the management of the system, while being highly democratic and oriented toward an international clientele, is cumbersome and inefficient, with the result that proposed additions and changes are being made too slowly and infrequently. During the last five years, this criticism has resulted in some significant movement toward change, partly aimed at reform of the existing framework, and partly directed toward radically new solutions to the problem of an international and universal system of information retrieval.

Reform

Since its beginnings, the UDC has been based on the principle of constant ongoing revision in order to keep pace with new developments and new conceptions of the universe of knowledge. Although this has resulted in a rather unwieldy committee structure which often impedes rather than advances needed revisions, every year hundreds of new and revised codes are added, many obsolete ones are deleted, and major expansions of existing main classes are effected. Of course, sometimes radical surgery would be easier to perform and would give better results, but piecemeal revision and updating are necessary because of the needs of present users, some of which have built up extensive files over the years. Lately, the processes of reform have been brought more in line with the requirements of modern information retrieval, and several specially appointed committees have tried to apply the insights gained from research into the theoretical foundations of classification. Among the tangible results of their work are the following:

1. The procedures for the proposal of additions, deletions or changes and their accomplishment by appropriate committees or experts has been streamlined, leading to a quicker publication of the results.
2. Most parts of class 3 *social sciences* have been largely remodeled, and now constitute not only the most detailed but probably also the best balanced schemes for this field, which is one of the most difficult to handle in any information retrieval system. The difficulties result from its diffuse, imprecise and constantly changing terminology, and because of the ideological differences and diametrically opposed conceptions held by sociologists, economists, educators and politicians in the West, in the communist countries, and in the Third World. The construction of the revised parts of class 3 was undertaken with the collaboration of experts from capitalist and communist countries alike, which should ensure that it will be a truly international tool for information retrieval in the social sciences.
3. Several large and important subject fields have undergone major revisions, most of which could be made *in situ,* i.e., without a change in the main code; among these are 51 *mathematics,* 52 *astronomy,* 624 *civil engineering,* 69 *building construction,* 796 *sport,* and 903 *archeology* (this one transferred from 930.26 and entirely new).

The Basic Medium Edition (BME)

For a long time, the UDC has been published in editions of varying scope. The full editions contain every code (estimated at more than 200,000); the first of these were two French editions, followed by a German one, and now there is also an almost complete (although not entirely updated) full edition in English. Partial full editions exist also in Czech, Polish, Portuguese, Russian, Serbo-Croatian, Spanish and Japanese. These editions are intended for subject experts who need minutely detailed codes for classing documents in their particular field, but they are not practical for classing documents ranging over all or most fields, e.g., in general library collections or for a comprehensive indexing service. Therefore, more than twenty abridged editions have been published over the years in as many languages, ranging in scope from 10 to 15 percent of the codes contained in a full edition. Incidentally, these abridged editions form a kind of multilingual dictionary, in which concepts and their denoting terms in various languages are linked by the same code numbers.

Unfortunately, abridged editions soon proved to be sufficient only for small libraries or for rather broad classification. In 1967, a medium-sized edition ("Handausgabe") was published in Germany, comprising about 30 percent of the codes in the full edition, and this was soon followed by a similar French "medium" edition. Although the decision about which codes from the full edition should be included in a medium-sized one cannot be based on percentages alone, and must be carefully considered for each class in the light of user needs and of characteristics of the pertinent literature, it is now generally agreed that an edition containing about one-third of the main codes, plus a complete set of auxiliary tables for the common facets, is the most versatile tool for the practical indexer and classifier.

The last English abridged edition was published in 1961, and is now hopelessly out of date. In light of the success of the German and French medium editions, it was decided not to issue another English abridged edition, but to forge ahead with a medium edition which, at the same time, would become the basic master edition on which all others would be modeled. The original goal to produce this Basic Medium Edition (BME) in 1976 as UDC's contribution to the Dewey centennial could unfortunately not be met, but it may be published in 1977. The amount of abridgment for each class has already been established by the general editor in close collaboration with existing committees and subject experts; it will probably have main tables containing about 50,000 codes, to which will be added complete tables of common facets; all additions and changes up until mid-1975 will be incorporated.

Preparations are presently being made to convert the codes of the BME and their English verbal equivalents into machine-readable form, to be later augmented by German, French, and possibly other language equivalents, and to update the resulting master file whenever revisions are being made. It is possible that this master file will be managed by the Library of the Eidgenössische Technische Hochschule in Zürich, where a machine-readable data base of this kind already exists in abbreviated form (mainly for technical and scientific subjects covered by this library).[4] A copy of the master file will also be kept at the headquarters of the International Federation for Documentation (FID) in the Hague, and the tapes will be made available to other users who could produce their own version of UDC tables for specialized purposes, or in languages not covered by the master tape.

The alphabetical index to the BME will be published separately at a later date, and will probably be constructed on the thesaurus principle, thus producing another variant of the system originally produced for the field of electrical engineering under the name of *Thesaurofacet.*[5] A pilot project for the construction of such an index has already been produced by Belgian experts for class 33 *economics,* and is considered to be better and easier to use than the conventional relative index of the type with which we are familiar in Dewey and in the English abridged edition of 1961. Another possibility is the computer-aided construction of index entries in a KWOC format, recently employed in the index to the Dutch abridged edition, which is much better than the computer-generated index to the German medium edition that was produced by simply extracting keywords from headings without any regard to related terms or synonyms.

A New Class 4

A reform measure not yet implemented is the creation of a new class 4. For more than a decade, this class has been vacant, its contents having been amalgamated with class 8, which now comprises both *literature* and *linguistics.* The intention had been to make an entire main class available for relocation of scientific and technical subjects now squeezed into the overcrowded classes 5 and 6. Several proposals for the repopulation of class 4 have been made; the most recent, as yet existing only in rough outline, has the following subdivisions:

4 *man and his natural environment; material resources*
41 *man as an individual; medical sciences; anthropology; psychology*
42 *general biology; botany; zoology*
43 *agricultural sciences; plants and animals*
44 *animal biology and husbandry* (if 43 for *plants and crops* only)
45 *mineral resources; mining and mineral dressing*
46 *materials; testing, sampling, etc.*
47 *handling and transport of materials and persons*
48 *management: business, household, etc.*

It is, of course, possible to quarrel with this proposal and its juxtaposition of major subjects as much as with any of the earlier proposals, but it seems to come close to the present general consensus on a helpful collocation of topics clustering around man and his environment. If finally adopted and suitably elaborated, it would make room for the reallocation of subjects now suffering from bad notation and unhelpful placement, among them *electrical, nuclear* and *transportation engineering.*

Drastic Revision and a New UDC

The implementation of reform in various parts of the UDC as outlined above will inevitably lead to a complete restructuring and possibly to a New UDC (NUDC). A committee on "drastic revision of the UDC" has been active during the past three years, and its members have produced various outlines for such a reconstruction. The latest version envisages the creation of General Facets which would be applicable throughout the system (similar to, but more systematic than, the present Auxiliaries) such as Attributes, Phenomena, Processes, Methods and Objects; subdivisions of the latter would be Matter, Persons, Organizations, Products, etc., each of which could be further subdivided as needed. There would also be a number of Subject Fields, roughly subdivided into Natural Sciences, Life Sciences, Engineering and Technology, Humanities, and Social Sciences, each further subdivided, but not to the sometimes excessive degree of detail now found in UDC. Common features in each Subject Field would be expressed by Special Facets, i.e., those applicable only to a particular field or topic. All this is, of course, by no means entirely new, and can in fact be traced back to the original ideas on synthesis of numbers as conceived by Dewey, but it would certainly result in a new universal classification scheme which would have little in common with the UDC as we know it now.

The new scheme is already well on its way, and at least some of the General Facets have already been elaborated in detail, or will be taken over more or less completely from the present UDC, e.g., the Materials Facet -03, with whose help any object can be classed according to the material of which it is made, independent of where in the UDC the object has been classed. Other General Facets are the Time Facet (now having the notation "...") and the Space Facet (...), both of which have recently been revised and expanded to cater to the needs not only of geographers and historians, but also of any classifier in need of time, place and space indications. A substantial part of the work with an NUDC will consist in weeding the existing schedules and eliminating direct subdivisions of main codes which can be better expressed by general or special facets. Doing so will make the whole system more flexible and amenable to cope with rapid changes both in science and technology and in the general conceptions of the world we live in.

It will be possible, of course, to handle the NUDC by computers for the purpose of automatic retrieval of information from large systems. The present UDC has shown itself to be amenable to automation, and more than sixty working systems (some of them experimental) have been designed and used.[6] Partial retrieval failures or other shortcomings of these systems were almost always due to the fact that the basically faceted structure of UDC is not uniformly applied throughout the system. Straight decimal subdivision of main codes (inherited from DDC) is often substituted for synthetic notation, and unnecessary duplication results from denoting recurrent concepts by different kinds of auxiliary notations in various parts of the UDC. The elimination of such incongruencies by judicious weeding of the tables and application of General and Special Facets will make the restructured UDC a much more reliable retrieval tool for mechanized systems.

Broad System of Ordering (BSO)

The worldwide information systems network created by Unesco under the name of UNISIST recommended in its basic policy statement that an internationally applicable classification system be adopted as a means to organize recorded knowledge independent of the many vernaculars in which it is now published all over the world. It was obvious that the UDC would be considered for this role, but it was also pointed out that it was not acceptable in the form in which it then existed. It soon became clear, however, that if anybody could design a suitable classification system, it would have to be the group of people who had the widest experience with an already existing international scheme. Thus, several prominent members of the Central Classification Committee of UDC, together with other experts, were entrusted with the task of designing a Broad System of Ordering with the instruction to create a tool capable of achieving three main objectives: (1) to serve as a connecting link and a switching mechanism between various information systems, services and centers, each of which may have its own indexing and retrieval language (natural or controlled, verbal or numerical, but in most cases incompatible with that of any other system); (2) to be used for internationally standardized "tagging" of subject fields and their main subdivisions, i.e., to serve as a shallow indexing tool; and (3) to be a referral aid for the identification and location of information sources, centers and services of all kinds.

A proposal for BSO was elaborated and submitted to UNISIST in early 1975 for approval and testing. The scheme contains about 2,000 headings, arranged in three levels of hierarchy; approximately 670 of these are in the natural and life sciences (including agriculture and medicine), 530 are in technology, and the rest, about 700, cover the social sciences, humanities and arts. The small number of headings in the BSO (fewer than those in the second edition of Dewey's scheme) was deliberately used in order to keep the system broad, as indicated by its name. BSO is not intended to supersede individual specific headings or codes in existing indexing languages, but to serve primarily as a switching language. An interesting feature in BSO is the separation of the natural sciences from their associated technologies, despite the often-voiced criticism of this arrangement in DDC, UDC and other classification schemes, and often attributed to the outmoded conceptions prevailing in the late nineteenth century. Both classificationists and subject experts agreed that, on the whole, the advantages of such a separation outweighed the disadvantages; they made an exception only for the life sciences, because of the close ties between biology and its applications in agriculture and medicine. Throughout the proposed BSO, care was taken to ensure that the individual elements could be freely combined in order to accommodate future developments and new knowledge without frequent drastic restructuring of the scheme. This feature would also compensate to some degree for the separation of sciences and technologies.

The scheme is now to be tested by experts in various fields, before final adjustments to the scope and specificity of headings will be made in the light of practical experience. The field trials will test the completeness of coverage and the appropriateness of indexing depth. Initially, the tests will not be aimed at the retrieval of specific documents, but rather at broad groups of documents and "blocks of information" by taking samples from the *World Inventory of Indexing and Abstracting Services* (published by FID in collaboration with the National Federation of Abstracting and Indexing Services, and available in machine-readable format), from other indexes in machine-readable format, and from national directories of information sources.

The designers of BSO wisely refrained from appending a notation to the tentative scheme, in order not to influence the conceptual structure by any constraints exercised by a preconceived ordering device. The notation will be assigned to the headings only after final confirmation of their scope and relative position in the scheme.

If and when this happens, the notation may not be purely numerical, and it may not even be decimal, so that on the face of it there seems to be little, if any, connection between BSO and UDC. Because of the broad nature of BSO, however, a system such as UDC with its greater detail and flexibility will be needed to supplement the "roof code" of BSO for the purpose of indexing and retrieving individual and specific documents. More important still, it is probably no exaggeration to say that without UDC, BSO may not have become a reality, or that it would at least have been vastly more difficult to design such a scheme from scratch. After all, the cumulative experience of hundreds of contributors, and the feedback provided by thousands of users throughout the world over a period of eight decades, together with insights gained from research into the theoretical foundations of classification during the last thirty years, has resulted in a tool that, despite its many shortcomings, remains the most universal, versatile and widely used system for indexing and retrieval of information. The UDC in turn would not have been possible, but for the genius of Dewey, whose scheme contained the basic building blocks on which all modern retrieval systems have been built.

Perhaps the new BSO will achieve, albeit on a very general level, for the subject organization of documents what has already been accomplished to a large extent in the closely related field of descriptive control by the International Standard Bibliographic Description (ISBD) and other appurtenant elements aimed at standardization in bibliographic control. It may thus become the capstone of the great conception which for 500 years has been the dream of bibliographers and librarians, and which only now is gradually taking shape, namely Universal Bibliographic Control—knowing the sum total of all knowledge that has been recorded in whatever form, and knowing what and where those records are.

REFERENCES

1. Dewey, Melvil. *Dewey Decimal Classification and Relative Index.* 12th ed. Lake Placid Club, N.Y., Forest Press, 1927, p. 40.
2. *Ibid.,* pp. 40-41.
3. Rigby, Malcolm. *Computers and the UDC: A Decade of Progress, 1963-1973.* The Hague, International Federation for Documentation, 1974. (FID 523)
4. Downey, Maurice W. "Data Collection and Transcription in the Cataloguing Section," *Libri* 22:58-76, 1972.
5. Aitchison, Jean, *et al. Thesaurofacet: A Thesaurus and Facetted Classification for Engineering and Related Subjects.* Whetstone, England, English Electric Co., 1969.
6. Rigby, *op. cit.*

ADDITIONAL REFERENCES

Foskett, Anthony C. *The Universal Decimal Classification: The History, Present Status and Future Prospects of a Large General Classification Scheme.* Hamden, Conn., Linnet Books, 1973.
Schmidt, A. F., and Wijn, J. H. de. "Some Possibilities for a New 'Reformed' UDC (Suitable for Extension of the Standard Reference Code)," *DK-Mitteilungen* 16:19-21, 1972.
Van der Laan, Andre, and Wijn, Jan H. de. "UDC Revision and SRC Project: Relations and Feedback," *Unesco Bulletin for Libraries* 28:2-9, Jan.-Feb. 1974.
Wellisch, H. "UDC: Present and Potential," *Drexel Library Quarterly* 10:75-89, Oct. 1974.

DEREK AUSTIN
Head
Subject Systems Office
The British Library
London, England

The Role of Indexing
in Subject Retrieval

On first reading the list of speakers proposed for this institute, I became aware of being rather the "odd man out" for two reasons. Firstly, I was asked to present a paper on PRECIS—which is very much a verbal indexing system—at a conference dominated by contributions on classification schemes with a natural bias, as the centenary year approaches, toward the Dewey Decimal Classification (DDC). Secondly, I feared (quite wrongly, as it happens) that I might be at variance with one or two of my fellow speakers, who would possibly like to assure us, in an age when we can no longer ignore the computer, that traditional library schemes such as DDC and Library of Congress Classification (LCC) are capable of maintaining their original function of organizing collections of documents, and at the same time are also well suited to the retrieval of relevant citations from machine-held files. In this context, I am reminded of a review of a general collection of essays on classification schemes which appeared in the *Journal of Documentation* in 1972. Norman Roberts, reviewing the papers which dealt specifically with the well established schemes, deduced that "all the writers project their particular schemes into the future with an optimism that springs, perhaps, as much from a sense of emotional involvement as from concrete evidence."[1] Since I do not believe that these general schemes can play any significant part in the retrieval of items from mechanized files, it appeared that I had been cast in the role of devil's advocate.

By tradition, the role of devil's advocate (and we should remember that every conference needs one) has to be defended by logical argument. I would therefore like to begin by stating some of my grounds for believing that a library classification, as this term is usually understood, cannot function equally well for the dual purpose of organizing shelves on the one hand, and searching machine-held files on the other. This will then serve as a useful introduction to the topic on which I was primarily invited to speak: the role of the verbal subject index in document retrieval, using PRECIS as the example with which I am familiar.

STRUCTURE AND FUNCTION IN LIBRARY CLASSIFICATION

The review by Norman Roberts quoted earlier referred to a collection of essays edited by Arthur Maltby, entitled *Classification in the 1970's.*[2] A rather more direct opinion of this work was expressed by an astute American reviewer, Jean Perreault, who regarded these essays as clear evidence that "the two major purposes of documentary classification, namely for shelf organisation and for mechanised retrieval, are *not* well served by a single system unless consciously modified to cater for the two purposes."[3] Perreault does not suggest how this modification might be carried out, though I strongly suspect that any alteration of a scheme to enhance its performance in one of these roles would almost certainly render it less effective in the other. To demonstrate this point, we can consider the relationship between structure and function in a classification scheme, starting with its obvious function of imposing order upon collections of documents. For this purpose, we can stipulate certain desiderata, of which the most important are probably:

1. brevity of notation—this point was heavily stressed by librarians in a survey of classification needs carried out by the (British) Library Association in 1966;[4]
2. reasonable collocation, or the bringing together of like-with-like on the shelves, while bearing in mind the disconcerting fact that no library scheme, however well conceived, can ever bring together all the documents which a given reader would regard as belonging to his special field of interest;
3. hospitality and specificity—with the introduction of these two complementary characteristics we can already begin to detect an element of strain (i.e., How can any scheme offer these two characteristics, and still retain a short notation?);
4. standardization—becoming increasingly important as international data exchange networks continue to develop. The acceptance of a classification scheme as a general standard could eventually mean that the librarian in

Chicago has no need to reclassify any work which has been handled already by his counterpart in London or Paris. Provided that a decision made in the country of origin of the document accords with standard practice, it should be possible to adopt that decision as soon as it becomes available, either in the form of a magnetic tape record, or via a telecommunication link directly into the foreign data base.

I should now like to consider a different set of desiderata: those which apply to a mechanized file intended for tracing relevant documents in response to users' inquiries. In this context, we could stipulate two important characteristics:

1. currency and hospitality—that is, we need the ability to identify quickly works on newly emerging concepts, or on new subjects which consist of familiar concepts combined in unfamiliar and even unexpected ways. A good deal of the literature we handle on a day-to-day basis contains emergent knowledge which belongs to one or the other of these two categories;
2. we need to identify, in the most *economical* way (which in computer terms means as *quickly* as possible) all the works which may have dealt with a specific concept. For this purpose, a given concept should ideally be represented by just one symbol which can then be used as the key to its retrieval from any part of the file.

If we now attempt to compare these two sets of desiderata—that is, those for a shelf-order system, and those for a mechanized file—we can, perhaps, begin to see why these different needs cannot be satisfied entirely by a single system. Let us consider, for example, the librarian's justifiable need for a short notation, and contrast this with the need, in a mechanized file, to identify each separate element in a compound subject by some unique symbol which could serve as the key to its retrieval from any part of the system. An enumerative classification, such as DDC or LCC, obviously serves the librarian very well in terms of notational economy. A great deal of conceptual information can be packed into a fairly simple class mark such as 621.3, which represents *electrical engineering*. However, this number is not particularly helpful if we consider it as an aggregate of concepts from the viewpoint of machine retrieval. The symbol .3, attached to the stem number 621, means *electrical* in this case, but it does not follow (as it should, ideally, in a mechanized system) that the mark .3 continues to express *electrical* throughout the rest of the schedules. In a different class context, such as 914, for example, an additional .3 denotes *Central Europe and Germany*.

In that case, a given symbol does not consistently represent the same concept. The converse is equally true; that is, a given concept is not represented consistently by the same symbol. In fact, it takes approximately one hundred different symbols to represent the concept *electrical* or *electricity* in the schedules of the eighteenth edition of DDC. Such a wide range of numbers is partly due to the fact that this scheme is generally enumerative, but it does not follow that the problem has been solved by the makers of faceted classifications. For example, a relatively simple concept such as *iron* is expressed by at least six entirely different numbers in the abridged edition of the Universal Decimal Classification, and by several different symbols in the Colon Classification. This does not mean that these schemes have no role to play in library organization, but it does cast at least some doubts on their effectiveness as tools for mechanized searching. I have tried, in a different paper, to set out the case for regarding these faceted schemes as less than satisfactory for present-day purposes on the grounds that, in trying to satisfy both the librarian and the data base manager, they may have attempted the impossible and succeeded in neither.[5]

THE CRG RESEARCH INTO A
NEW GENERAL CLASSIFICATION

I might point out that this opinion represents more than a theoretical viewpoint. It is also based on some personal experience in trying to devise a scheme which could function equally well for both library arrangement and mechanized retrieval. An opportunity to explore this ground arose in connection with the NATO-funded research into a new general classification scheme which was carried out by the Classification Research Group (CRG) in London during the 1960s. Partially for the reasons I have outlined, the CRG decided that an entirely new approach to classification was needed—one which, it was hoped, would lead to a scheme which could function equally well for both library arrangement and the identification of works on specific concepts.

It was assumed from the beginning of this research that any new scheme should be founded upon the basic postulates for an analytico-synthetic classification established by Ranganathan. These postulates are themselves based on two assumptions which together constitute the keystone to modern classification theory: (1) any compound subject is amenable to analysis into discrete conceptual elements, each of which (at least in theory) could be identified by its own unique symbol; and (2) the compound subject, regarded as a whole, could then be reconstituted out of these parts in accordance with a general formula, and the formula itself could be based upon a single set of logical principles which would apply across the whole spectrum of knowledge.

These postulates are all very well in theory, but what about the practice? At the time when the CRG research began, no one had actually attempted to take these ideas to their logical conclusion and construct an entirely analytico-synthetic classification. Even Ranganathan's Colon Classification is firmly based on a set of main classes, and the notation which represents a given concept can vary from one main class to another. Furthermore, Ranganathan's formula for number building, based on the general categories of Personality, Matter, Energy, Space and Time, is not so generalized at it first appears. In particular, the primary facet, Personality, has caused problems for both teachers and practitioners. Since this is the factor which has to be cited first when building a compound subject from its parts, it is therefore the factor which determines where documents on that subject will be shelved.

In practice, however, it has been found that the interpretation of Personality depends upon the main class structure of the scheme in use; even in the Colon Classification system, this can vary from one class to another. Unfortunately, a good deal of modern literature, even at the monograph level, severely strains the concept of main classes. When faced by a subject such as "the use of computers to handle the payroll of teaching staff in American universities," the interpretation of Personality will certainly vary with the frames of reference of the user (as well as the librarian) depending on whether the user is computer-oriented, is an accountant, a personnel manager, or a university administrator.

These were the kinds of challenge, which appear to be endemic in both enumerative and faceted classifications, which stimulated the CRG research. The solutions we explored can best be considered as simultaneous attacks on two different but related fronts. The first might be called the semantic approach, and was concerned with the organization of concepts (individual units of information) into basic categories to which they appeared to belong in a definitional sense, without taking any account of the ways in which these concepts might occur in different compound subjects, in the sense in which *iron*, for example, belongs to a category called *metals*, and *beauty* to a general class of *human subjective judgments*. Once a concept had been assigned to its general class, it would then have been identified by a single notational symbol which would have served two purposes: (1) to label that concept in a once-and-for-all fashion, so that the symbol could be used for locating documents on that concept from any part of a data base; and (2) it would show, through its hierarchically expressive structure, the general class of ideas to which the concept belonged. The other approach we considered is more closely related to syntax than semantics. This was a search for what might be called a set of generalized rules which would constitute a classificatory "grammar," insofar as they would determine the order in which concepts should be set down when building any compound subject out of its parts.

The first of these tasks—the assignment of concepts to general categories—obviously called for an explicit act of classification, although not in the library sense. We were here concerned with imposing order on a universe of concepts, not on a universe of subjects. For this reason, I would prefer to use the term *categorization* to describe what we attempted, leaving the term *classification* to be used in its familiar or library sense. In terms of methodology, our general approach to this universe of concepts was not radically different from that employed by the maker of a library classification. Each of these tasks calls for a basically similar technique. Certain principles of division have to be established, and these must then be introduced one at a time, each principle being exhausted before a new one is introduced. We first divided concepts into two basic kinds, those which indicate Things, and those which are the Attributes of things. Each of these classes was then further subdivided. The general category of Things, for example, was separated into two new classes, called Naturally Occurring Entities and Artificial Entities; the latter category was again divided into concrete artifacts (such as *chairs* and *aircraft*), and mental constructs (such as *systems of belief* and *theoretical models*). A similar operation was also carried out for the general cateogry of Attributes. If there had been time to complete this work, the final product would have been what might be called a macrothesaurus dealing with the basic concepts, as they occur in modern literature, which form the quanta from which all compound subjects in any field can be constructed.

I should, perhaps, stress that this is not an entirely new approach to the organization of knowledge. Thesauri, as such, have a long and respectable history, with Roget's serving as the obvious model for the kind of macrothesaurus we are now considering. It is also worth noting that several library classification systems, with DDC as the classic example, already operate in this way to some extent. Apart from the fact that compound subjects can be built by using the *add* instruction, certain classes of general concepts, especially those which are likely to be needed at any point in the schedules, have already been assigned to general categories. These form the auxiliary schedules which now occupy a separate volume in the current edition of DDC, and from which the classifier extracts, as he needs them, commonly occurring factors such as bibliographic forms, places, method-ologies, and so on. The approach considered by the CRG would simply have taken this idea to its logical conclusion—that is, *all* the concepts in the schedules would, in effect, have been assigned to the auxiliary schedules, then notated on a permanent basis, ready for use in number-building whenever the appropriate literature appeared.

The second problem faced by the CRG was that of devising a general formula, based on teachable and logical principles, for building compound subjects out of their parts. We had, of course, started with the classical PMEST formula of Ranganathan, but this was found to be inadequate in some respects. We therefore extended this model in various ways. Following the work of Vickery,[6] we defined the parts of a subject more explicitly in terms of their grammatical roles or functions. For examples, Wholes were distinguished from Parts, and it was stipulated that the whole must always be cited before the part. We also identified specific elements of subjects, such as the product of an action, the object upon which the action was performed, the action itself, and its agent. In order to achieve a reasonable level of consistency among classifiers, each of these roles was identified by a numerical code (called an operator) which was given a built-in filing value. When building a compound subject out of its parts, each separate piece of notation representing a specific concept would have been prefixed by an appropriate operator, and the filing value attached to the operator would have ensured, for example, that the whole was consistently set down before the part, that the object or recipient of the action was written before the action itself, and the action before the agent. In effect, we were searching for a generalized grammar of classification—one which could be used as a mental model for regulating the order of concepts in any compound subject. In devising this model, we had deliberately disregarded traditional disciplines as these are usually understood. Nevertheless, the order of concepts had still been selected with a view to providing some kind of helpful collocation in a pan-disciplinary library or bibliography.

It would be foolish to claim that anything resembling a new general classification arose from these efforts. Nevertheless, at the end of the research (when we had used up the £5,000 awarded to the CRG by the NATO Science Foundation), I think we had at least demonstrated the feasibility of the approach we had been exploring, both toward the construction of a general thesaurus, and toward the establishment of a generalized grammar for subject building. Near the end of the project, a provisional notation was applied to the outline categories of concepts which had been developed, and the number-building techniques were applied to a sample collection of research reports. The results were then studied by the members of the CRG, who considered them from various viewpoints. From the viewpoint of collocation, the results were surprisingly acceptable. Obviously, the general formula we had developed did not produce groupings of the kind which are usually associated with the traditional disciplines found in schemes such as DDC. Nevertheless, we appeared to have achieved helpful groupings, especially in those emergent fields which tend to cut across the older disciplines. However, there was still one factor we could not ignore. Although this system might have proved well suited to the searching of machine-held files, the resulting class numbers were completely unsuitable for library purposes, simply because they were far too long and complicated. As Jack Mills pointed out when reviewing this work: "the code system used . . . conveys the structure of the system succinctly for machine manipulation . . . although it is obvious that the system does constitute a general 'library classification' in the accepted sense."[7]

THE DEVELOPMENT OF PRECIS

Fortunately, this was not the end of the story. During the CRG search for a number-building formula, concepts had been organized in various ways to test a range of hypotheses. In a number of cases, we had actually used words rather than notational symbols to represent specific concepts, partly because a word conveys a more obvious and immediate message than a symbol, and also because in many cases we were dealing with concepts which had not yet been admitted into the thesaurus. These experiments in term manipulation became more than a matter of expediency, and assumed the status of a new research project when the decision was made, in 1969, to produce the *British National Bibliography* (BNB) directly from our own MARC tapes.

From its first issues, BNB has appeared as a classified bibliography; that is to say, full catalog entries for all British monograph output have been printed under their DDC class numbers in the "front end" of the bibliography, and this systematic arrangement has been supported by one or more separate indexes giving access under the names of authors, titles, subjects, etc. It is necessary, at this point, to stress a lesson of MARC which has still not been fully appreciated by many librarians: MARC, if applied correctly, should mean the end of the concept of the main entry. Provided that all the essential components of a full catalog entry have been assigned to their correct fields in a record, so that each is uniquely identified, the librarian can, through a simple instruction to the computer, ask for these data to be organized in any way which satisfies his requirements. This kind of provision is endemic in MARC itself; nevertheless, it was some time before we fully realized the potential of the system. When BNB first became involved with MARC, our exchange tapes were made as an extra operation, and the national bibliography itself was still being produced by traditional means. It then became clear that many of the sequences found in BNB could, in fact, be extracted directly from the MARC records. For example, it was a simple matter to print full catalog entries under DDC class marks as the front end to the bibliography, since all the necessary data are uniquely tagged in MARC records. Some of the supplementary indexes could also be produced in this way, especially those giving the names of authors, titles, etc. However, when BNB first became involved with MARC, no satisfactory means existed for producing a subject index directly from these records. The decision was therefore made in 1969 to set up a special research project to study the machine production of a subject index, as a necessary preparation for the fully automated production of BNB.

Quite naturally, we tried first to automate the production of the chain index which had been a familiar feature of BNB for some twenty years, but for various reasons this proved to be abortive. We also studied a range of alternative indexing techniques which had already been designed for use with computers, but none seemed entirely capable of producing an index to the standards we felt were necessary in a national bibliography. We therefore made what was probably a courageous decision, and set out to explore some new approach to the production of a subject index directly from machine-readable data. This is the research which led to PRECIS.

Certain desiderata for this new index were established as guidelines at the start of the project, and others were added as the work progressed. The principal characteristics for the index can be summarized under five main headings:

1. The computer, not the indexer, should produce all of the index entries, so that a large part of the clerical drudgery of index-making would be handled by the machine. The indexer's task would be limited to preparing an input string of the terms which are the components of index entries, together with instruction codes which indicate to the computer how these terms should be organized into entries; all the entries themselves would be constructed by the machine.
2. Each of the entries constructed in this way should be equally coextensive. In other words, each entry should express in a summary form the full subject of the document as perceived by the indexer. This should be seen in contrast to the chain index, where only the final entry is actually coextensive with the subject of the work in question, and also to a system of subject headings, where a compound subject may have to be expressed by two or more different headings, none of which by itself expresses the whole of the subject.
3. The system should be based on a single set of logical relationships among concepts; these should apply to subjects across the whole spectrum of knowledge. This would mean that terms in input strings, and in the entries produced from these strings, should be organized according to a kind of indexing grammar which would remain valid in fields as diverse as physics and metaphysics. Obviously, this grammar would not necessarily reflect the order in which concepts are introduced into the schedules of any one

classification scheme. However, this notion of classificatory neutrality was also regarded as important in a system carrying a range of different class marks such as MARC, since the same alphabetical index could then be applied to classified sequences organized by any of the schemes in the data base.

4. Index entries should be meaningful according to what might be called the normal frames of reference of the user. In other words, they should not be based on a librarian's conception of grammar, which accepts an inverted heading, such as *bridges, concrete,* as though it were everyday English. Instead, we should try to come closer to natural language so that the uninitiated reader can use the index with a minimum of instruction.

5. To complement the entries produced from input strings, the system should also be provided with means for constructing references among terms such as synonyms and higher generics, which are semantically related to index entry terms. These *see* and *see also* references would be extracted by quoting a suitable code from a machine-held thesaurus.

On the face of it, this may appear to be a complex set of criteria; considered on a very elementary level, however, it can be seen that we were actually concerned with only two different kinds of relationships among concepts. Furthermore, both of these had already been studied during the CRG research into a general classification. The earlier work had dealt with the search for a general formula for regulating the order of concepts in a compound class number; we were now concerned with a general model for regulating the order of terms in input strings and index entries. We might call this the search for a generalized syntax for an indexing language. Also, during the CRG research we had studied the ways in which concepts might be organized into categories within a macrothesaurus; we now had the task of creating a machine-held thesaurus of this kind to serve as the source of *see* and *see also* references in a printed index. This could be termed the semantic approach to an indexing language.

Examples of output from each of these sides of the index system can be seen in the extract from a typical PRECIS index which appears in figure 1. At the top of column 3, the user is redirected by a *see* reference from the term *pelecypoda* to its preferred synonym *bivalves.* This is one kind of semantic relationship. A different kind can be seen at the top of the middle column, where the term *particles* is linked, through a *see also* reference, to the names of various species such as *alpha particles, atoms,* and so on. The same term, *particles,* also appears farther down in the middle column, but this time it functions as part of an index entry and is syntactically related to terms such as *beams* and *scattering.* In this particular index, produced by the British Universities Film Council, the user is then referred, through a UDC number,

Papyri
Ancient Greek papyri. Conservation & interpretation 091(38)
Parades. 50th birthday of Hitler, Adolf. Germany
By Nationalsozialistische Deutsche Arbeiter Partei 943.082
Parades. Circuses
— *Animation films* 791.83
Parades reviewed by Mao Tse-Tung. China
Parades to celebrate 17th anniversary of communist government 951.0
Paraffins *See* **Alkanes**
Parainfluenza. Man
Pathogens: Viruses. Effects on mammalian cells in vitro 576.858.7
Paralysis
See also
Myasthenia gravis
Paramecium 593.171.4
Paramoeba eilhardi
Effects on cell nuclei of amoebas 576.89
Paranormal phenomena
See also
Divination
Magic
Mamu
Spirits. Paranormal phenomena
Parasites
See also
Diphyllobothrium latum
Echinococcus granulosus
Ectoparasites
Worms. Parasites
Parasites
Fleas, hookworms & rat mites. Behaviour 576.8.095
Parasites. Alder wood wasps
Hymenoptera 595.79:576.89
Parasites. Cyclorrhapha
Mormoniella 595.77
Parasites. Ephelota gemmipara 593.176
Parasites. Fish
Diphyllobothrium latum. Life cycle 595.121
Parasites. Herbivores
Lancet flukes. Vectors: Ants 595.79:595.122
Liver flukes. Vectors: Mud snails 595.122:594.3
Parasites. Larvae. Cabbage butterflies
Apanteles 591.34:576.89
Parasites. Livestock
Echinococcus granulosus. Life cycle & control 636.089
Parasites. Man
Echinococcus granulosus. Life cycle & control 614.44
Head lice 616-095:576.895.75
Plasmodium. Vectors: Mosquitoes 593.19
Parasites. Sheep
Worms 595.1:636.31
Parasitic diseases
See also
Diseases caused by flukes
Helminthic diseases
Parents
See also
Mothers
Parents
Interpersonal relationships with children. Role in moral development of children 159.922.7
Role in learning in babies 159.922.72
Separation from babies — *Study examples: Babies in foster care* 159.922.7
Separation from babies — *Study examples: Babies in nursery care* 159.922.7
Separation from children, 2-3 years — *Study examples: Children in foster care* 159.922.7
Parents. Botswana. Shakawe; India. Andheri; New Guinea. Buk; Lancashire. Colne & Surrey. Esher
Interpersonal relationships with children — *Sociological perspectives — Comparative studies* 392.31
Parents. Great Britain
Choice of schools 371.2
Paris. France
Chinese theatre — *Performances — Extracts* 792.09
Commune, *1871* 944.081"1871"
National libraries: Bibliothèque Nationale *(France)* 027(44.36)
Students. Protest movements, *1968* 323.23(443.6)
Theatre. Companies: Comédie Française. Performances of Bourgeois gentilhomme 792.09
Theatre. Companies: Comédie Française. Performances of Femmes savantes 792.09
Theatre. Companies: Comédie Française. Performances of Le Tartuffe 792.09
Theatre: Théâtre de France. Rehearsals of Hamlet with Barrault, Jean Louis 792.09
Theatre: Théâtre National Populaire — *Rehearsals & performances — Extracts* 792.09
Paris Peace Conference, *1919. Treaty of Versailles See* **Treaty of Versailles,** *1919*
Parks
See also
National parks
Parliaments
See also
Great Britain. *Parliament*
Partial differential equations
See also
Euler's equations
Lagrange's equations
Particle accelerators
See also
Linear accelerators
Particles
See also
Alpha particles
Atoms
Charged particles
Electrons
Molecules
Moving particles
Muons
Photons
Powders
Particles
Beams. Scattering. Use in determination of structure of atomic nuclei 539.1.08
Counting & size measurement. Use of electronic equipment 621.38
Parties. Politics *See* **Political parties**
Parturition. Cats 591.16:599.742.7
Parturition. Cows. Cattle. Livestock 636.082.456
Parturition. Rabbits 591.16:599.325
Contraction of uterus 591.16:599.325
Uterine contraction after parturition 591.16:599.325
Uterine contraction before parturition 591.16:599.325
Parturition. Red kangaroos 591.16:599.22
Parturition. Sows *See* **Farrowing**
Pascal, Blaise. French philosophy
— *Critical studies* 190(44)
Passavant's bar. Man
Arteries 616.321
Passenger transport services
See also
Bus services
Passenger vehicles
See also
Cars
Passeriformes
See also
Cactospiza pallida
Cutthroat finches
Geospizid finches
Gouldian finches
Swallows
Passfield, Beatrice Webb, *Baroness See* **Webb, Beatrice,** *Baroness Passfield*
Pasteurs et troupeaux. Hugo, Victor. *Study examples*
Poetry in French. Romanticism — *Study examples: Hugo, Victor. Pasteurs et troupeaux, Lamartine, Alphonse de. Lac, Le & Vigny, Alfred Victor, comte de. Maison du berger — Critical studies* 840-1
Pastimes *See* **Recreations**
Pastures. Australia
Improvement. Role of legumes 633.3
Pathogens. Dysentery. Man
Entamoeba histolytica 616.993.12
Pathogens. Ectromelia. Mice
Viruses. Effects on mammalian cells in vitro — *For medicine* 576.858
Pathogens. Herpes simplex. Man
Viruses. Effects on mammalian cells in vitro 576.858.1
Pathogens. Parainfluenza. Man
Viruses. Effects on mammalian cells in vitro 576.858.7
Pathogens. Poliomyelitis. Man
Viruses. Effects on mammalian cells in vitro 576.858.2
Pathogens. Vaccinia. Cattle
Viruses. Effects on mammalian cells in vitro — *For medicine* 576.858.1
Pathogens. Vesicular stomatitis. Mammals
Viruses. Effects on mammalian cells in vitro — *For medicine* 576.858.1
Pathology
See also
Diseases
Paths. Electrons. Uniform magnetic fields
Curvature. Use in measurement of electron mass 537.533
Patients. Mental hospitals
Aggression 616.89-008.444.9
Paving. Motorway M6. Lancashire
Concrete paving 625.84
Pavlov, Ivan Petrovich
Theories of conditioned reflexes in animals — *For medicine* 591.182
Theories of reflexes in man 612.833
Pay *See* **Remuneration**
Peace
See also
Armistices
Pacifism
Peace Pledge Union. Great Britain
Lansbury, George. Political speeches, *1937* 942.085(042)
Pears, David Francis
Theories of free will & determinism 123
Peasants. Rural regions. North-east Brazil
Nomadic peasants. Social conditions 362(81)
Peat industries. Fuel industries. Ireland *(Republic)* 622.271
Peck order. Flocks. Chickens 591.55:598.61
Pedestrian areas *See* **Vehicle-free areas**
Pediatrics *See* **Paediatrics**
Pediculati
See also
Phrynelox scaber
Peek Frean and Company
Factories, *ca 1906* 664.681(091)
Peel, *Sir* **Robert,** *bart.* Great Britain
1810-1850 942.073/.081
Pekingese dogs. Livestock
Urinary tract. Calculi. Cystotomy 619:616.62
Pelecaniformes
See also
Flightless cormorants
Pelecypoda *See* **Bivalves**
Penal system
See also
Approved schools
Prisons
Pendulums
Coupled pendulums. Energy transfer 531.539.2
Coupled pendulums. Equal masses 531.539.2
Coupled pendulums. Normal modes 531.539.2
Forced vibration & resonance 531.53
Penicillin
Effects on Proteus 576.8.097
Effects on Proteus — *Time-lapse films* 576.8.097
Effects on Streptobacillus moniliformis 576.852
Production. Flat flask method 615.779:002
People's Liberation Army of China *See* **China.** *People's Liberation Army*
Peppered moths. Industrial regions. Great Britain
Variation 575.3/.7:595.78
Perca *See* **Perch**
Perception
See also
Appreciation
Illusions
Motion perception
Visual perception
Perception. Animals 591.51
Perception. Man 159.937
Perceptuo-motor skills. Babies
Coordination 159.922.7
Perch
Feeding behaviour 597
Percomorphi
See also
Archerfish
Haplochromis
Perch
Percussion instruments
See also
Drums. Percussion instruments
Percussion techniques. Making. Blades. Stone Age cutting tools 930.26
Performing arts
See also
Acting
Cinema films
Dancing
Mime
Music
Theatre
Performing arts. West Germany
Professional education: Folkwang Hochschule 378.9:78/79
Periodic phenomena
See also
Oscillators
Rhythms
Periodic table
See also
Periodicity
Periodicals on political events
Labour Monthly — *Personal observations* 05
Periodicity. Chemical elements 541.9
Peripheral equipment
See also
Terminals. Computer systems
Peripheral nervous system. Dogs 591.18
Perissodactyla
See also
White rhinoceroses
Persecution and assassination of Jean-Paul Marat as performed by the inmates of the asylum at Charenton under the direction of the Marquis de Sade. Weiss, Peter. Drama in German
Performances by Royal Shakespeare Theatre Company — *English texts* 792.09
Persia *See* **Iran**
Persian Gulf
Petroleum deposits. Drilling 622.1
Personal appearance
See also
Clothing
Personnel
See also
Personnel *under* Names of specific industries & professions
Crews
Employment
Industrial relations
Manpower
Personnel management
Supervision — *Study examples: Coal industries* 658.3-052.24
Persons questioned by police. Great Britain
Rights. Law 351.74.085
Perspiration. Man 612.792
Peru
Marine birds. Social behaviour 598.4(85)
Pesticides
See also
Herbicides
Pests
Bed bugs. Control 614.44:595.754
Insects. Biological control & chemical control 632.7
Pests. Australia
Argentine ants. Control 632.93:595.79
Pests. Potatoes
Eelworms. Control 632.651.32
Pests. Soils
Control 631.4:632.93

Figure 1. Extract of PRECIS Index

to a classified sequence where full details of the appropriate films will be found. However, I should point out that this is just one of several options available in PRECIS. In some cases the entry may refer to a separate file of subject headings which have been derived mechanically from the PRECIS input strings. One or two organizations also use PRECIS as a one-stage index—that is, they print the relevant citation directly below each index entry.

I cannot attempt to describe in detail all the stages in the production of a PRECIS index—that would require a series of papers. However, I would like to deal at least briefly with the basic mechanics of the system, partly to demonstrate the extent to which we met the basic requirements for a printed index considered earlier, and also to show how this indexing system relates to a general classification. I shall deal separately with the two aspects of the system, and consider first the syntactical relations between terms in index entries, then briefly touch on the semantics and the making of a machine-held thesaurus. Syntax itself can be considered from two different viewpoints: (1) the format and structure of index entries, and (2) the organization of terms into the strings from which the entries are produced.

THE PRECIS ENTRY FORMAT

When we set out to establish a suitable format for PRECIS, we found that we had to depart, in some respects, from the concept of a single-line entry which is typically found in systems such as the chain index, KWIC, and subject headings. The reasons for this can be illustrated by referring to the string of terms, and some hypothetical entries, which are shown in figure 2. The string:

FRANCE · TEXTILE INDUSTRIES · SKILLED PERSONNEL · TRAINING

represents a typical PRECIS input, and justifies some explanation. In the first place, these terms have been organized deliberately so that they form what we call a context-dependent sequence. This means that each term in the string sets the next term into its obviously wider context, in the sense in which *France,* for example, establishes the environment in which the *textile industries,* and therefore the rest of the subject, were considered by the author. The next term, *textile industries*, identifies the context in which *skilled personnel* were considered, and this new term establishes the class of persons to whom the act of *training* was being applied. It is worth pointing out that no attempt has been made to organize these terms in such a way that their order reflects their relative importance as shelving factors; we are principally concerned with expressing the meaning of the subject, and we leave the job of indicating shelf position to the classification scheme.

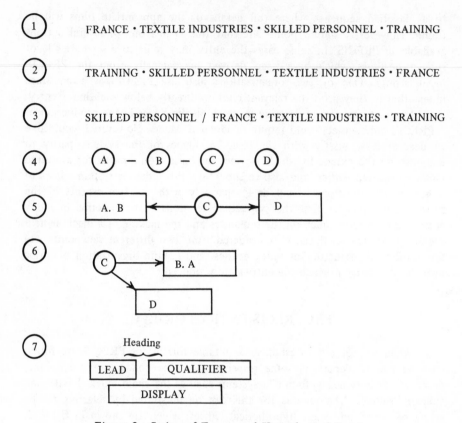

Figure 2. String of Terms and Hypothetical Entries

As a natural consequence of arranging these terms in a context-dependent order, they also form what we call a one-to-one related sequence. This means that each term is directly related to the next term in the string. Both context dependency and one-to-one relations occur in natural language itself, of course, and it may be worth mentioning that the order used in PRECIS was derived from a study of sentence structures. We regard these one-to-one relations as particularly important in conveying the meaning of a subject statement; indeed, in the present example, these relationships are so strong that the meaning of the original string remains unchanged even when the order of terms is reversed, as:

TRAINING • SKILLED PERSONNEL • TEXTILE INDUSTRIES • FRANCE

It therefore follows that either of these strings could function as an index entry which satisfies most of the criteria considered earlier: they are equally coextensive, and they both convey the same message according to common frames of reference. Both could also be derived, by a very simple algorithm, from a single input string.

However, we start to encounter problems when we consider the production of an entry under one of the middle terms, such as *skilled personnel*. It would be a simple matter to instruct the computer to lift this term out of its place in the string and print it at the start of the entry, as shown at position 3 of figure 2. An element of ambiguity, however, has then been created: when reading this entry, we can no longer tell with certainty how the *skilled personnel* are related to the rest of the terms. Are they being trained, or are they employed in training others? It is not a difficult matter to deduce how this ambiguity arose. When this term was shifted from its original position, the mind automatically closed up the space that was left, and created a new set of one-to-one relationships. In a situation such as this, the problem can be expressed as a question: How can we maintain the original one-to-one relationships in an index entry without distorting the meaning, and without losing any of the terms in the process?

The approach we adopted is shown in the form of a diagram at position 4:

$$A - B - C - D$$

These four letters represent a sequence of four terms organized as a context-dependent and one-to-one related sequence. As we saw, the problem arose when we tried to make an index entry under one of the middle terms, such as C. As shown at position 5, this is due to the fact the term C is related simultaneously to the terms on either side; that is, B (which sets C into its wider context), and D (which is itself context-dependent on C). In order to make these relationships explicit on the printed page, we devised the two-line and three-position format which is shown at position 6. In this case, the term C functions as the user's access point to the index, and this is followed on the same line by those terms which set the lead into its wider contexts. The final term, D, is indented below on a second line, but remains explicitly related to the entry term C.

The layout of terms seen at position 6 shows an obvious two-line and three-position structure, which has now become a typical feature of a PRECIS index. These parts have been separately named, as shown at position 7. The *lead* is the term which functions as the user's access point, and this is automatically printed in roman bold to give it emphasis. The *qualifier* follows on the same line, and contains those terms which set the lead into its context, while the *display* holds the terms which are context-dependent on the lead. Terms in the qualifier and display may be printed in ordinary roman or italic, depending on how they are coded in the input string. The lead and qualifier together constitute what is called the *heading*. If two or more different strings give rise to the same heading,

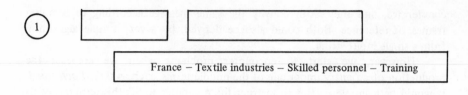

France – Textile industries – Skilled personnel – Training

FRANCE
Textile industries. Skilled personnel. Training

TEXTILE INDUSTRIES. France
Skilled personnel. Training

SKILLED PERSONNEL. Textile industries. France
Training

TRAINING. Skilled personnel. Textile industries. France

Figure 3. Terms Organized in Standard Format

so that only the displays are different, the computer automatically cancels the second and subsequent headings, and organizes the displays as an alphabetical column (see figure 1), where the term *particles* (near the top of the middle column) has two displays, one starting with the term *beams,* and the other with the term *counting.*

The adoption of this format did more than resolve the problem of maintaining the one-to-one relationships between terms. It also gave us the basis for a fairly simple program which would allow us to generate mechanically a full set of entries out of a single input. This is performed by an operation known as *shunting;* the choice of this name may become clear if we consider the example of index entry construction which is shown in figure 3. At the top of this page we can see the three basic positions in a PRECIS entry, with a set of terms marshaled in the display position. The lead has not yet been occupied, and no entry has yet been produced. At the first stage of the operation, the first term in the display is shunted into the lead, and the remaining terms are then shifted left to a standard indentation position; this gives us the first entry, under the term *France,* which appears in position 2. In generating the next entry, the term *France* is shunted across into the qualifier, and its place in the lead is taken by the next term, *textile industries*; again, the rest of the terms in the display shift across to the standard indentation level. This operation could be repeated twice more, to give us the entries under the terms *skilled personnel* and *training.* In this particular case, all of the terms in the input string passed through the lead position to give a total of four entries, but it should be pointed out that the generation of entries is not left entirely to the computer. It is, in fact, always under the control of the indexer, who can stipulate, in the form of instruction codes written as prefixes to each of the terms in the string, which terms should appear in the lead, or in any other part of the entry.

The entries shown in figure 3 represent terms organized in what is called the *standard format.* This format, which is produced by a straightforward application of shunting techniques, accounts for most of the entries in any PRECIS index. Two other formats are also available, but I shall not attempt to describe these here—they are fully explained in some of the technical accounts of the system.[8]

THE TREATMENT OF COMPOUND TERMS

The procedures shown in figure 3 demonstrate the treatment of a typical compound subject—that is, a subject which consists of a string of several terms. We also found that a basically similar technique could be applied to a compound term—that is, a term which has to be expressed in more than one word. The treatment of a term of this type *(fibre reinforced plastics)* is shown in figure 4.

In order to explain this procedure, it is first necessary to make a distinction between the different components of this term. In particular, we need to distinguish clearly between the noun, which is called the *focus*, and the adjectives, which are called *differences.* The focus (the word *plastics* in the present example) identifies the general class of concepts to which the term as a whole belongs. The term *difference* is used in its strictly logical sense to indicate some characteristic which specifies a subclass of the focal concept. In the present example, we have two differences, *fibre* and *reinforced,* each of which has its own logical function. The word *reinforced* functions as what we call a direct difference—it qualifies the focus, and defines a special subclass of the universe of *plastics* called *reinforced plastics.* The word *fibre,* however, has a rather different function, since it does not directly qualify the focus (that is, these are *not* fibre plastics), but instead qualifies the adjective *reinforced* in terms of the material used as reinforcement. It therefore functions as what we call an "indirect difference." This distiction is shown in the diagram at position 2 in figure 4.

Since these logical functions affect the correct form of term in an index entry, they must be indicated clearly to the computer. This is expressed by

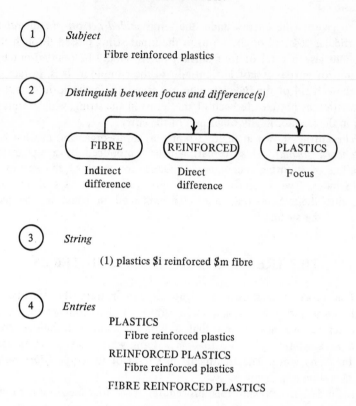

Figure 4. Treatment of Compound Terms

codes which are written as prefixes to each part of a compound term in the input string. An example of an input is shown at position 3 in figure 4:

(1) plástics $i reinforced $m fibre

where the focus, *plastics,* is prefixed by one of the role operators which we shall be considering later, while its status as a lead is indicated by a check. The code $i, which precedes the word *reinforced,* conveys two instructions to the computer: (1) it indicates that this is a direct difference, and (2) it shows that this word should appear in the lead. The code $m, which precedes *fibre,* also indicates a lead, but specifies that this word functions as an indirect difference. The output from this string is shown at position 4, and it can be seen that each of these entries is fully coextensive with the original concept. If the term in the lead is incomplete, as it is in the first and second entries, the whole term is printed, in natural-language order, in the display position.

Using these procedures, it is not possible to produce an inverted heading such as *plastics, reinforced.*

THE SCHEMA OF ROLE OPERATORS

So far we have considered the basic mechanics of entry construction, but we have not yet faced the problem of trying to ensure that a team of indexers will consistently achieve the same order of terms in their input strings. As I mentioned earlier, terms in an input string have to be arranged so that they form a context-dependent sequence. However, this is no more than the statement of a guiding principle. We need something more definite if we are to ensure that a team of different and quite human indexers (including the same indexer on different occasions) will consistently achieve this order.

To this end, the indexers work within the constraints of a kind of grammar. This is represented in the schema of role operators shown in figure 5. In many respects, this schema possesses some of the functions of the system developed during the CRG research. One of these operators has to be written as a prefix to each of the terms in an input string, and the operators then have two functions: (1) the principal codes (that is, the numbered or main-line operators seen at the top of the list) have built-in filing values, and it is these which determine the overall pattern of terms in a string; and (2) the codes act as computer instructions, and determine not only the format of the index entries, but also the typography of each term and its associated punctuation.

It would be quite impossible in the time available to describe in detail the workings of a scheme such as this, which is capable of dealing with compound subjects at any level of complexity. At least I can try to demonstrate how the system operates in practice, using the role operators to carry out an analysis of the subject we considered earlier: the training of skilled personnel in the French textile industries. This analysis is shown in figure 6.

During their initial training, indexers are taught to carry out their analyses in a step-by-step fashion, and are advised first to test each subject for the presence of an action. If an action concept is present, it usually determines how the rest of the subject should be handled, in much the same way that the verb tends to dominate the sentence in traditional grammar. In the present example, it is clear that an action is present in the term *training.* This term could therefore be written first, and prefixed by the operator "2," which represents an action or its effects, as shown at position 2:

Main line operators		
Environment of observed system	0	Location
Observed system (Core operators)	1	Key system: *object of transitive action; agent of intransitive action*
	2	Action/Effect
	3	Agent of transitive action; Aspects; Factors

A —————————————————————————————————

Data relating to observer	4	Viewpoint-as-form
Selected instance	5	Sample population/Study region
Presentation of data	6	Target/Form

Interposed operators		
Dependent elements	p	Part/Property
	q	Member of quasi-generic group
	r	Aggregate
Concept interlinks	s	Role definer
	t	Author attributed association
Coordinate concepts	g	Coordinate concept

B —————————————————————————————————

Differencing operators		
(prefixed by $)	h	Non-lead direct difference
	i	Lead direct difference
	j	Salient difference
	k	Non-lead indirect difference
	m	Lead indirect difference
	n	Non-lead parenthetical difference
	o	Lead parenthetical difference
	d	Date as a difference

Connectives		
(Components of linking phrases; prefixed by $)	v	Downward reading component
	w	Upward reading component

C —————————————————————————————————

Theme interlinks		
	x	First element in coordinate theme
	y	Subsequent element in coordinate theme
	z	Element of common theme

Figure 5. PRECIS—Schema of Role Operators

(1)　Subject:　Training of skilled personnel in the French textile industries

(2)　Check for the presence of an action. Write the appropriate operator
　　　　　　(2)　training

(3)　If the action is transitive, and the object is present, code the object as 'key system'
　　　　　　(1)　skilled personnel
　　　　　　(2)　training

(4)　If the key system is part of a whole, code the whole as key system; use 'p' to
　　　　identify the part
　　　　　　(1)　textile industries
　　　　　　(p)　skilled personnel
　　　　　　(2)　training

(5)　Establish the environment
　　　　　　(0)　France
　　　　　　(1)　textile industries
　　　　　　(p)　skilled personnel
　　　　　　(2)　training

(6)　Entries in 'standard format' (assuming a lead on each term)
　　　　　　FRANCE
　　　　　　　　Textile industries. Skilled personnel. Training

　　　　　　TEXTILE INDUSTRIES.　France
　　　　　　　　Skilled personnel. Training

　　　　　　SKILLED PERSONNEL.　Textile industries. France
　　　　　　　　Training

　　　　　　TRAINING.　Skilled personnel. Textile industries. France

Figure 6. Analysis of a Compound Subject

(2) training

The indexer next determines whether the action is transitive or intransitive; if (as in this example) the action is transitive, he establishes whether the object is also present. In this case, the act of *training* is being applied to the *skilled personnel,* who therefore represent the object. This concept is frequently coded as the key system, as shown at position 3:

(1) skilled personnel
(2) training.

However, this particular example contains a circumstance which causes a change to be made in this coding. In fact, the *skilled personnel* are part of another system (the *textile industries*), and this whole/part relationship has to be expressed by noting an operator "p" (which introduces a part or property indicator) in front of the name of the part. The numbered operator, "1," is then assigned to the name of the whole, which gives us the revised string seen in position 4:

(1) textile industries
(p) skilled personnel
(2) training

One more concept remains to be coded. This is the term *France,* which establishes the environment in which all the rest of the subject was considered, and therefore should be introduced by the operator "0." The final version of the string is shown at position 5:

(0) France
(1) textile industries
(p) skilled personnel
(2) training

It can now be seen that we have achieved in a fairly mechanical way exactly the same order of terms as in the earlier analysis, when this subject was considered only from the viewpoints of context-dependency and one-to-one relationships. It is only fair to point out that an experienced indexer would *not* go through the stages of this step-by-step analysis. Instead, he would write the correct string in an almost intuitive fashion, without necessarily being aware of the mental processes involved. The entries produced from this input are shown at position 6.

THE SEMANTIC ASPECTS OF PRECIS

I shall turn now to a different side of the system—that is, to the construction of the thesaurus which serves as the source of *see* and *see also* references in the printed index. This introduces a different set of routines and relationships, many of which involve classification in its taxonomic (rather than its library) sense; I will deal with these only briefly. I should start by pointing out that PRECIS works with an open-ended vocabulary; that is, a new term can be admitted into the system at any time, as soon as it has been encountered in a document. Any term marked as a lead in an input string is assigned—as part of a separate operation—to a position in a random-access file.

This position is indicated to the computer by writing a special number as part of each thesaurus input record. This number (the Reference Indicator Number, or RIN) identifies the address where the term will be stored. This address will later be written in a special field on an indexing form, where the presence of this number acts as a machine instruction, and leads automatically to the production of a full set of *see* and *see also* references directing the user toward the term which actually occurred in an index entry.

In figure 7 we can see a batch of thesaurus input records which have been prepared by an indexer, and are ready to be keyboarded and put into the computer. These are the cards which might be written if the indexer encountered the term *penguins* in a string for the first time, assuming that none of the other associated terms had previously been admitted into the system. The input record for *penguins* appears at the bottom of the sequence, and it can be seen that a number of data are recorded on this card. These include special codes, such as $m and $o, which indicate that the term *penguins* is related, in clearly specified ways, to terms which are held at other random file addresses in the computer, such as its synonym, *sphenisciformes,* and the higher generic term *birds.* The codes used for this purpose actually record, in machine-readable form, a range of semantic relationships which has now been established by the International Standards Organisation, and is recorded in a new international standard, IS 2788. These codes and their associated relationships are shown in figure 8; we can see at position 2 that they also determine the kind of reference which should be printed. The code $m produces a *see* reference from a nonpreferred term to its preferred synonym, while $n and $o both generate *see also* references.

Not all the data on these input records have to be keyboarded. It would be pointless, for example, to keyboard the terms from which references have to be made: it is enough to indicate to the computer the addresses at which these terms have been stored. If we turn to the bottom of figure 7, we can see the relatively small amount of data which is actually assigned to the computer when the card containing the term *penguins* is being processed. Once keyboarding is finished, the input cards are returned to the indexer, who then stores them alphabetically to form a term authority file.

Perhaps it is difficult at first to see any coherent pattern in the set of input records shown in figure 7. Nevertheless, this set of cards contains all of the semantic information needed to record within the computer the network of logically related terms shown in figure 9. Once a network of this kind has been established, it can be used in various ways. For example, the address of any term in the network can be quoted as part of an indexing record as soon as an appropriate document is encountered, and the necessary *see* and *see also* references will then be produced automatically. If we had set up this network

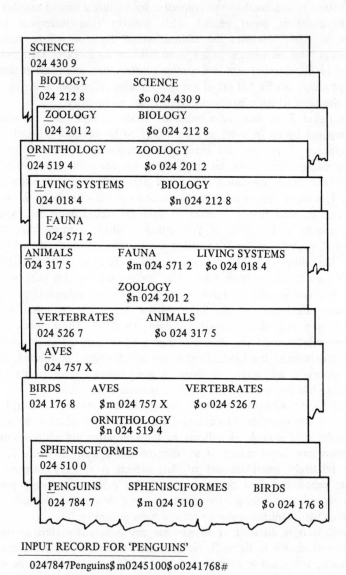

INPUT RECORD FOR 'PENGUINS'

0247847Penguins$ m0245100$ o0241768#

Figure 7. Thesaurus Input Records

(1)   RELATIONAL CODES USED TO LINK TERM ADDRESSES (RINs)

Relationships based on IS 2788

$m   = EQUIVALENCE RELATIONSHIP
          Synonyms
          Quasi-synonyms

$o   = HIERARCHICAL RELATIONSHIP
          Genus-species
          Hierarchical whole-part

$n   = ASSOCIATIVE RELATIONSHIP

(2)   MACHINE INSTRUCTIONS BUILT INTO CODES

$m   = PRINT *See* REFERENCE, i.e. Aaa *See* Bbb

$n ⎱
$o ⎰ = PRINT *See also* REFERENCE, i.e.
                                    Aaa
                                  See also
                                      Bbb
                                      Ccc

Figure 8. PRECIS Thesaurus

for *penguins*, and we later handled a work on *vertebrates,* we could immediately produce references such as:

Animals		Zoology
see also	and	*see also*
Vertebrates		Animals

simply by quoting the RIN 024 526 7 in the appropriate field on the indexing record. We can also quote any of these addresses to link new terms to the names of categories which are already on the file—we need to set up the network only once, then leave the rest to the computer.

THE MANAGEMENT ASPECTS OF PRECIS

Finally, some of the management aspects of PRECIS merit attention. In view of the present conference, particular notice should be taken of its relationship to some of the other subject data appearing on current British MARC records. This immediately introduces the concept of a packet of subject data, which can best be explained through reference to the work-flow diagram which appears in figure 10.

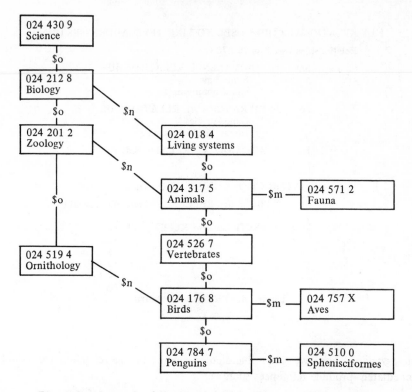

Figure 9. Network of Terms Linked by Thesaural Relationships

When documents are processed in the British Library, descriptive and subject cataloging are handled by separate teams of specialists, and a document enters the subject division after it has been cataloged descriptively. Each document is accompanied by a worksheet containing details of author, title, etc., recorded in the appropriate MARC fields. This worksheet, however, contains no fields for the recognized subject data, such as the PRECIS string or the DDC class mark. It does, however, contain one small box which will later be occupied by a number which will function as the link between the document record and all the appropriate subject data held in a separate file inside the computer.

As soon as a document is received from the catalogers, it is handled first by the PRECIS team. They formulate its subject, then check for a precedent in their master file of all past index entries, using any appropriate term as an access point. Let us assume that an indexer, after examining a document,

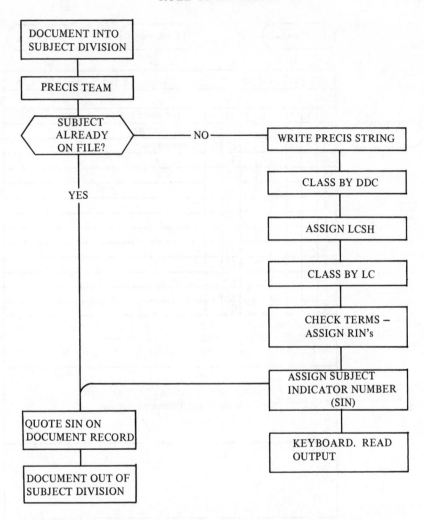

Figure 10. Work-flow through Subject Division of British Library

cannot find an exact match in the file of past decisions. The PRECIS indexer must then move to the right side of the work-flow diagram, to the point where the indexer writes the PRECIS string. This is recorded in a special field (Field 690) on the subject form which is shown in figure 11; the example shows the string for a document about a programming language called BASIC.

The document and the index form then move on together to the DDC team. Working from the string, and if necessary the document, this group

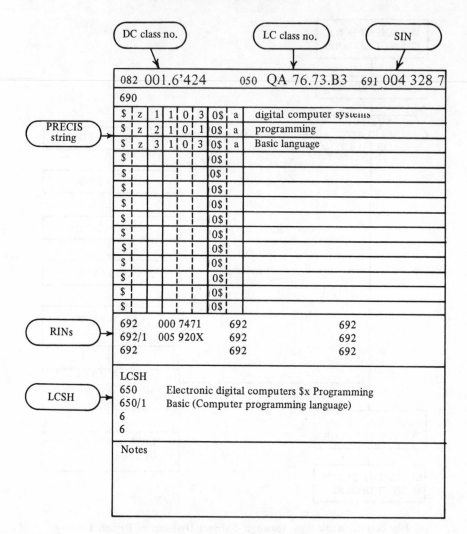

Figure 11. Sample of Indexing Input Form

assigns the appropriate class number, and records this in Field 082 in the upper left corner of the indexing form. In the majority of cases, they do not expect to find an exact place in the DDC schedules for the subject expressed in the string. A careful analysis of our working methods has shown that only some 15 percent of PRECIS strings can be matched exactly by DDC numbers. We do not regard this in any way as a serious problem. We recognize a clear distinction between the function of an index and that of a shelf-order scheme. The index entry should tell us what the document is about; the class number then supplements this information by indicating where it appears on the shelves.

The document and form then travel from team to team through the rest of the subject division—i.e., down the right side of the flow diagram in figure 10—and at each step, a different decision is recorded on the worksheet, such as the LC class number, Library of Congress subject headings, and the Reference Indicator Numbers (or RINs) which direct the computer to the machine-held thesaurus. Finally, the form is checked by a junior indexer, who ensures that all the necessary fields are occupied and then strikes out the next available random file address number from a machine-produced list. This is the Subject Indicator Number (inevitably shortened to SIN) which is written in Field 691 on the top line of the indexing form. The SIN identifies the address in a machine-held file at which all these subject data will be stored, as a package, for future use. The same number is also transcribed onto the catalog form, and then becomes the link between the document record and all its appropriate subject data.

The subject form goes on to the keyboarding section, and the data are submitted to the computer, which first carries out a series of validation checks; if these are satisfactory, it then assigns all the data to disk. It also responds by producing a full set of authority file cards of the kind shown in figure 12. These are read for errors such as spelling mistakes, and if they are satisfactory they are filed as a reference tool for the indexers and classifiers. It should be noted that each of these cards contains the whole packet of subject data, including the SIN itself—this is the number 004 3281 which appears on the left side immediately below the index entry.

Let us now return to the work-flow diagram in figure 10, and visualize a different situation. Let us assume this time that after examining the document, the indexer checks the authority file and finds that the subject, as he perceives it, has already been handled in the past. In that case, he can transcribe the SIN directly onto the catalog record, and the process is then completed. The document and its catalog worksheet can now be routed out of the subject division down the left side of the flow diagram. We have kept very careful statistics of the extent to which this left-hand route is used, and calculated that some 55 percent of BNB's total throughput was handled in this way from a three-year-old authority file. Obviously, from a manager's viewpoint, this represents a worthwhile savings of time and intellectual effort.

Figures 13-16 show some figures relating to indexer performance and index evaluation, as well as a survey of the present and potential users of PRECIS. Unfortunately, this list is already outdated. I feel that the most satisfying aspect of this survey of users is its sheer diversity. This applies first

Digital computer systems
  Programming. Basic language

0043281   082010 001.6'424

690000 $z11030$adigital computer systems$z21010$aprogramming
$z31030$aBasic language

692000 0007471 692000 005920X

650000 Electronic digital computers $x Programming
650000|Basic (Computer programming language)
050000 QA76.73.B3

Programming. Digital computer systems
  Basic language

0043281   082010 001.6'424

690000 $z11030$adigital computer systems$z21010$aprogramming
$z31030$aBasic language

692000 007471 692000 005920X
650000 Electronic digital computers $x Programming
650000 Basic (Computer programming language)
050000 QA76.73.B3

Basic language. Digital computer systems
0043281   082010 001.6'424

690000 $z11030$a digital computer systems$z21010$aprogramming
$z31030$aBasic language

692000 0007471 692000 005920X
650000 Electronic digital computers $x Programming
650000 Basic (Computer programming language)
050000 QA76.73.B3

001.6'424   QA76.73.B3

0043281

690000 $z11030$adigital computer systems$z21010$aprogramming
$z31030$aBasic language

692000 0007471 692000 005920X

650000 Electronic digital computers $x Programming
650000 Basic (Computer programming language)

Figure 12. Diagnostic Printout on Continuous Card Stationery

1 *Indexing Rates*

Indexing rate (i.e. string writing) is approximately 30 documents per working day of seven and one-quarter hours, i.e. the average time required to string a document on a new theme is about 18 mins. This figure represents 'elapsed working time', as opposed to stop-watch times, which would be 37-50 percent shorter.

Manipulation coding accounts for less than 10 percent of the total string writing time.

2 *Statistical properties of strings*	*Averages (mean)*
Number of strings per document	1
Number of terms per string	2.7
Number of lead terms per string	1.9

3 *Operation of the RIN and SIN systems*

A. Proportion of documents handled by quoting existing SIN's from a three year file (1971-73)   55%

B. Number of terms in thesaurus after three years   27,000

Figure 13. Indexing Performance Figures Collected at BNB

1 *Test environment*

PRECIS index to 584 journal articles in the field of management.

100 questions; 1 relevant document per question; each question searched once.

28 researchers, mainly students.

2 *Success rate of searches*

No. of successful searches (relevant document retrieved).	83
No. of unsuccessful searches (relevant document missed).	17
Recall ratio	83%

3 *Search times*   *Average per question (to nearest 15 secs.)*

	Mean		Median	
	Mins.	Secs.	Mins.	Secs.
Successful searches	1	30	1	00
Unsuccessful searches	4	00	3	00
All searches	1	45	1	00

Figure 14. Research at Liverpool Polytechnic

Note on symbols: (a) = form and/or frequency of output
                    (b) = production: computer or manual
                    (c) = 1-stage or 2-stage index
                    (d) = if 2-stage, classification or other address system

A) CATALOGUES OF LIBRARIES OR LIBRARY NETWORKS

1 East Sussex Public Libraries – *(a) COM; (b) computer; (c) 2-stage; (d) DC*

2 London Borough of Hillingdon Libraries – *(a) COM; (b) computer; (c) 2-stage (d) DC*

3 Sheffield College of Education – *(a) card; (b) manual; (c) 1-stage*

4 Polytechnic of Central London – *(a) card, may experiment with COM; (b) manual, but computer planned; (c) 2-stage; (d) DC*

5 Stockwell College of Education (London) – *(a) COM; (b) computer; (c) 2-stage; (d) DC*

6 Media Resources Centre (Inner London Education Authority) – *(a) card; (b) manual, but computer planned; (c) 2-stage; (d) DC*

7 Aurora High School Library *(Ontario, Canada)* – *(a) card; (b) manual; (c) 1-stage*

B) BIBLIOGRAPHIES

1 Australian National Bibliography – *(a) printed & cumulating; (b) computer; (c) 2-stage; (d) DC*

2 British National Bibliography – *(a) printed & cumulating; (b) computer; (c) 2-stage; (d) DC*

3 British National Film Catalogue – *(a) printed & comulating; (b) computer; (c) 2-stage; (d) UDC*

4 A/V Materials for Higher Education *(British Universities Film Council)* – *(a) printed; (b) computer; (c) 2-stage; (d) UDC*

5 HELPIS (A/V materials) – *(a) printed, intermittent; (b) computer; (c) 2-stage; (d) UDC*

6 HELPIS-MEDICAL – *(a) printed, intermittent; (b) computer; (c) 2-stage; (d) UDC*

7 Film Catalogue *(College Bibliocentre, Ontario)* – *(a) printed & cumulating; (b) computer; (c) 2-stage; (d) broad subject headings + serial numbers*

8 British Education Index *(from January 1976)* – *(a) printed & cumulating; (b) computer; (c) 2-stage; (d) PRECIS S/H*

Figure 15. Users of PRECIS

A) CATALOGUES OF LIBRARIES OR LIBRARY NETWORKS

  1 Wollongong University *(NSW) – (a) card; (b) manual; (c) 1-stage*

  2 S.G.M.E. *(Dept. of A/V Materials, Ministry of Education, Quebec)–(a) printed, French; (b) computer; (c) 2-stage; (d) Lamy-Rousseau classification of A/V materials*

  3 Department of the Environment *(GB) – details not settled*

  4 British Library Reference Division *(formerly British Museum Library) – (a) COM, cumulating; (b) computer; (c) 2-stage; (d) PRECIS S/H*

  5 Université de Rouen, Section Sciences – *(a) printed or COM, French; (b) computer; (c) 2-stage; (d) thesis serial number or PRECIS S/H*

B) BIBLIOGRAPHIES

  1 British Catalogue of Music – *(a) printed & cumulating; (b) computer; (c) 2-stage; (d) details not settled*

C) BACK-OF-THE-BOOK INDEXES

  1 Public Record Office (London) – *indexes to calendars etc*

  2 Scottish Record Office (Edinburgh) – *indexes to calendars etc*

AGENCIES PLANNING PILOT PROJECTS, OR
ENQUIRING FOR TRAINING OR PROGRAMS

1 Malaysian National Bibliography

2 South African National Bibliography

3 South African Council for Scientific & Industrial Research

4 Danish Library Centre

5 ONTERIS (Ontario Educational Research Information Service)

6 British Library (Library Association Library)

7 Indian Library Science Abstracts

8 National Film Board of Canada

Figure 16. Pilot Projects

to the size of the organizations involved—they range from a high school in Canada to two national bibliographies. It also applies to the media being indexed, which range from monographs, through audiovisual materials, to archives held in two public record offices. It is, I think, worth recording that none of these factors has affected the use of the system.

REFERENCES

1. Roberts, Norman. "Review of *Classification in the 1970's," Journal of Documentation* 28:184, June 1972.

2. Maltby, Arthur, ed. *Classification in the 1970's.* Hamden, Conn., Linnet Books, 1972.

3. Perreault, Jean M. "Review of *Classification in the 1970's," International Classification* 1:47-48, 1974.

4. Davison, Keith. *Classification Practice in Britain.* London, Library Association, 1966.

5. Austin, Derek. "Differences between Library Classifications and Machine-based Subject Retrieval Systems." In *Proceedings of the Third International Study Conference on Classification Research, Bombay, 1975.* The Hague, FID. (In press.)

6. Vickery, Brian C. *Classification and Indexing in Science.* 3d ed. London, Butterworths, 1975.

7. Mills, J. "Progress in Documentation: Library Classification," *Journal of Documentation* 26:138, June 1970.

8. Austin, Derek. "The Development of PRECIS," *Journal of Documentation* 30:47-102, March 1974.

9. _____. *PRECIS: A Manual of Concept Analysis and Subject Indexing.* London, BNB, 1974.

PAULE ROLLAND-THOMAS
Associate Professor
Ecole de Bibliothéconomie
Université de Montréal, Canada

The Role of Classification in Subject Retrieval in the Future

It always seems befitting that the last speaker at a conference should gaze at a crystal ball and predict the future of the subject that has been discussed; I feel I should quote Confucius by saying that I do not invent, but transmit.

In the last ten years, since the Elsinore Conference on Classification Research, classification theory and practice have produced a large body of literature and contributed to meetings such as this one. Major futuristic works, especially *Classification in the 1970's,*[1] which was published early in this decade, provide the reader with a clear insight of what the future holds for each topic covered. J. Mills states of Bliss's *Bibliographic Classification* that "as a library classification scheme *per se,* the prospect is clear and bright," but "from the point of view of its future use, the prospect is less predictable."[2] Bibliographic Classification (BC) is being revised because some ninety libraries use it and need a revised edition. Presently, no BC class numbers are provided from centralized cataloging services such as *British National Bibliography,* MARC tapes, etc. However, Mills asserts that if demand warrants it: "This might involve the development of a 'switching language' whereby the subject analysis and description implicit in the production of PRECIS index entries ... could be translated quickly and economically into BC numbers."[3]

Gopinath writes that the third version of the Colon Classification (CC) is tending to become a freely faceted analytico-synthetic scheme:

157

It is now possible for the notational system of CC to place any new main subject, or non-main subject—simple or compound in any facet—in the helpful position determined by the idea plane. . . . Thus during the next decade the development of CC will be approximate to the ideal of a freely-faceted model of classification.[4]

According to Sarah Vann, the flexibility of notation in Dewey's Decimal Classification (DDC) will contribute to its internationalization:

This flexibility is to be 'controlled' through the inclusion of notes telling where to class subjects displaced. How long the 'official' Dewey will remain official in use, therefore, is highly speculative until further study is made. It can be assumed, however, that the use of the basic text both by the *British national bibliography* and the Decimal Classification division of the Library of Congress will continue to insure authoritative interpretation of notation.[5]

This prompts me to question the desirability and the practical value of a truly international scheme; varied cultures, national differences, distinct systems of values (even among countries in the Western world) have already shown that DDC is inadequate in some areas, namely the 100s, 200s, and 300s.

J.P. Immroth has invested a lot of energy, thought and research on the Library of Congress Classification (LCC).[6] He deserves credit, I believe, for the first groundwork in building a theoretical approach to LCC, (fragile as it may be). I feel that the future of this scheme lies in its keeping up with the development of knowledge in its own enumerative manner and not in trying to imitate other schemes. The wealth of words contained in the schedules, the indexes to the schedules, and the lists of subject headings should allow for further research on the homologation and structural model building of the scheme and its ancillaries.

The Universal Decimal Classification (UDC) development program for the 1970s has been described by G.A. Lloyd.[7] Funded partly by the International Federation for Documentation (FID) and partly through UNESCO, the program may be considered in four phrases, in addition to the normal revisions. They are:

1) immediate elaboration of a UDC "roof scheme" capable of fulfilling the role of international switching language in multilingual and multidisciplinary information systems, especially of an international or large-scale nature;
2) extended studies on the use of UDC combined with coordinate-indexing schemes, thesauri or special-subject classifications, and the

compilation of appropriate concordances, as means to improving information retrieval systems generally;

3) short-term priority projects, mainly FID-funded, to improve or remedy defective or deficient parts of the existing UDC schedules;

4) further perspectives of structural and notational improvements of a more far-reaching nature.[8]

Although Vickery's paper on classificatory principles in natural-language indexing systems[9] presents a sound explanation of the underlying classificatory technique in indexing, no new ventures in this particular area are foreseen.

In his paper, "Prospects for Classification Suggested by Evaluation Tests Carried Out 1957-1970," E.M. Keen questions the benefits of classificatory index languages on the ground that their logical foundations may be at fault.

> In providing controlled languages their artificiality and complexity introduce new opportunities for misunderstanding and error. But another answer may be that the logical foundation presupposes a false view of the objectives of document retrieval systems. Users rarely require to see every single fully and marginally relevant document in a particular file, and they do not always expect that every non-relevant document in the file can be withheld.[10]

He concludes that the next decade will see different kinds of information retrieval systems—manual, mechanized and new ones approaching automation. Keen deduces:

> On considerations of retrieval performance there is ample evidence that, in the kind of situations covered by tests so far, relatively uncontrolled languages used at the indexing stage cannot be improved on by controlled languages, and that in many cases even the use of controlled language aids at the search stage will not be necessary.[11]

For the sake of thoroughness, I will summarize Derek Austin's viewpoints as presented in his paper on trends toward a compatible general system.[12] In this paper, he has outlined and discussed postulates and findings of the Classification Research Group as they relate to that group's approach to classification. Plans for research into a new general classification scheme were laid down at the London Conference in 1963.[13] Throughout the years, the plans have evolved from a fairly conventional faceted classification scheme to the assignment of concepts "in a once-and-for-all basis to general categories from which they can be selected as needed in the building of any compound subject."[14]

PRECIS, as Austin writes, "should be seen rather as an interesting by-product of the continuing search for a general classification scheme."[15] Its strings have been rotated to produce sets of entries that are meaningful in languages other than English. Recent developments in linguistics (namely Chomsky's school) have contributed to classification research insofar as it "supports the hypothesis of a deep syntactic structure which is common to all language systems."[16] Therefore, the goal of the CRG research is to produce a "metalanguage which is capable of expressing any subject as a string of notated elements which is neutral with respect to: (a) the placing of the subject in various standard shelf order classifications, (b) the categorial framework of the user of the system, and (c) the words and syntax of any one natural language."[17]

Robert Freeman concludes his discussion of "Classification in Computer-Based Information Systems of the 1970's" with the statement:

> The matter of switching among existing classifications and indexing languages used in machine-readable data bases probably will continue to be subject of considerable effort throughout the 1970's. A variety of classifications will continue to thrive in the context of computer-based systems, both as file-partitioning and as detailed subject searching devices. Large-scale use of automatic classification techniques is probably at least a decade away.[18]

We are so close in time to these projections that I find it difficult to assess them. Since no single classification scheme or indexing system can take care of all library situations satisfactorily, the development and improvement of what seem to be competing systems will be with us for some time.

Maltby wrote that "there are a number of fundamental questions which profoundly concern the future of classification in general libraries, particularly if by the term 'classification' we really mean a rational sequence of the maximum utility and not simply a convenient pigeonholing system." He believes that "there is an increasing gulf between the type of classification needed for book arrangement and that required for information retrieval."[19] This quotation points to the lack of rigorous usage of terms in librarians' professional jargon. We have often used interchangeably the terms *informational retrieval* and *subject retrieval*, treating them as synonyms or near-synonyms. This has given rise to much confusion in teaching classification as well as in applied classification. Many fine minds have formulated their own definitions using one term and ignoring the other one, or using the two terms synonomously. I believe that as librarians, we should be reminded of Henri Bergson's warning: "On est libre de donner aux mots le sens qu'on veut, quand on prend soin de le définir."[20]

John Metcalfe concludes an article entitled "When is a Subject Not a Subject?" with the statement that "'subject' has not proved a satisfactory term in information retrieval because of ambiguity in its use in information at large."[21] The term is nevertheless here to stay in communication with library users, but generates confusions in meaning with distinctions between the general and the specific, and between object and aspect. "Isolate has had some use to distinguish one of its meanings, but not without ambiguity of what Kaiser called Concrete and Process and what Cutter with more certain breadth of meaning called object and aspect."[22] For himself, Metcalfe intends to continue the distinction between object and aspect. By doing so, he endorses dialectical epistemology: the knowing subject and the known object—aspect, as he uses it, being a restriction at a conscious level of what we want to know about the object. This can be applied to the daily library environment as information retrieval from a subject-matter embodied in a document. I believe that most library classifications have succeeded to some extent in providing subject retrieval by mapping out or listing subjects, but many failed, save those that have introduced facet analysis or similar devices, to produce information retrieval from subjects. The editors of the *Dewey Decimal Classification* made an interesting and necessary distinction between *subject* and *discipline* as a useful device in applying that particular classification scheme. In that case, *subject* would be equivalent to *concept,* and *discipline* would fit the concept in such *a priori* classification schedules.

Robert Fairthorne writes: "The problem of helping those who are ignorant, in detail, of what people have said about things, is therefore solved by defining 'aboutness' in extension. That is by listing the things that are mentioned in a document...."[23] But the mere listing of things or entities does not reveal what is said about them, because it is irrelevant to the reader who is necessarily ignorant of what is said. Fairthorne distinguishes two kinds of "aboutnesses": (1) extensional "aboutness" takes into account the environment of the use and the production of a document (thus it is a relation, not an attribute); and (2) intentional "aboutness," which clearly cannot be determined from the study of the text alone: "It entails knowledge of how it is going to be used by what class of readers."[24] While not applying entirely William James's pragmatism to library classification, this last quotation from Fairthorne is suggestive not only of a classification of knowledge or the determination of the "aboutness" of a document, but also of a classification of readers. Shera stressed that "the study of *habits of use* is requisite to the act of classifying," for "there can be no universal library classification because there is no universal library user."[25]

The term *user habits* is a catchall to cover the behavior of all kinds of readers, from pre-readers to scholarly users. We must know more about our readers as individuals seeking information and recreation; we must know more about them as members of a socioeconomic group; we must know more about the civilization or culture to which they belong, and about the values which they cherish. It would be a gross error to overlook differences among peoples and nations even in the Western world; too often library classifications have been forced upon certain groups of readers, making the use of classification as an effective information retrieval tool almost impossible to achieve.

The use of classifications for retrieval is not an invention of modern Western man; primitive peoples have through the ages devised taxonomies and classifications for their own benefit. These were by no means mere intellectual exercises, but were implements for their survival, both physical and spiritual.

Many distinguished ethnologists have collected and interpreted primitive peoples' classifications, but none has given so much attention to their theories as the great French philosopher and anthropologist Claude Lévi-Strauss. He synthesizes the examination both of the structure of primitive thought and of the complexity of the organization of primitive collective life. In his book, *The Savage Mind,*[26] Lévi-Strauss deals extensively with classifications of primitive peoples. At first glance, languages of American Indians and other primitive peoples include few terms to express concepts; lacking words like *tree* or *animal,* their classifications are, as a rule, very detailed and enumerative. Krause claims that Indians classify and name living organisms in two main categories: useful and harmful.[27] Anything that does not fall under one of these two categories makes up a third category which we could consider neutral. The study of languages will reveal that names are assigned to things according to the particular needs of each community.

The theoretical foundations of totemic classifications, if we may be allowed to use this term, are quite simple: classifications are devised to bring order into the universe. According to Lévi-Strauss, "classifying, as opposed to not classifying, has a value of its own, whatever form the classification may take."[28] Classification is based on observation leading to a systematic inventory of relations and connections that leads, sometimes, to correct scientific results. One interesting example is classification by smell; modern chemistry has revealed that the presence or absence of carbon, hydrogen, oxygen, sulfur, and/or nitrogen will affect smell and taste. Botany separates onions, garlic, cabbage, turnips, radishes, and mustard (some belonging to the *liliaceae* and others to crucifers), but the olfactory sense confirms that these plants all share one element, sulfur. Simpson has stated that the demand for organization is a need common to art and science and, in consequence, "taxonomy, which is ordering par excellence, has eminent aesthetic value."[29]

Any classification is superior to chaos, even when it is based on external and artificial characteristics; it is a step toward rational ordering and is a tool that makes the building of a memory possible.

Among American Indians, the Navaho, who claim to be great classifiers, have divided living beings into two categories: those endowed with speech and those that are not; the latter includes animals and plants. Animals are then divided into three groups: running, flying, and crawling.[30] These species are a far cry from Western zoological taxonomies. Reichard writes that, "since the Navaho regard all parts of the universe as essential to well-being, a major problem of religious study is the classification of natural objects, a subject that demands careful taxonomical attention."[31] Of the Guarani of Argentina and Paraguay, Dennler states:

> In general, native terms can be said to constitute a well-conceived system, and, with a pinch of salt, they can be said to bear some resemblance to our scientific nomenclature. These primitive Indians did not leave the naming of natural phenomena to chance. They assembled tribal councils to decide which terms best corresponded to the nature of species, classifying groups and sub-groups with great precision. The preservation of the indigenous terms for the local fauna is not just a matter of piety and integrity; it is a duty to science.[32]

Lévi-Strauss regrets that ethnologists disregard these classifications by concluding that they were of no value whatsoever for the study of primitive peoples. He finds that these classifications bear a close resemblance to those devised in ancient times and in the Middle Ages by such men as Galen, Pliny, Hermes Tresmegistus, and Albert the Great, and are very close to Greek and Roman plant emblematism.[33]

The study of totemic classifications is fascinating; characteristics of such classifications are quite different from one culture to another. Lévi-Strauss states that: "The terms never have any intrinsic significance. Their meaning is one of 'position'—a function of the history and cultural context on the one hand and of the structural system in which they are called upon to appear on the other."[34] They are built on dichotomies based on values and usefulness and are hierarchical. "The truth of the matter," writes Lévi-Strauss, "is that *the principle underlying a classification can never be postulated in advance. It can only be discovered a posteriori* by ethnographic investigation, that is, by experience."[35]

It would be tempting to conclude that totemic classifications are mere listings used to build a collective memory, but relationships between terms make them workable. These relations are most commonly based on contiguity or on resemblance. Formally, contiguity and resemblance play an important part in modern classifications of knowledge; as Lévi-Strauss says in regard to Simpson's remarks:

> contiguity for discovering things which "belong both structurally and functionally ... to a single system" and resemblance, which does not

require membership of the same system and is based simply on the possession by objects of one or more common characteristics, such as all being "yellow or all smooth, or all with wings or all ten feet high."[36]

Other kinds of relationships may be found on either the sensible level or the intelligible level. Relations will vary from one culture to another; in fact, these civilizations could be labeled richer or poorer "on the basis of the formal properties of the systems of reference to which they appeal in the construction of their classifications."[37] The totemic classifications are not only conceptualized, but lived. By pointing out some aspects of Lévi-Strauss's work on totemic classifications, I am not suggesting that we should avail ourselves of primitive classifications, but that we might draw from these "savage minds" their concern for usefulness, both physical and spiritual, relevant to our late-twentieth-century, post-industrial society.

We are now familiar with Piaget, Bärbel and Inhelder's findings on classification or, more precisely, on classifying. In a contribution to the Shera Festschrift entitled "The Contribution of Classification to a Theory of Librarianship," D. J. Foskett summarizes the Geneva school's findings on classification. There are two ways of forming a class: (1) by analysis (or the separation) of things from a collection by naming their specific properties, and (2) by synthesis (or the grouping) of things which share certain properties. It is clear that separating and grouping can be done on the basis of more than one property or set of properties: "Thus the processes of forming concepts involve multiplicative classifications, or lattices, and not just single hierarchies. Mastery of these processes brings the ability not only to form classes, but also to identify the relations between objects that exist in the real, material world."[38]

The problem of relations, even though Farradane[39] hoped to have solved it twenty years ago, is still very much with us. The PRECIS system's relational operators are effective inasmuch as they are used with that method of indexing, but would they be as effective in another classificatory and/or indexing environment?

In a recent article on the future of classification, Phyllis Richmond wrote: "We do not yet have an organizing philosophic basis for current thought in the late twentieth century. The philosophy may be here but unrecognized, or it may be in process but has not yet emerged publicly."[40] She regrets that the Classification Research Group has no philosophical system for the projected New General Classification. They give their attention to Francis Bacon's Reason only, leaving aside for the time being, we hope, Memory and Imagination.[41] The future of classification in subject retrieval may lie not only in developing a philosophical basis, but also in determining in which way the different fields of knowledge are interrelated by deciphering the structures of knowledge that comprise knowledge itself.

In a remarkable book edited by Jean Piaget, *Logique et connaissance scientifique*,[42] Piaget rejects what he calls static classifications, which he considers artificial. The problem is to find epistemological filiations and analogies between different forms of scientific knowledge, and the epistemological meaning of these relations, as classification is considered as a search for noetic filiations.

Piaget posits that the dependency relation among the sciences necessarily leads to a linear classification. In reviewing some classifications from Bacon to Kedrov, he finds that according to Spencer's empirical epistemology, knowledge comes from the object itself, the forms of the object or phenomena. Knowledge concerning itself with forms only will produce a linear series, where the first term will be the most abstract and the last the most concrete. Spencer seems unaware that the abstract can be drawn not only from the object, but also from the actions of the subject.

Piaget recalls that an epistemology is a kind of a dialectical situation between a subject and an object. The object is known only through the subject and the latter knows itself in relation to the object. The setting of the foundations of logic and mathematics must therefore lie with the subject, and the building of a science of the subject requires biology, physics and mathematics. Auguste Comte's intent was to set a linear classification, but epistemologically his system suggests circularity. Relations between genesis and structures are the main problems to be faced in establishing a classification scheme. Are structures a result of a genesis? If so, how do we explain genesis without referring to structures? The first link contains the axiomatic sciences, and the last contains sciences of genesis (or as Comte calls them, *dynamiques*).

Cournot had divided knowledge according to structures and genesis. Disregarding Bacon's human faculties, his classification goes from the least historical—mathematics—to the most historical—the humanities. He also introduced a third dimension: the technical or practical series.

The latest classification of the sciences has been elaborated by the Soviet epistemologist, B. Kedrov. Kedrov rejects what Piaget calls static classifications, where a continuity is provided from one science to the other, and he also rejects classifications based on usefulness. Kedrov starts with what he calls the principles of objectivity and of subordination (or development from inferior forms to superior forms). One must consider primarily Kedrov's dialectics as a methodology, not as a philosophy. If one considers dialectics as a methodology stemming from the humanities, or more exactly from psychology and sociology, the method can go back to the starting point of logic/mathematics to provide structures for the physical sciences and to

I.	Logic/mathematics
II.	Physical sciences
III.	Biological sciences
IV.	Psycho-sociological sciences
A.	Domaine matériel (material scope)
B.	Domaine conceptuel (conceptual scope)
C.	Domaine épistémologique interne (internal epistemological scope)
D.	Domaine épistémologique dérivé (derived epistemological scope)

Table 1. Piaget's Epistemological Levels.

contribute to a total circular system of the sciences. The problem is not one of a structure to be given to a classification of the sciences (classifiers and classificationists cannot modify the real world); the problem is rather whether the sciences, in their spontaneous evolution, will reveal linear and hierarchical structures or cyclic and interdependent structures. Is knowledge developing as a living organism where all organs are interconnected, or is it developing by subordination in a preferred field?

Piaget has worked for more than thirty years on his proposed system of classification. His hypothesis is that the system of the sciences bears a circular structure, not a linear structure. He divides knowledge into four broad classes: I. logic/mathematics; II. physical sciences; III. biological sciences; IV. psycho-sociological sciences, including linguistics, economics, etc. (see Table 1).

At first glance, the proper order would appear to be I, II, III, IV, with a possibility of an internal interaction between IV and II, and I and III, discarding, therefore, a I to IV fixed sequence ending at IV. This is not an arbitrary order; there are relations between the classes. The meaning and the nature of these relations must be defined, for it would otherwise be totally absurd to link mathematics to psychology: while the latter relies on experimentation, the first relies on deduction. Piaget develops the hypothesis of the circle of the sciences by distinguishing different kinds of dependence: "reduction" or filiation between the sciences.

A first distinction must be recognized before establishing relations between different fields of knowledge and the use of these relations to build a natural classification (*natural* meaning here "adapted to the nature of these relations without any reference to the distinction between nature in general and ideal or transcendental realities").

The distinction lies between the *domaine matériel*—the material scope or matter of a science, i.e., the set of objects with which it concerns itself (for example, numbers and functions for mathematics; bodies, energies and organs for physics and biology) and the *domaine conceptuel*—the conceptual scope or set of theories or organized knowledge of a particular science about its object (for instance, the theory of numbers, the theories of masses and energies, the description and interpretation of biological organs, the analysis of mental phenomena). The material scope will be labeled IA, IIA, IIIA, IVA; and the conceptual scope IB, IIB, IIIB, IVB. It is perfectly acceptable to relate the material scope of IA *logic mathematics* and IVA *psycho-sociology;* this has been done by empiricists who have "reduced" logic/mathematics to language; Piaget, however, derives them from the general coordinations of action.

On the other hand, it would be rather clumsy to relate the conceptual scope of IB *logic/mathematics* to IVB *psycho-sociology;* the mathematician does not consult a psychologist before formulating a theory of numbers or complex functions. It is therefore possible to draw a circular classification at the level of material scope, but the conceptual scope remains linear. It is worth noting that classificationists have more or less taken this dichotomy into account when devising their systems. When Comte discards psychology and inserts its object in biology and sociology, he deals with the material scope. The observations, theories and experiments belonging to the conceptual scope are not altered whether psychology is classed in biology or sociology.

One might say that most classifications are concerned with the *material scope* exclusively. However, knowledge about a science is not developed on one level only; different levels of knowledge proceed from the conceptualization (B) of its object (A) to an inquiry into that conceptualization, which in turn leads to a critical examination, or to the internal epistemological scope. This third level will be assigned the letter C and is defined as the set of theories whose objectives are the criticism or the study of the foundations of the conceptual scope. The four main classes of this level will thus be: IC, IIC, IIIC, and IVC.

The study of the foundations of a science will eventually yield general epistemological problems such as the part of the subject and the contribution of the object to knowledge. A fourth level, D, *derived epistemological scope,* will accommodate the general epistemological results of comparing one science with other sciences. The problem will then deal with relations between the subject and the object. It is therefore essential that this level—ID, IID, IIID, IVD—be considered separately, because IVD concerns itself with psychogenesis and sociogenesis, and thus constitutes an indispensable part of genetic psychology. Obviously, epistemologies C and D refer equally to the material scope A and to the conceptual scope B, because their concern is the critical examination of concepts B in relation to their object A. Classifications according to B and C will remain linear, whereas a cyclic structure will be found in A and D, since the study of the subject in the building of the logico/mathematical structures is already an object in IVD.

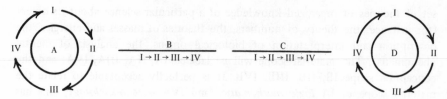

Figure 1. Piaget's Circle of the Sciences.

Piaget concludes that a dynamic classification of the sciences takes into account the four levels of knowledge because they are interdependent. He then exhibits the relations between the subject and the object. Relations of succession may differ according to the levels considered: for levels A and D the order appears circular, while for B and C it appears linear. On the hypothesis of a circular order of the sciences, Piaget distinguishes two kinds of relations: causal and implicative. The causal relations belong to the physical and biological sciences—to their material object. On the other hand, mental states such as feelings, values, and obligations are not causes, but imply something; we call them, therefore, implicative relations. If the circle of the subject and the object produces a cyclic structure to the whole of the sciences, it is because there is a dialectic or circular relation between classification systems based on causality and those based on implication.

Having defined these types of relations, Piaget distinguishes six types of dependence. These are: (1) unilateral reduction of a science or causal theory to another; (2) reduction by interdependence of sciences or causal theories; (3) correspondence between a causal system and an implicative system until the first is assimilated by the second; (4) correspondence between a causal system and an implicative system, with a search towards an isomorphism or a structure; (5) interdependence by abstraction between two implicative systems; and (6) reduction by axiomatization of two implicative systems.

Piaget's basic concept of the relations among the sciences can be expressed by the drawing of a circle: it takes its origin in logic/mathematics and closes also in logic/mathematics. He concludes that the material scope (A) is circular, given the fifth and sixth types of dependence, where logic belongs equally to levels A and D. The conceptual scope (B) is linear; logic tends to consider all circles as vicious. The internal epistemological scope (C) is linear, for approximately the same reasons as were applicable for B. Finally, the derived epistemological scope (D) is circular. Piaget grants that the limits between C and D might be somewhat difficult to determine. The epistemological results obtained in C in a given science may prove valid in another science. The circularity of A and D remains hypothetical until the types of dependence have been set and proved to exist. The proof of the circularity of both A and D is obtained by the application of Piaget's dialectical epistemology: the subject knows the object through his own action performed on the object, and knows itself insofar as it is affected by the object. Empiristic philosophy draws knowledge from the object alone; aprioristic philosophy from the subject alone.

I am very much aware that Piaget's circular classification might be indeed difficult to apply to a practical library and information-oriented environment, but I believe it is worth investigating. Regarding knowledge per se, his system has set its own limitations; it does not provide for knowledge that is not scientific, such as practical knowledge, beliefs, opinions, values, and what Erikson calls "intimacy with the domain," which includes knowledge acquired by connoisseurs of the fine arts and music, sports fans, serious collectors, etc.

These considerations, some far-fetched, should not deter us from trying to cope with the more mundane, day-to-day problems that we face in libraries. Among these problems is the "tandem"—close *vs.* broad classification exists only in library situations where the classification scheme serves two purposes: shelf location and subject analysis (in its broadest meaning). Theoretically, there is no physical limit to minute classification in catalogs, whether manual or automated. But if the classification scheme selected serves as a location device, truncation is possible without more or less loss of meaning if the notation is hierarchically expressive—whatever applies to the whole applies to the parts. I cannot imagine truncation applied to other types of notations that do not express hierarchy without severe loss of meaning.

In November 1973, the Library and Learning Resources Service of the City of London Polytechnic conducted a survey in which problems on automation brought questions on the length of DDC-18 class numbers as allocated by the *British National Bibliography* (BNB). In this survey, it was decided to investigate the possibility of truncating numbers in a select group of classes which reflect the collections held by that particular institution, without too much loss of information. Results of the study indicated that:

> Specificity of classing is a principle well established in texts on classification and in practical classification as carried out by LC and BNB. Truncating numbers either on a rigid basis of X digits after the decimal point or using the prime marks as suggested in the DC 18 Editor's Introduction (vol. 1, p. 41) inevitably reduces specificity and merges topics.[43]

The surveyors found that one of the features of class 300 and especially 330, 380 and 350 were long numbers resulting from additions from the Area Tables and the use of "add as" instructions, particularly in 300 and 380. They also felt that: "the 5- and 7-digit levels are unacceptable and that if truncation is to take place it should be at the 9-digit level. . . . If we take into account the fact that class numbers are not always coextensive with the subject matter, then the true picture is even worse."[44]

The surveyors recommended that more research is needed to determine the relative costs of:

1. The extra staff and user effort in searching a non specific catalog and shelves.
2. The extent to which users do not find a book because of long class numbers (unable to memorize or writing it down wrongly).
3. The extent to which users are put off from using the catalogue.
4. The difference in staff tidying and shelving times.[45]

The results of such an investigation would apply exclusively to a library environment where the three following conditions would be met: (1) open shelves, (2) classification is used for shelf location and subject analysis (in its broadest meaning), and (3) the scheme used is DDC or another scheme whose notation is decimal or lends itself to truncation without loss of meaning. It would also entail reassessment of the research and educational value of open stacks, self-service, and browsing.

Maltby has stated that: "there is an increasing gulf between the type of classification needed for book arrangement and that required for information retrieval. . . . The dichotomy is now too certain for any one scheme to be viewed with confidence as a classification for all situations."[46] He writes further that: "Broad classification, apart from the effect on cataloguing and the uncertainty of interpretation as to just what constitutes 'broad shelf arrangement; is at best often little more than a ruined shell of the scheme represented."[47]

The classified catalog is not theoretically bound to an exact matching of class numbers on books and catalog cards. In libraries maintaining this kind of catalog, the books may be arranged on the shelves in any orderly fashion; it may be by accession number, it may be by a classification scheme totally different from the one selected for the catalog, or according to the classification scheme used in the catalog, matching exactly the principal class number assigned to the catalog, or a broader class number than the one selected as the principal number for the catalog.

It is not within the scope of this paper to analyze the components of the classified catalog, nor its virtues and weaknesses; eminent librarians such as Shera and Egan,[48] Ranganathan,[49] and R. F. Kennedy[50] have treated with great intellectual rigor this tool for subject retrieval. I will, however, comment briefly on the few remaining or recently closed classified catalogs on this continent.

Among the most important classified catalogs recently closed are those of the Boston University Library and the National Library of Canada. Each of these catalogs was constructed quite differently: the Boston University catalog was a far cry from the rules on the construction of a classified catalog as set forth by Shera and Egan and by Ranganathan; LCC class numbers were used in the classified list, and LC subject headings were used for the index, matching as far as possible the class numbers assigned to the classified file.[51]

The National Library of Canada catalog was begun in 1961 and closed in 1974. It was "arranged in Dewey Decimal Classification order [with] indexes in English and French established according to the technique of chain indexing."[52] LCC class numbers were assigned to books.

According to Margaret Hazen, the Boston University Library catalog "had a serious drawback—namely, the difficulty of keeping the subject records current,"[53] resulting in a serious backlog. The development of LC MARC tapes and "the introduction of cooperative cataloging by member libraries in the OCLC [Ohio College Library Center] system provided a possible method for achieving speed and efficiency in subject—and general—cataloging."[54] Boston University became a member of the New England Library Network, accepting LC call numbers and subject headings, and began an alphabetic subject catalog. Standardization is the main reason behind the abandonment of the classified catalog. The same reason prevailed in the closing of the National Library of Canada catalog:

> The decision was made because of the need for greater standardization and the ensuing possibility of sharing cataloguing information, thus providing access to the collection more rapidly and decreasing cataloguing costs. . . . Although the classed catalogue has proved to be an efficient subject retrieval tool, it could not hold against the current trends.[55]

In Quebec, where the classified catalog enjoyed some popularity, large and small libraries have converted or are considering converting or closing their classified catalogs. Again, the reason is standardization: to bring, for the time being, research and academic libraries in line with Ontario libraries as members of UNICAT/TELECAT (a program of cooperative cataloging based on OCLC) with the addition of a bilingual (English and French) union file.

If we claim that subject indexing is equivalent to classification, then alphabetical subject catalogs will not alleviate defective classification. J.E. Daily has written: "One must assume that language, in its broadest sense, affects the subject indexing and that there is no distinct difference between classification, which is identified by its structure of notation, and the alphabetical list, however organized. Subject indexing is a classification process."[56] The *Encyclopédie*[57] is an alphabetical dictionary, but Diderot states that references between words are the most important part of the work; the intent of the "renvois" is obviously classificatory.

The future of classification for information retrieval lies in the confrontation of economics and the intrinsic value of research and its application. Valuable advances have been made and successfully applied in the classification and subject indexing of science and technology. Unfortunately, the humanities and the social sciences have been poorly served, and deserve more investigation in order to provide meaningful subject access. Any new venture is costly, and the economics will weigh heavily in adopting or rejecting systems applicable to a particular library. This is why standardization, regardless of its worth, has gained so many supporters.

REFERENCES

1. Maltby, Arthur, ed. *Classification in the 1970's.* Hamden, Conn., Linnet Books, and London, Clive Bingley, 1972.

2. Mills, J. "The Bibliographic Classification." *In* Maltby, *op. cit.,* p. 27.

3. *Ibid.,* p. 50.

4. Gopinath, M. A. "The Colon Classification." *In* Maltby, *op. cit.,* p. 70.

5. Vann, Sarah K. "The Dewey Decimal Classification." *In* Maltby, *op. cit.,* p. 108.

6. Immroth, J. P. "Library of Congress Classification." *In* Maltby, *op. cit.,* pp. 125-43.

7. Lloyd, G. A. "Universal Decimal Classification." *In* Maltby, *op. cit.,* pp. 147-65.

8. *Ibid.,* p. 156.

9. Vickery, B. C. "Classificatory Principles in Natural Language Indexing Systems." *In* Maltby, *op. cit.,* pp. 169-91.

10. Keen, E. M. "Prospects for Classification Suggested by Evaluation Tests Carried Out 1957-1970." *In* Maltby, *op. cit.* p. 209.

11. *Ibid.,* pp. 209-10.

12. Austin, D. "Trends Towards a Compatible General System." *In* Maltby, *op. cit.,* pp. 213-48.

13. *Some Problems of a General Classification Scheme* (Report of a Conference held in London, June 1963). London, Library Association, 1964.

14. Austin, *op. cit.,* p. 215.

15. *Ibid.,* p. 214.

16. *Ibid.,* p. 246.

17. *Ibid.,* pp. 246-47.

18. Freeman, Robert R. "Classification in Computer-Based Information Systems of the 1970's." *In* Maltby, *op. cit.,* p. 262.

19. Maltby, A. "Classification—Logic, Limits, Levels." *In* Maltby, *op. cit.,* pp. 11, 12.

20. Bergson, Henri. *La pensée et le mouvant: essais et conférences.* Paris, Alcan, 1934, p. 201, note. ("We are free to give whatever meaning we wish to words, once we have taken care to define them.")

21. Metcalfe, John. "When is a Subject Not a Subject?" *In* Conrad H. Rawski, ed. *Toward a Theory of Librarianship: Papers in Honor of Jesse Hauk Shera.* Metuchen, N.J., Scarecrow Press, 1973, p. 336.

22. *Ibid.*

23. Fairthorne, Robert A. "The Symmetries of Ignorance." *In* Rawski, *op. cit.*, p. 264.

24. *Ibid.*, p. 265.

25. Shera, Jesse H. *Libraries and the Organization of Knowledge.* D. J. Foskett, ed. Hamden, Conn., Archon Books, 1965, pp. 92, 110.

26. Lévi-Strauss, Claude. *The Savage Mind (La pensée sauvage).* London, Weidenfeld and Nicolson, 1966.

27. Krause, Aurel. *The Tlingit Indians.* E. Gunther, trans. Seattle, Univ. of Washington Press, 1956, p. 104.

28. Lévi-Strauss, *op. cit.*, p. 9.

29. Simpson, George G. *Principles of Animal Taxonomy.* New York, Columbia University Press, 1961, p. 4.

30. Lévi-Strauss, *op. cit.*, p. 39.

31. Reichard, Gladys A. *Navaho Religion; A Study of Symbolism* (Bollingen Series No. 18). 2 vols. New York, Pantheon Books, 1950, p. 7.

32. Dennler, J. G. Quoted *in* Lévi-Strauss, *op. cit.*, p. 44.

33. Lévi-Strauss, *op. cit.*, p. 42.

34. *Ibid.*, p. 55.

35. *Ibid.*, p. 58.

36. *Ibid.*, p. 63.

37. *Ibid.*

38. Foskett, D. J. "The Contribution of Classification to a Theory of Librarianship." *In* Rawski, *op. cit.*, pp. 174-75.

39. Farradane, J. E. L. "The Psychology of Classification," *Journal of Documentation* 11:187-201, Dec. 1955.

40. Richmond, Phyllis A. "The Future of Classification," *Drexel Library Quarterly* 10:111, Oct. 1974.

41. "Classification Research Group, Bulletin No. 10," *Journal of Documentation* 29:51-71, March 1973.

42. Piaget, Jean, ed. *Logique et connaissance scientifique* (Encyclopédie de la Pléiade, vol. 22). Paris, Gallimard, 1967.

43. City of London Polytechnic. Library and Learning Resources Service. *The Length of DC18 Class Numbers: Investigation in Selected Subject Areas.* London, City of London Polytechnic, Nov. 1973, 1. 2.

44. *Ibid.*, 1. 3.

45. *Ibid.*

46. Maltby, *op. cit.*, p. 12.

47. *Ibid.*, p. 19.

48. Shera, Jesse H., and Egan, Margaret E. *The Classified Catalog.* Chicago, ALA, 1956.

49. Ranganathan, S. R. *Classified Catalogue Code.* 5th ed. Bombay, Asia Publishing House, 1964.

50. Kennedy, R. F. *Classified Cataloguing: A Practical Guide*. Cape Town, Balkema, 1966.

51. Hazen, Margaret H. "The Closing of the Classified Catalog at Boston University," *Library Resources & Technical Services* 18:220-25, Summer 1974.

52. "Closing of the Classed Catalogue," *National Library News, Canada* 7:9, Jan.-Feb. 1975.

53. Hazen, *op. cit.*, p. 221.

54. *Ibid.*, p. 222.

55. "Closing of the Classed Catalogue," *op. cit.*

56. Daily, Jay E. "Classification and Categorization." *In* Allen Kent and Harold Lancour, eds. *Encyclopedia of Library and Information Science*. Vol. 5. New York, Marcel Dekker, 1971, p. 44.

57. Diderot, Denis, and D'Alembert, Jean, eds. *Encyclopédie: ou, Dictionnaire raisonné des sciences, des arts et des métiers*. 17 vols. Paris, Briasson, 1751-65.

ADDITIONAL REFERENCES

Flavell, John H. *The Developmental Psychology of Jean Piaget*. Princeton, N.J., Van Nostrand, 1963.

Hymes, Dell H., ed. *Language in Culture and Society: A Reader in Linguistics and Anthropology*. New York, Harper and Row, 1964.

Lévi-Strauss, Claude. *Anthropologie structurale*. Paris, Plon, 1958.

─────────. *Anthropologie structurale deux*. Paris, Plon, 1973.

─────────. *Le totémisme aujourd'hui* (Mythes et Religions). Paris, Presses universitaires de France, 1969.

Wellisch, Hans, and Wilson, Thomas D. *Subject Retrieval in the Seventies: New Directions* (Proceedings of an International Symposium held at the Center of Adult Education, University of Maryland . . . May 14-15, 1971) (Contributions in Librarianship and Information Science, No. 3). Westport, Conn., Greenwood Press, 1972.

Contributors

DAVID BATTY had experience as a librarian before he served as Head of the Department of Information Retrieval Studies, College of Librarianship, Wales, from its foundation in 1964 to September 1971. In 1971, he joined the faculty of the Graduate School of Library Science, McGill University. His programmed texts for the 16th through 18th editions of DDC are well known to library school students. He has made numerous other contributions to the literature of librarianship.

JOHN P. COMAROMI has served as a school librarian and as a circulation librarian. He has been a cataloging instructor at the University of Michigan and the University of Oregon, and currently teaches in that subject area at Western Michigan University. His Ph.D. dissertation for the University of Michigan was concerned with the history of DDC; Forest Press has published that history. He serves as a member of the Decimal Classification Editorial Policy Committee. In the summer of 1975 he traveled 10,000 miles to visit libraries using the DDC as principal investigator of the survey of the classification's use in the United States and Canada.

MARGARET E. COCKSHUTT has served in a variety of teaching and administrative positions at the University of Toronto School of Library Science since 1949. Currently she is an Associate Professor at the school and Academic Secretary for the Graduate Department of Library Science. The latter position entails responsibility for all the academic programs of all students and for liaison with the School of Graduate Studies. She is the author of a number of professional articles relating to cataloging, filing, classification, and education for librarianship. Among her many professional

175

activities should be mentioned her membership on the Decimal Classification Editorial Policy Committee.

MARY ELLEN MICHAEL has served as a Research Associate, Library Research Center, Graduate School of Library Science, University of Illinois at Urbana-Champaign and as a librarian. She served as co-author of *Planning and Evaluating Library System Services in Illinois* and her *Continuing Professional Education in Librarianship and Other Fields; A classified and annotated bibliography, 1965-1974* was published in 1975.

JOEL C. DOWNING is currently Director, English Language and Copyright Services, Bibliographic Services Division, the British Library, arriving at that position after work experience in London's public library system and responsibilities with the *British National Bibliography*. He has been a member of the Library Association's Cataloguing Rules Sub-committee since 1951. In 1965, he assisted David Batty and Peter Lewis in the founding and development of the Cataloguing and Indexing Group of the Library Association. He has served as chairperson of that group since 1971. From 1967 to 1970, he was secretary of the IFLA Committee on Cataloguing, and is currently a member of the Joint Steering Committee for the Revision of the *Anglo-American Cataloguing Rules*. Since 1970, he has served as the British representative on the Decimal Classification Editorial Policy Committee.

GORDON STEVENSON has been a faculty member of the School of Library and Information Science, State University of New York at Albany, since 1970. He holds a Ph.D. in Library Science from the Graduate Library School, Indiana University, Bloomington. He has contributed articles to library publications, including "The Historical Context: Traditional Classification since 1950" in *Drexel Library Quarterly*, October 1974. An active member of the American Library Association, he has served on the Catalog Code Revision Committee.

PETER R. LEWIS has been a frequent visitor to the United States since 1968 when he first represented British interests in discussions with the American Library Association and the Library of Congress concerning the maintenance of the *Anglo-American Cataloging Rules*. From 1968 to 1971, he was chairperson of the British Cataloguing Rules Committee. He was also chairperson of the Library Association Committee which published *Non-Book Materials Cataloguing Rules* (1972). He represents the British Library on the Joint Steering Committee for Revision of AACR and serves as the chairperson of the committee.

HANS WELLISCH has held various library positions in Sweden and Israel, and since 1969 has been a faculty member of the College of Library and Information Services, University of Maryland. In 1975, he received a Ph.D. from the University of Maryland. He is the author of several books and more than forty articles in library journals.

DEREK AUSTIN worked in public libraries for a number of years, usually as a reference librarian or a subject specialist, learning, as he says, "the hard way how to *use* indexes and classifications, and generally being disillu-sioned with existing schemes." From 1963 to 1967, he served as subject editor at the *British National Bibliography*, "learning as a practitioner just how difficult it is to make a good index or classification." Under the auspices of the NATO Science Foundation and the Classification Research Group, he worked on research into general principles for a new bibliographic classifica-tion from 1967 to 1969. From 1969 to 1973 he served as Principal Investigator for the PRECIS Project (UK MARC) trying to translate the general principles into practice. Since 1974, he has served as Head, Subject Systems Office, The British Library.

PAULE ROLLAND-THOMAS has been a cataloger in school and university libraries as well as the Deputy Librarian, Reference Library, National Film Board of Canada. Since 1961, she has been teaching in the areas of technical services, cataloging and classification at the School of Library Economy, University of Montreal. She is a doctoral candidate in philosophy at the University of Montreal, where her dissertation topic is "Cultural Classifications." The French edition for Canadian libraries of the *Anglo-American Cataloging Rules* (1967) and the revised chapter 6 of the code (1974) were prepared under her direction.

Index